MAAT PHILOSOPHY
VS.
FASCISM AND THE POLICE STATE

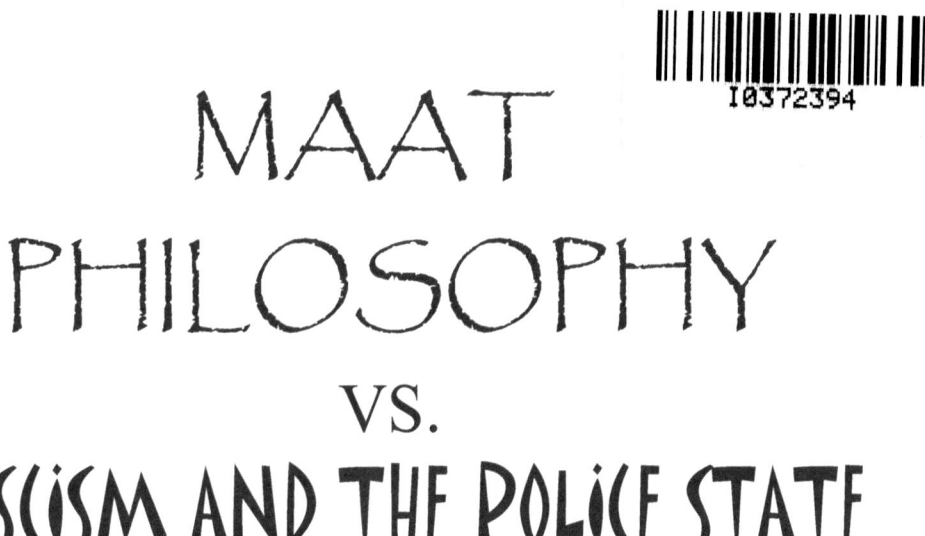

Understanding Modern Fascism and the Police State through Lessons from Ancient Egyptian Government Based on Maat Philosophy

"MAAT is great and its effectiveness lasting; it has not been disturbed since the time of Osiris. There is punishment for those who pass over its laws, but this is unfamiliar to the covetous one....When the end is nigh, MAAT lasts."
-Ancient Egyptian Proverb

Maat Philosophy Versus Fascism and the Police State

Sema Books
P.O.Box 570459
Miami, Fl. 33257

www.Egyptianyoga.com

© 2013 By Reginald Muata Ashby

All rights reserved. No part of this book may be used or reproduced in any manner whatsoever without written permission (address above) except in the case of brief quotations embodied in critical articles and reviews. All inquiries may be addressed to the address above.

Ashby, Muata
Maat Philosophy in Government Versus Fascism and the Police State
ISBN: 978-884564-87-1

TABLE OF CONTENTS

Preface: Where is Society Presently? 6

    Secrecy and The Loss of Constitutional Guarantees of Freedom of the Press and the Establishment of Citizens Spying on Citizens, and the American Stasi 32

    Assessment of Where We are Now 34

    Possible Actions In Response to the Current Negative Economic Conditions 40

    New Worldwide Environmental Threat 41

Chapter 1: Introduction to Maat Philosophy 50

    Who is Maat? Maat as a Secular and Non-Secular Philosophy 50

    What is True Virtue? 53

    The Source of Ethics in Maat Philosophy 58

    MAAT as the Spiritual Path of Righteous Action 59

    Maat as a Legal Basis for Laws and Law Enforcement 66

Chapter 2: Introduction to Fascism 68

    Government based on Fascism 71

    Government based on Maat Philosophy 72

    The Economic Objective of Capitalism and the Objective of Fascism: The Wealth Disparity and Income Inequality 74

        Bail-Outs and Bail-Ins 83

        The Fatally Flawed Economic System: Crony Capitalism (Fascism) 87

Chapter 3: The Modern Police State 95

    The Hard Police State and the Culture of Exceptionalism 124

Chapter 5: The Illusion of the American Dream and the Reality of a Corporate backed Police State 132

    The Corporate Soft Police State as a tool of Fascist Government and Economic Policy to Control the Compliant Masses 133

    Leadership for the Fascist Government 150

    The President Monarch, Indefinite Detention, Kill Lists and Intimidation of Citizens and Non-citizens Worldwide with the Threat of Reprisals 156

    Absence of Religious Criticism in the Face of Fascistic Politics and Economics 168

Chapter 6: Corporate Media, and Criminality at the Top, Neglect and Abuse of the Poor, and the Attack On Truth-tellers and Whistleblowers 172

    Wealth and Income Imbalance and Poverty as a Source of Crime 176

    Poverty as a Choice by Society as a Group 180

        USA: Rich in Name Only 186

The Triumph of Capitalism for the Wealthy and the Failure of Capitalism For Everyone Else –by Design 188

        What does Ancient Egyptian Maat philosophy say about the issue of hoarding wealth? 192

        Failure by Design: The Illusion of The "Broken" System 193

        The Illusion of Constitutional Government and The Reality of Corporate Government 196

Chapter 7: Maat Philosophy as a foundation for Good Government and a Well Ordered Society that Does Not Need a Police State 200

    Ancient Egyptian Police 207

    Maat Philosophy and Ancient Egyptian Law 209

    A Maatian Paradigm of Leadership 211

    The Maatian Ideal of Just Government and Leadership for the Balanced Ethical Human Personality and the Worldly Personality Types that Compose Present day Non-Maatian Societies 217

        Examples of Unrepentant Deception and Disregard for Fellow Human Beings 226

        An Example of Duplicity to undermine confidence in Government and give the impression that people suffering from the Wealth and Income Imbalances are unjustified. 228

        An Example of Duplicity and Disregard for the spirit of the Law 232

        Two Examples of Protecting Criminals, and Becoming an Accomplice with their Crimes by Not Acting Within One's Power to Uphold Justice and Disregard for the Letter and Spirit of the Law 234

        The Delusion of the USA as the "Best Country in the World" 235

    Conclusions 239

Epilog 241

    Politics, Government, Leadership, Virtue and Dictatorship in Modern Society 241

    Conclusion 249

    Finally 255

        A Last Word on the Term "Ethical Conscience." 257

INDEX 259

Other Books From C M Books 266
Music Based on the Prt M Hru and other Kemetic Texts 298

PREFACE: WHERE IS SOCIETY PRESENTLY?

FALL 2013

This preface may be considered as a complementary volume to the Books *Collapse of Civilization* and the EBOOK- White Paper: *Malfeasance and Immorality* and *Introduction to Maat Philosophy* by Muata Ashby.[1] Before we explore the world of Maat Philosophy and the modern conception of the Police State and its underlying sociopolitical/economic foundations in fascism, we will first look at a snapshot of where the western society, and in particular, the USA, is currently so that we can have a backdrop to the discussion that will follow. I have been a student and researcher as well as practitioner of Maat Philosophy for several years. I thought this was a propitious time, with all that is going on in society, to put forth this volume and show concrete examples of how Maat Philosophy can inform us of the negative aspects of social order and also about the higher way of thinking that can leads society to prosperity, peace and the fulfillment of its citizens.

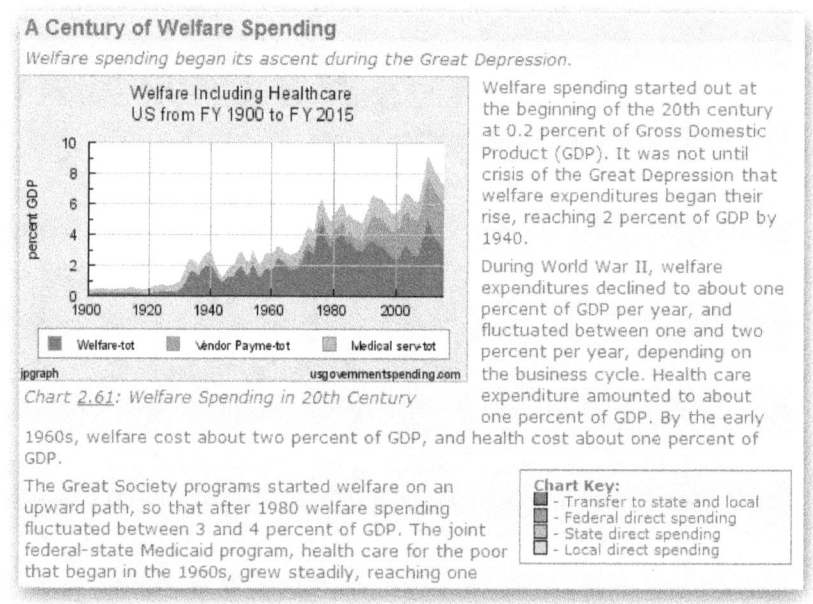

US Welfare Spending History from 1900[2]

Since 2004 I have been following political and economic issues closely and recent events seem to indicate we are at a tipping point wherein the politics and economics

---

[1] www.Egyptianyoga.com/catalog
[2] http://www.usgovernmentspending.com/welfare_spending

of the western countries, in particular the USA, are likely heading sooner or later [probably sooner than later] for a major collapse. What occurred in 2008 and since may be characterized as a crash and cushioned depression, which occurs periodically in a capitalist system of economy but would have been a major collapse were it not for the bailouts by the Federal Reserve bank and the US Government sustaining a sizable portion of the population with welfare and food stamps.

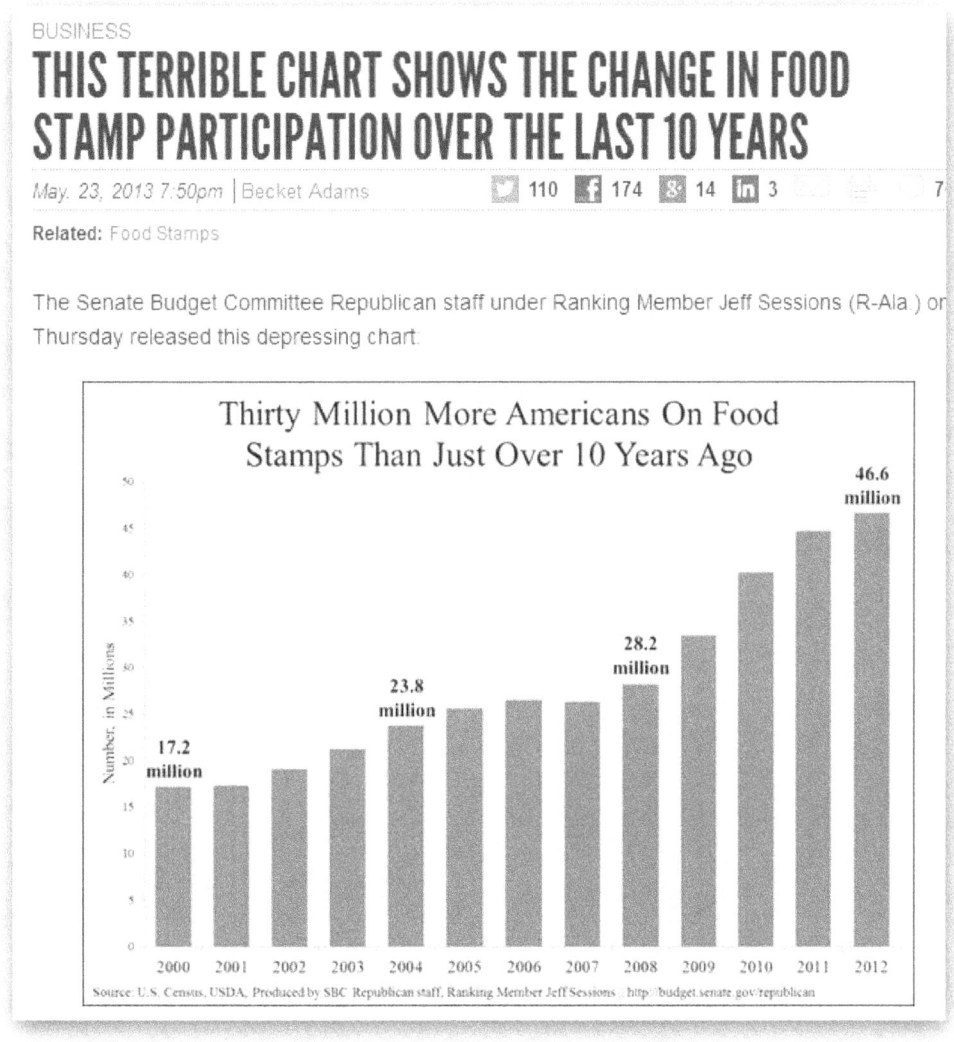

Food Stamp Participation Over the Last 10 Years[3]

---

[3] http://www.theblaze.com/stories/2013/05/23/this-depressing-chart-shows-how-many-more-americans-are-now-on-food-stamps-compared-to-10-years-ago/

However, those bailouts of the major banks in 2008 did not solve the problem and were only stop gap measures. The bailouts, to save the banks and the wealthy, did not help ordinary people and have made the initial situation worse and the eventual collapse much harder than it would otherwise have been. The usual destruction of wealth through inflation and the debt banking system that impoverishes the masses while making the banks and wealthy wealthier, has been compounded by massive transference of wealth through the bailouts (more than 20 Trillion $) by the US government and the Federal Reserve (central bank of the USA). Since in the current capitalist debt, fractional reserve banking system all money is created by banks at the same time they create debt, then it follows that using the money is associating oneself with debt to its issuer and consequently since the creditor controls the debtor it is a system of subservience to the owners or rather issuers of capital. In other words, this is a system that controls through debt and that control is tantamount to serfdom and serfdom is slavery without the chattel component. It is a kind of slavery in which the wealthy control by pulling financial strings instead of driving chain gangs. Force is only used when a significant portion of the population misbehaved, which cannot be handled by the prison industrial component of the society that is also owned by the capitalists. So the procedure is not to use force first but rather to use deception followed or coupled with coercion first, by inspiring loyalty to "the greatest country that ever existed" where supposedly all have equal opportunity to succeed and attain the "American Dream" through "hard work" and "upward mobility." If coercion fails, then ridicule, through the media, is used. If ridicule and ostracizing fails then the police are used to suppress protest and the prison system is used to detain.

It's not entirely a hereditary aristocracy and hereditary serfs; but the circumstances, genes, and connections that a person is born with do have a marked impact in this country.[4]

People are so overwhelmed by the "rat race", of working constantly to pay bills that are always increasing, that they purposely turn away from politics and turn to mindless entertainments and drugs to alleviate their stresses. They are hard-pressed to follow and substantively understand and respond to how the politicians, colluding with corporate leaders and the wealthy investors, set the laws and economic policies against them. Consequently, they are rendered powerless to do anything substantial to change their situation. As a result, their minds become weak and malleable to the manipulations of the media either to buy unnecessary objects or support politicians and policies that are against their best interests. They idolize and become enamored with Hollywood and sports celebrities, become intimidated by the power elite at work, in political policies and on the streets in the form of the police. The media also promotes the constant bombardment of the population with patriotic messages and contradictory facts, which maintain confusion, which produces inaction. If the deception of well being through obeying the power elite and buying unnecessary objects or believing in the mindless drivel of the news or Hollywood or sports media fails, then coercion is used in such a way that a neocolonial system can be setup within pockets of the country such that some members of the society, such as lawyers, judges, police, politicians and others, are given certain privileges and more wealth than the masses, for the service of keeping the masses in their place. The western

---

[4] http://www.businessinsider.com/social-mobility-is-a-myth-in-the-us-2013-3

economies are setup in such a way as to make it possible for a minority (the power elite of the society) to amass great wealth along with an apparently altruistic ideal of philanthropy. This fraud of philanthropy and charitable donating has the effect of legitimizing the ideal of a power elite and the necessity to go to them for support and or sponsorships. Therefore, only the initiatives and or policies, that they decide to support, will have the chance to become effective political actions. This arrangement of economics has the effect of allowing the power elite to control society by supporting only the groups and initiatives they want to support while appearing charitable in the process. It also has the effect of allowing them to control those whom they donate to and prevent other ideas and initiatives by not donating to them and through politics not allowing politicians to support certain initiatives. The donors also get the benefit of tax deductions and another benefit, the donations they sometimes make can close a gap between the inadequate government funding of social programs that if left unfunded would lead to rioting and threaten to more seriously fray the social bonds that hold the society together and maintain the elite position of the power elite. A recent example of this issue occurred during the government shutdown of 2013 when the republican party members forced a federal government shutdown and many members of the population became upset, especially veterans seeking to visit war memorials and others wishing to visit parks were turned away and the media began to focus on them. Rich donors started giving to open up those facilities so as to avoid the bad press coverage focusing on the republican party and the rich members of society who are being stingy, greedy and callous. The hypocrisy is that they supported the party that shut down those facilities and with their special position as wealthy elite they tried to manipulate public opinion by shifting the focus away from their party which had caused the shutdown in the first place.

Private donations to allow Mount Rushmore to reopen[5]

Clearly, the western form of philanthropy is a fiction and a fraud, a self-serving way of appearing to help members of society that in reality benefits the wealthy. The Maatian form of philanthropy was the first known in human history that formally implemented a policy of charity for all members of society. It went beyond the idea of a safety net and included the ideal of helping a person not only survive but to have a foundation in life to also be able to self-actualize, to progress and have an opportunity to develop themselves and discover the meaning of life.

---

[5] http://rapidcityjournal.com/news/private-donations-to-allow-mount-rushmore-to-reopen/article_695c8008-2474-5cd4-be8d-a92325b77446.html

The subsidies by the rich, of select groups in the society, is also the source of think tanks and talking heads on cable channels, the recurring" hoards of "experts" that always support the party line or the line that best serves the wealthy and power elite. These are people who either advocate policies they do not agree with but do so because they are getting paid or allow themselves to believe the party line even though they know it is a lie. Some examples of persons who are in the public sphere and promote ideological views admittedly not out of personal conviction or ethical conscience but out of desire to entertain and make money, can be found in liberal as well as conservative media including MSNBC and Fox News; these are persons who advocate points of view to manipulate the public into supporting the government policies and politicians or opposing them and at the same time make money entertaining the public and occupying their attention, deluding, lulling them into a false sense of security by instead of educating and passing on ethical, moral and truthful information, they instead support and reinforce their audience's prejudices. Alternatively, they stoke anger, hatred for entertainment value, to sell their products and books but also to support the fascistic elements of the society, which they are a part of. Others in this class include politicians (all of them)[6], who tout points of view that are dictated by their donors, the power elite, who can destroy them politically at will. The high rate of incumbency and the high rate of the revolving door between industry is not just an example of inbred politics of the wealthy but it is also indicative of and a hallmark of fascism. Fascism is the collusion between corporations, the power elite and the officials of government to serve the needs of the wealthy, the power elite of the society. Such persons who work for the government and or media, men and women who tout ideologies that are unjust but are nevertheless self-serving and or supportive of the positions of wealthy donors, may be considered personalities overcome by greed and lust for power, adulation and admiration of the rich and powerful or as sociopaths who do not care for anyone other than themselves while other personalities who work in government willingly prostitute themselves and their ideals for the money, all the while knowing they are peddling lies in the media or in politics that will hurt the weak and or the poor or the ignorant.

---

[6] The designation "all" is used because since the entire system of government is corrupt, criminal and a fraud, serving only the needs and dictates of the BNCVBNVVBNMCVBNMKL;DSDJKLMN=][POUYGFRHJOIKP=-877 all who work or desire to work in such a system are also corrupt, and criminal. This includes the president, congress and their aids and lobbyists.

Maat Philosophy Versus Fascism and the Police State

President Bush, VP Cheney, and Speaker Pelosi at the 2007 State of the Union address

Like the legendary Roman emperor Nero, whose lusts and the corruption of his wife and ministers along with the plutocratic oligarchy, in the form of the Roman senate, led Roman society from prosperity to ruin, so too the American empire leaders, men and women of both parties, applaud as the country, and indeed the world, moves towards political and economic ruin due to exploitation of the citizenry and world population through corporatism/fascism and oppression of other countries through colonialism, neocolonialism and now "neo-liberalism"[7] and globalization.[8] A question that should be foremost in the mind, as we explore the themes of this book, is why and or how is it that Ancient Egypt avoided a fall into corruption, despotism and malfeasance that led to the downfall of Ancient Rome and is apparently leading the USA and Western Europe into decline and fascism?

---

[7] NEO-LIBERALISM includes but is not limited to: Free market fundamentalist economics, **Laissez-faire economics**, corporations are people, trade without tariffs, opening world markets for exploitation by multinational corporations, trickle-down economics (free money to the rich), globalization of these ideas and economic models through political coercion, war, bribery of government officials, saddling countries with debt and then imposing "structural adjustment" (austerity on the masses) while giving bailouts to the rich and corporations, low taxes for the rich and high taxes for the poor, lenient laws for the wealthy and corporations and harcsh laws for the masses.

[8] Methods or spreading nep-liberals ideas and policies around the world. Not to be confused with "globalism", the idea that humanity is part of a "global" community and people should treat each other as a family.

Maat Philosophy Versus Fascism and the Police State

Let's begin our exploration with an Ancient Egyptian Proverb to set the tone of our discussions. What does Ancient Egyptian Maat Philosophy say about ethics in politics?

> "If you are an official of high standing, and you are commissioned to satisfy the many, then hold to a straight line. When you speak don't lean to one side or to the other. Beware lest someone complain, saying to the judges, "he has distorted things", and then your very deeds will turn into a judgment of you."
> -Ancient Egyptian Proverb

photo of the September 11 attack on the World Trade Center.

The events of the terrorist attack in New York city on 9-11-2001 (whether or not it was an actual attack from foreigners or an attack orchestrated by members of the US government) have facilitated the ushering in of what can be described with the term a "soft police state" including unlawful mass surveillance, widespread suppression of political and economic dissent, unprecedented persecution and prosecution of whistleblowers, massive corporate frauds and a two tiered justice system (one for the wealthy and one for the rest of the population) and suspension of the rule of law for the super rich, the politicians, and the national security agencies and now restriction of financial freedom and later to come, restrictions in freedom of movement. A complete collapse of the economy would likely lead to economic, social and political chaos and inevitably harden the current soft police state we have at this moment. A hard police state would mean restrictions in travel and movement, restrictions of financial freedom, devaluation of currency, widespread violent crime, mass incarcerations and detentions as well as extrajudicial or more corrupt judicial dispensations of the law, possibly leading to martial law and not just ignoring the constitution, which is what we have now, but complete abrogation of it and full <u>worldwide</u> corporate rule. Incidentally, if the new Trans Pacific Partnership (TPP) treaty is approved it will abrogate the constitution in favor of international corporate commercial law which will place corporations above consumers and consumer rights and above the USA constitution.

Essentially, trade treaties like the TPP, and its counterpart Atlantic Treaty, are evolutions of other treaties such as NAFTA and are expressions of a strategy of one world government or control through the legal and financial system of the world with the backing of the police state, but without the high profile of instituting an actual world government with a president. In this manner, the one world control can be instituted subversively by control through international finance and debt and corporate law, which will supersede the national and local laws. This means that those who control corporate law, the owners of capital and corporations, will become the absolute rulers and the government leaders become mere objects for public focus of displeasure and anger, while deflecting the attention from the real power behind the scenes.

The Trans-Pacific Partnership.[9]
The TPP is often referred to by critics as "NAFTA on steroids"

The acceptance and implementation of the TPP would mean a faster decline in wages which would also lead to economic collapse and greater social disorder. Additionally, new wars may emerge due to fights over resources or as a means to distract from the dire social, political and economic consequences of allowing the politics and economics to deteriorate to the current extent. such an event would lead to hardening of the soft police state and the possibility of more actual terrorist attacks, domestic or international, prompting more calls for a hard police state with loss of more civil rights. The continued relentless pursuit of dominion over the resources of other countries and the malfeasance (fraud and lack of regulation of corporations) of the Federal Reserve bank of the USA (maintaining low rates and giving trillions of virtually free dollars to corporations and world banks) have been the only factors sustaining the

---

[9] http://www.democracynow.org/2013/10/4/a_corporate_trojan_horse_obama_pushes

economy, albeit artificially, though eventually those solutions (crony capitalism) will be unsustainable since the money printing will eventually affect the value of the currency (US Dollar) adversely or the bond market adversely, or when the confidence of investors ,in the US dollar or US bond market and economy fails, or when the derivatives market in the shadow banking system fails, when any of these happens the collapse can suddenly begin in earnest.[10]

The big banks

Who are the "investors" or bondholders, that invest in the USA economy by holding USA Treasury Bills issued by the US government? Who would be dumping the US debt (bonds) if the confidence was lost in the US economy and its ability to repay the debt? Who would sell the bonds if they thought that their value would be reduced by the Federal Reserve Bank having to raise interest rates? Who would sell the bonds if they thought that the FED would stop supporting the market by "Quantitative Easing" (QE), (euphemism for collective bailout by the whole population), as occurred earlier in 2013 when the FED hinted they would stop)? The chart below displays the answer. Quantitative easing is free money for the main banks and does not help the general economy.

---

[10] **Book References detailing the Economic Conditions**:
Conquer the Crash by Robert Prechter
The Five Stages of Collapse by Dimitri Orlov
The Great Depression Ahead by Harry S. Dent Jr.
Strategic Relocation by Joel M. Skousen
The Great Bust Ahead by Daniel A. Arnold
The Great Deformation by David Stockman
Rich Dad's Advisors: Guide to Investing In Gold and Silver by Michael Maloney

INTERET REFERENCES
www.PRN.fm
http://www.youtube.com/watch?v=iicyi2Vcal8
http://www.youtube.com/watch?v=jlZZ-87iPyg
http://www.youtube.com/watch?feature=player_detailpage&v=tj2s6vzErqY#t=1084s
http://www.youtube.com/watch?v=DyV0OfU3-FU&feature=c4-overview-vl&list=PLE88E9ICdipidHkTehs1VbFzgwrq1jkUJ

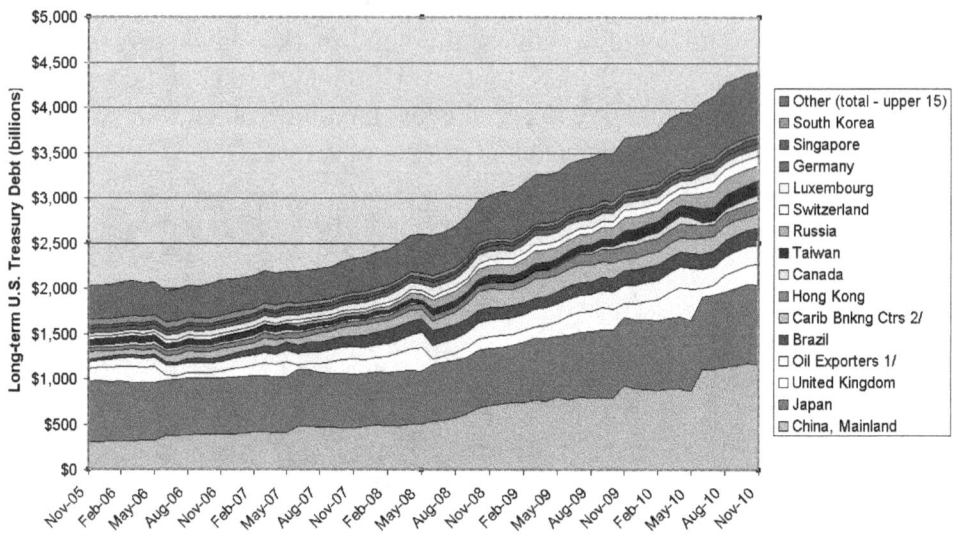

Composition of US Long-Term Treasury Debt held by foreign states, Nov. 2005–Nov. 2010. June figures are results of comprehensive Treasury Department surveys.[11]

Another scenario that would lead to an economic collapses is the incapacity of the masses to sustain spending to uphold even the current fragile and feeble state of the economy because banks are no longer able to give loans because the masses cannot repay them anymore as they did during the boom years before the 2008 crash. Most jobs are now part time jobs and lower paying jobs so people are making less money and working more, holding more than one job and because of inflation their money buys less. From 1980 to 2008 the economy was sustained by consumers (70% of all spending). However, since wages stagnated beginning in the early 1980's, and new income was taken by the wealthy members of society, where did the money come from to sustain consumer spending of the masses when wages stopped increasing to keep up with inflation? It came from loans (mortgage, car, credit card, student loans, etc.). Corporations and banks gave out loans liberally and consumers spent money liberally but it was merely a ponzi scheme (new loans supporting new spending and paying off old loans) that ended when prices elevated beyond the capacity of consumers to sustain spending in real estate and consumer goods even with secured loans like second mortgages or unsecured loans like credit cards. Having used their homes to access spending money, and now with the inability to get more loans, or more income, and with the housing market stagnating, the mortgage loans failed in massive numbers and that began the massive foreclosures around the country and the world especially in Europe and the USA that is still (in 2013) negatively affecting the economy, preventing growth and causing wealth loss. As loans failed and the real estate market collapsed the jobs

---

[11] https://en.wikipedia.org/wiki/National_debt_of_the_United_States

and companies relying on the real estate industry failed and Wall Street banks, that made the bad loans they should not have made, started to fail which is when they were bailed out.

Wealth and Income Imbalance

This peak in consumer incapacity to sustain the real estate ponzi scheme setup by the big banks, caused a collapse in the fraudulent repackaged mortgage loan market that they had setup and sold to investors around the world knowingly containing the foundation of the unsustainable loans they had made. This is referred to as the bursting of the real estate bubble (2007-2008). This ponzi scheme and the subsequent bailouts destroyed consumer wealth and continues to stagnate the economy. In recent years the Federal Reserve bank of the USA has been re-inflating the real estate bubble and it is again at an unsustainable level and poised for another crash.

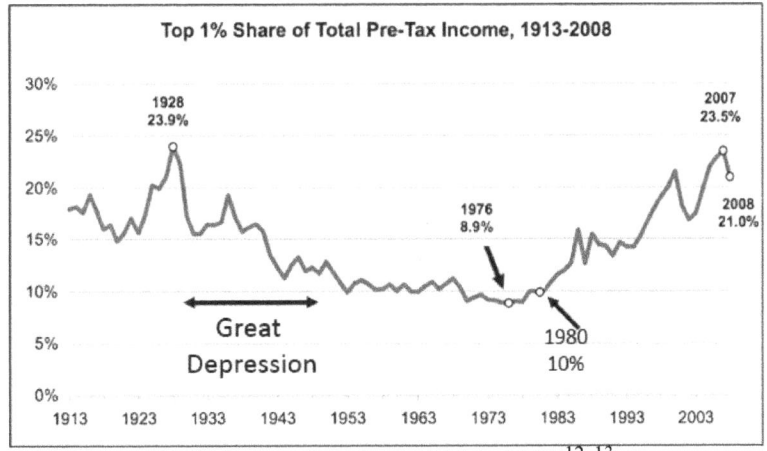

U.S. inequality from 1913–2008[12]/[13]

Source: Thomas Piketty and Emmanuel Saez, "Income Inequality in the United States, 1913-1998," Quarterly Journal of Economics, 118(1), 2003. Updated to 2008

Coincidentally, 2007 marked a second high point, within the last 100 years, in the disparity between the rich and poor in terms of wealth and income inequality. In 1927-28, the wealth disparity and bank malfeasance led to a crash in the economy (in 1929) and a severe depression. During the "Great Recession" years, that followed the 2008 crash, (between 2009 and 2010) the disparity was reduced, until 2013 when it was announced that the disparity again surpassed its

---

[12] Chart was made using data initially published as Thomas Piketty and Emmanuel Saez (2003), *Quarterly Journal of Economics*, 118(1), 2003, 1–39. Data (and updates) shown at http://inequality.org/income-inequality
[13] http://emlab.berkeley.edu/users/saez. - See more at: http://inequality.org/income-inequality/#sthash.0uOCoVsB.dpuf

previous record set in 2007 so this is another risk source that can lead to another crash and collapse. These issues also apply to the European union.

Post-1980 rise in inequality

Most current discussion of income inequality in America centers on its rise since the mid to late 1970s, the so-called "Great Divergence". According to the United States Census Bureau, it reported that the income inequality between the richest and poorest people grew to its widest in 2011, as the census recorded 46.2 million people living in poverty.[14]

Where has the income gone?

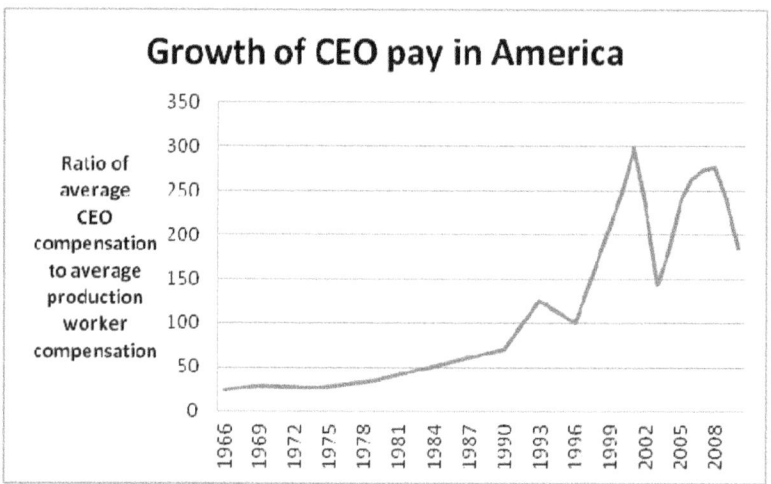

Ratio of average compensation of CEOs and production workers, 1965–2009. Source: Economic Policy Institute. 2011. Based on data from Wall Street Journal/Mercer, Hay Group 2010.[15]

Lisa Shalett of Merrill Lynch Wealth Management found that real average hourly earnings in the US "are essentially flat to down, with today's inflation-adjusted wage equating to about the same level as that attained by workers in 1970", despite the fact that "for the last two decades and especially in the current period", productivity has "soared". The benefits of productivity during this cycle had gone "almost exclusively to corporations and their very top executives."[16]

---

[14] Cathrine Dodge; Mike Dorning (12 September 2012). "Rich-Poor Gap Widens to Most Since 1967 as Income Falls". *Bloomberg*. Retrieved 6 November 2012.
[15] More compensation heading to the very top: 1965–2009. May 16, 2011.
[16] Wall Street Bolshevism, Part 3| Timothy Noah| tnr.com| 5 October 2011

Maat Philosophy Versus Fascism and the Police State

The above confirms that especially since the early 1980's there has been a concerted effort to lower real wages and increase corporate income and compensation to CEO's and the owners of corporations. "Offshoring" jobs (closing businesses and factories and hiring lower wage workers and building factories in other countries with low wage workers) to low wage countries such as China has been an integral part of the strategy of reducing wages. This has had the effect of de-industrializing the USA and thereby decreasing manufacturing jobs and increasing lower paying service jobs. This has also had the consequence of forcing the masses to access loans and work two or more jobs in order to make enough money to sustain the same lifestyle. The concern is that as occurred in 1927-1929 and in 2007, that a tipping point will be reached wherein the economy would again collapse because of the inability of the masses to sustain the level of spending that in turn sustains small and large businesses.

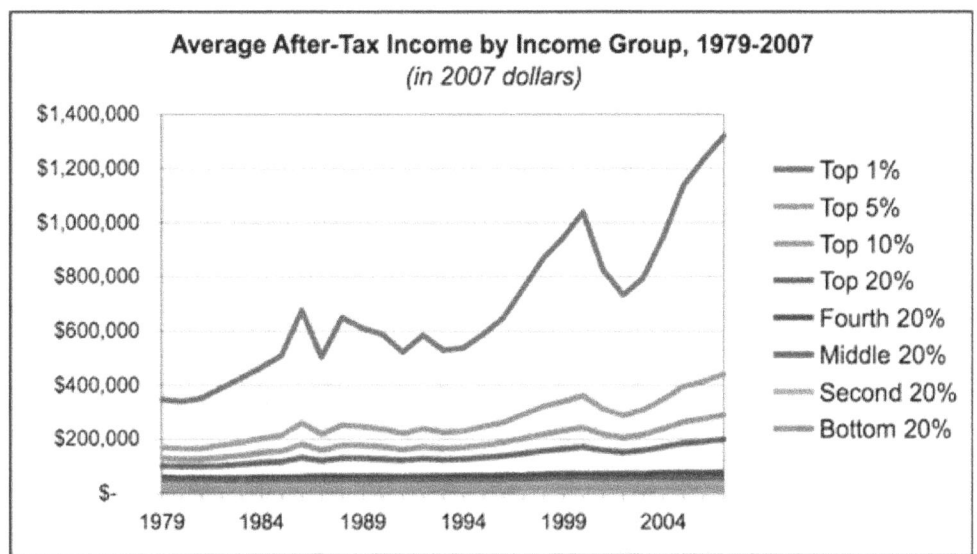

Source: Congressional Budget Office, Average Federal Taxes by Income Group, "Average After-Tax Household Income," June, 2010.

The chart above demonstrates the dramatic disparity between the 1% of the population and the 99% of the population in terms of where income has gone in the last 28 years; this despite the fact that workers work more hours than other industrialized countries and their productivity per hours worked has gone up.

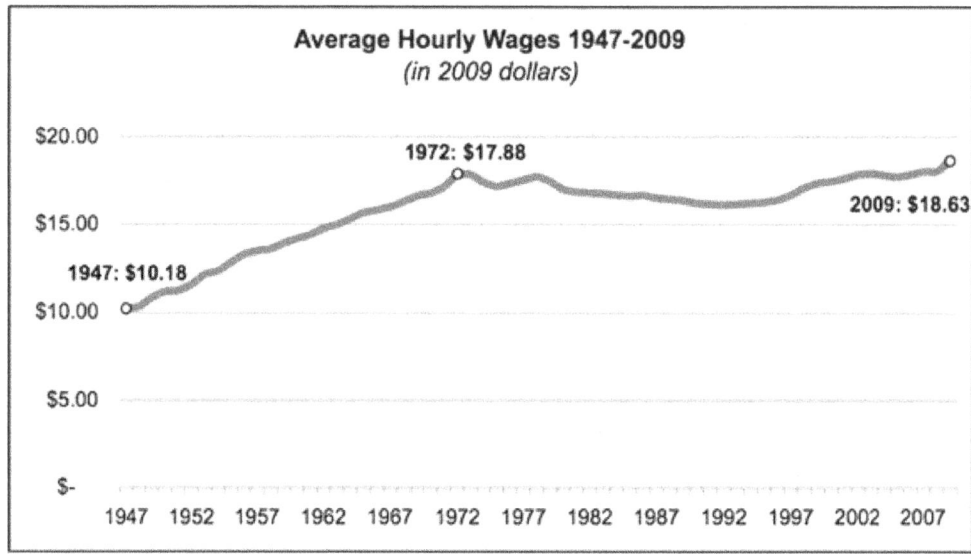

Source: Economic Policy Institute, "Wages and Compensation Stagnating," 2011, based on Bureau of Labor Statistics data.

The chart above shows that income in terms of wages, has remained essentially the same for the last 37 years.

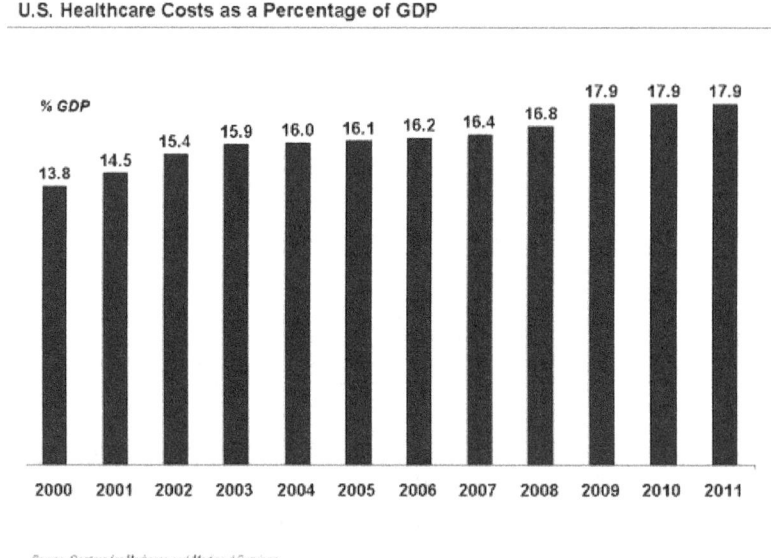

Healthcare Costs as a Percentage of GDP 2000-2011

Another area that deserves mention in this summary introduction is healthcare. In the book *Collapse of Civilization and the Death of American Empire* by Muata Ashby, Healthcare was one of four main topics, crisis challenges humanity is facing, that were covered as a looming source of medical, public health, social, political and economic failure. Healthcare is an important issue because it is more than 17% of the economy. Currently, the healthcare industry in the USA is based on a model of company or workplace provided healthcare and for-profit healthcare providers (MEDICAL INDUSTRIAL COMPLEX composed of: doctors, insurance companies, drug companies, medical supply and equipment companies and hospitals). The profit motive in the for-profit healthcare industry insidiously causes healthcare providers to seek ways to minimize the service and charge more for the services in order to make a profit off of the suffering and illness of the population. This means that instead of there being an incentive to promote public health there is instead an incentive to promote care and management of disease instead of cures. It has led to a situation in which the members of the medical industrial complex have setup a system whereby inflated charges and unnecessary services are performed, causing unnecessary pain and financial hardship, drawing wealth out of the population, even as health outcomes are worse than other industrialized and even some less developed countries. This is why the current system is more profitable than other industries and is a leading contributing cause of the economic downfall of the country. The main problem with healthcare as it is carried out in the USA is that it is allowed to exist as a profit oriented industry whereby drug companies, insurance companies and related medical supply companies are allowed to engage in price gauging and control the delivery of services under the guise of free enterprise. In fact there is severe collusion with lawmakers in the fact that they allowed lobbyists to write the law which conveniently has no competition between the companies as the system is setup by the new Affordable Care Act (ACA) instituted by President Obama and the congress. As it stands now, even more income will be given to corporations, instead of going to a single payer, socialized medicine program that would reduce costs, as other single payer programs around the world have done.

Weaponized Profits: The US Health Care System by Donna Smith[17]

After refusing to put forth a single payer healthcare system or even a public option as a choice for healthcare, at the behest of corporate leaders, which polls had indicated was the preferred choice of the general public, the new healthcare act was touted by the president and others in congress and the industry as a repair of the existing healthcare industry and was promoted by the president and congress as a step towards better, more widely available and affordable healthcare, as of the Fall of 2013 it became evident that the ACA or "Obamacare" was turning out to not be as affordable as advertised and would be a complete capture of the healthcare industry by the corporation's (healthcare industrial complex).

Many people think the new "Affordable Care Act" (Obamacare) is an improvement since some policies were changed, such as not allowing insurance companies to drop people due to having preexisting conditions. However, there are fatal flaws in the program that in the end will not fix the problem of costs or the problem of harm by the medical industrial complex due to medical errors, dangerous drugs, malfeasance, etc.

---

[17] https://www.commondreams.org/view/2013/09/22

Maat Philosophy Versus Fascism and the Police State

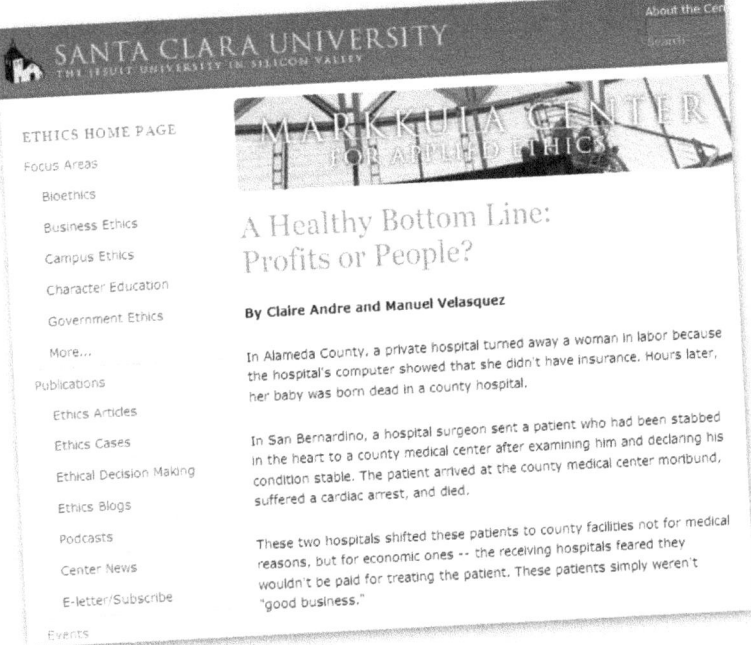

A Healthy Bottom Line: Profits or People?[18]

In fact, the problem of costs has not been addressed, in the "Affordable Care Act" (Obamacare), with proven solutions (which are opposed by the industry because they reduce profits) and the issue of corporations controlling the delivery of services and providing inferior and more expensive care has been made worse because now the new law forces more people (from the public, as customers) to be involved with a corrupt and fascist medical industry. From the standpoint that the "Affordable Care Act" does not make healthcare affordable, the naming of it as such is to be considered as an Orwellian[19] tactic. The corruptions not fixed include, price gauging and reduction of services and coverage by insurance companies, doctors performing unneeded surgeries for profit, drug companies putting out drugs they know are harmful but doing so anyway for profit and without fear of reprisals or criminal prosecution or

---

[18] http://www.scu.edu/ethics/publications/iie/v1n4/healthy.html

[19] In Orwell's novel, all citizens of Oceania are monitored by cameras, are fed fabricated news stories by the government, are forced to worship a mythical government leader called Big Brother, are indoctrinated to believe nonsense statements (the mantra "WAR IS PEACE, SLAVERY IS FREEDOM, IGNORANCE IS STRENGTH"), and are subject to torture and execution if they question the order of things.[http://civilliberty.about.com/od/historyprofiles/g/orwellian.htm]
"Orwellian" is an adjective describing the situation, idea, or societal condition that George Orwell identified as being destructive to the welfare of a free and open society. It connotes an attitude and a policy of control by propaganda, surveillance, misinformation, denial of truth, and manipulation of the past, including the "unperson" — a person whose past existence is expunged from the public record and memory, practiced by modern repressive governments. Often, this includes the circumstances depicted in his novels, particularly *Nineteen Eighty-Four*. [https://en.wikipedia.org/wiki/Orwellian]

financial loss, allowing companies to reduce workers to part-time status so they do not need to provide healthcare for their workers. and many others. So the ACA does not solve the healthcare crisis and actually eventually will hasten the economic problems of the country.

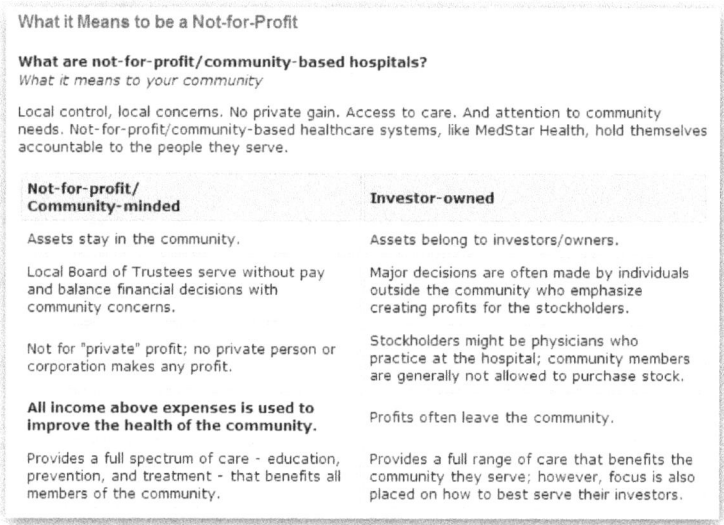

What it means to be a Not-for-Profit[20]

Even though the USA lags behind other industrialized nations in terms of healthcare, the corporate controlled media and congress and president, continue to advocate for a system that, just as the banking system pays fees to the banks unnecessarily, the ACA unnecessarily gives money to intermediary corporations, the insurance companies, when they are not necessary at all and the existing Medicare system could accommodate the entire population at minimal cost. The USA Medical system costs more than any other healthcare system in any other industrialized nation. The reason why the current system continues to be advocated is that it is profitable to the medical industries and to the politicians that take bribes (political contributions) from those industries. Again, the profit motive is affirmed over the health and well being of the population. The statistics below display the depth of the degradation of a society that allows the malfeasance and shoddy healthcare system to hurt and kill untold millions of persons in the population.[21]

> As shown in the following table, the estimated total number of iatrogenic deaths—that is, deaths induced inadvertently by a physician or surgeon or by medical treatment or diagnostic procedures— in the US annually is 783,936. It is evident that the American medical system is itself the leading

---

[20] http://www.medstarhealth.org/body.cfm?id=555663
[21] http://www.webdc.com/pdfs/deathbymedicine.pdf

cause of death and injury in the US. By comparison, approximately 699,697 Americans died of heart disease in 2001, while 553,251 died of cancer.[22]

Table 1: Estimated Annual Mortality and Economic Cost of Medical Intervention[23]

Condition	Deaths	Cost	Author
Adverse Drug Reactions	106,000	$12 billion	Lazarou(1), Suh (49)
Medical error	98,000	$2 billion	IOM(6)
Bedsores	115,000	$55 billion	Xakellis(7), Barczak (8)
Infection	88,000	$5 billion	Weinstein(9), MMWR (10)
Malnutrition	108,800	———	Nurses Coalition(11)
Outpatients	199,000	$77 billion	Starfield(12), Weingart(112)
Unnecessary Procedures	37,136	$122 billion	HCUP(3,13)
Surgery-Related	32,000	$9 billion	AHRQ(85)
Total	783,936	$282 billion	

---

[22] U.S. National Center for Health Statistics. National Vital Statistics Report, vol. 51, no. 5, March 14, 2003 .

[23] 3. For calculations detail, see "Unnecessary Surgery." Source s: HCUPnet, Healthcare Cost and Utilization Project. Agency for Healthcare Research and Quality, Rockville , MD. Available at: http://www.ahrq.gov/data/hcup/hcupnet.htm . Accessed December 18, 2003 . US Congressional House Subcommittee Oversight Investigation. Cost and Quality of Health Care: Unnecessary Surgery . Washington , DC : Government Printing Office;1976. Cited in: McClelland GB, Foundation for Chiropractic Education and Research. Testimony to the Department of Veterans Affairs' Chiropractic Advisory Committee. March 25, 2003 .
7. Xakellis GC, Frantz R, Lewis A. Cost of pressure ulcer prevention in long-term care. Am Geriatr Soc . 1995 May;43(5):496-501.
6. Thomas, EJ, Studdert DM, Burstin HR, etal. Incidence and types of adverse events and negligent care in Utah and Colorado. Med Care. 2000 Mar;38(3):261-71. Thomas, EJ, Studdert DM, Newhouse JP, etal. Costs of medical injuries in Utah and Colorado . Inquiry . 1999 Fall;36(3):255-64. [Two references.]
7. Xakellis GC, Frantz R, Lewis A. Cost of pressure ulcer prevention in long-term care. Am Geriatr Soc . 1995 May;43(5):496-501
8. Barczak CA, Barnett RI, Childs EJ, Bosley LM. Fourth national pressure ulcer prevalence survey. Adv Wound Care . 1997 Jul-Aug;10(4):18-26. 9. Weinstein RA. Nosocomial Infection Update. Emerg Infect Dis . 1998 Jul-Sep;4(3):416-20.
10. Fourth Decennial International Conference on Nosocomial and Healthcare-Associated Infections. Morbidity and Mortality Weekly Report. February 25, 2000 , Vol. 49, No. 7, p.138.
11. Burger SG, Kayser-Jones J, Bell JP. Malnutrition and dehydration in nursing homes: key issues in prevention and treatment. National Citizens' Coalition for Nursing Home Reform. June 2000. Available at: http://www.cmwf.org/programs/elders/burger_mal_386.asp. Accessed December 13, 2003 .
12. Starfield B. Is US health really the best in the world? JAMA . 2000 Jul 26;284(4):483-5. Starfield B. Deficiencies in US medical care. JAMA . 2000 Nov 1;284(17):2184-5
13. HCUPnet, Healthcare Cost and Utilization Project. Agency for Healthcare Research and Quality, Rockville , MD. Available at: http://www.ahrq.gov/data/hcup/hcupnet.htm . Accessed December 18, 2003
49. Drug giant accused of false claims. MSNBC News. July 11, 2003 . Available at: http://msnbc.com/news/937302.asp?0sl=-42&cp1=1. Accessed December 17,2003
85. Tunis SR, Gelband H. Health care technology in the United States . Health Policy . 1994 Oct-Dec;30(1-3):335-96
112. Injuryboard.com. General Accounting Office study sheds light on nursing home abuse. July 17, 2003 . Available at: http://www.injuryboard.com/view.cfm/Article=3005. Accessed December 17, 2003 .

Consider how many people died in the World Trade Center attacks of 2001, around 3000; now consider how many people die because of the greed, incompetence and ignorance related to the healthcare system. Now consider the trillions of dollars that have been mobilized to combat terror and nothing for health prevention or studies to devise ways to improve the system or at least stop the errors and accidents that would stem the tide of iatrogenic deaths. Yet nothing substantial is being done about the healthcare system. Knowing the statistics presented above, the unnecessary pain and suffering as well as financial graft being allowed by the present healthcare system, it is shameful that the system is still allowed to exist. This signifies collusion between and corruption, by political leaders and corporate leaders, who are instituting and managing the system as well as those who support them. That demonstrates depraved indifference to human life and human suffering, all for the purpose of having a system that profits those who manage and own it.

Depraved Indifference Law & Legal Definition

> To constitute depraved indifference, the defendant's conduct must be 'so wanton, so deficient in a moral sense of concern, so lacking in regard for the life or lives of others, and so blameworthy as to warrant the same criminal liability as that which the law imposes upon a person who intentionally causes a crime. Depraved indifference focuses on the risk created by the defendant's conduct, not the injuries actually resulting.[24]

In a corrupt society, a society that conducts its affairs based on a corrupting societal philosophy, the ideology of the societal philosophy is paramount even in the face of contrary facts and evidence of the failure of the ideology. In the case of the USA the corrupting societal philosophy is the ideology, that profit and the market are more important than the quality of life of the population as a whole. The ideology is that capitalism and the profit motive and individual self-interest are the best ways to conduct social, government and economic activities and human relationships. Since that societal philosophy of profit over quality of life is inherently flawed, that is, prone to causing suffering, imbalances, failure, crashes and collapse, as evinced by the market and collapse of 1929 and the crash of 2008 (and many others previous) and since it is admittedly flawed (by the head of the Federal Reserve bank[25]) and considering that it is permitted to exist even though the flaws are known, it follows that such a culture will deteriorate due to the corruption. With such a corrupting foundation that allows control by a plutocracy (wealthy minority), the dictates of the corporatists (plutocrats/power elite), will be followed by government leaders, who are beholden to and financially supported by that same power elite segment of the

---

[24] http://definitions.uslegal.com/d/depraved-indifference/
[25] http://www.pbs.org/newshour/bb/business/july-dec08/crisishearing_10-23.html
http://theflawmovie.com/synopsis.html

population (super rich / multi billionaires). That power to dictate laws in favor of themselves was demonstrated by the passage of the ACA[26], which was against the will of the majority of the population and according to the dictates and for the benefit of the power elite. Since, non-profit healthcare exists successfully in every other industrialized nation, and works better (provides better general health and longevity of the population) than the for-profit healthcare system in the USA, those who constantly use scare mongering to instill fear about public, non-profit health care are merely working in the interests of those who profit from a for-profit system.

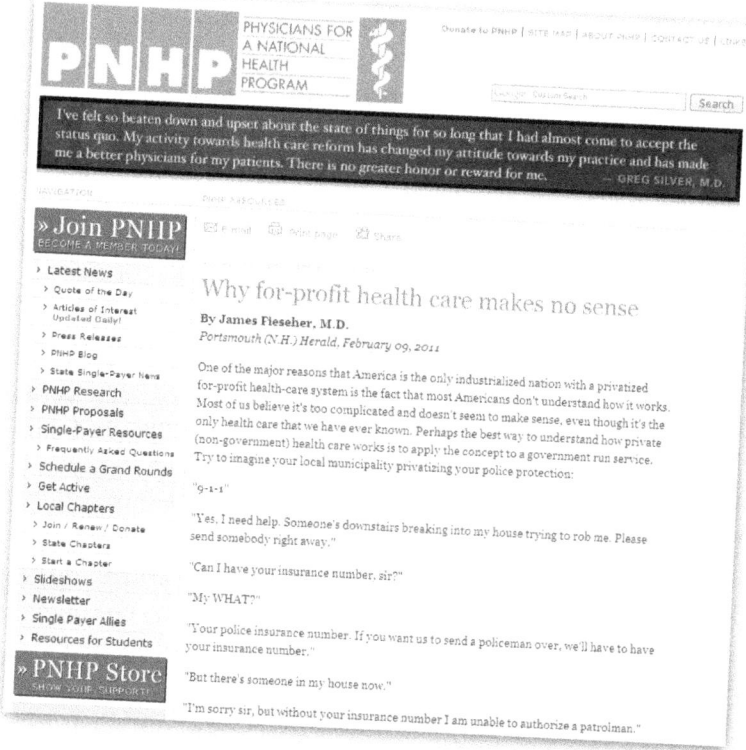

Why for-profit health care makes no sense.[27]

For-profit healthcare makes no sense from a social health standpoint and from efficiency or economic cost control standpoints but it continues because it makes financial sense for the corporate healthcare providers. As long as the government is under the control of those forces, the policies and industry procedures and laws passed by the government leaders will continue to favor those moneyed interests above the needs of the population and above common sense and even scientific facts. As long as the goal is more power and wealth going to corporations and as long as those corporations can dictate policies and

---

[26] Afordable Care Act [Obamacare]
[27] http://www.pnhp.org/news/2011/february/why-for-profit-health-care-makes-no-sense

laws by controlling presidents, congress and the legal branch through bribery (legalized campaign donations) and funding the political parties, so long the fascist imposition of policies and laws that benefit the power elite will continue.

(26) "I have not caused any one to weep."
(29) "I have not worked grief, I have not abused anyone."

-Ancient Egyptian Precepts of Maat

From a Maatian Philosophy perspective the ideal of profit in healthcare is of course immoral but from an economic standpoint it is inefficient, wasteful, corrupting and ineffective. Maat philosophy extols balance and peace and this ideal is what the Ancient Egyptian doctors sought to reestablish. They discovered that ill health is due to imbalances in life and therefore the balance needs to be reestablished in order to restore health. Imbalance comes from wrong ways of living that are stressful and in which people consume foods that are poisonous. Therefore, lifestyle, natural, herbal and dietetic remedies are important in Ancient Egyptian medicine. However, since modern culture is founded in mass consumption and processed foods, which are poisonous and inflammatory and since these natural treatments cannot be patented and used to make exorbitant profits, they are not discussed or considered by the establishment. Additionally, since the relief from illness and suffering would be more effective than prescribing medicines to alleviate symptoms, which would not resolve the issue and would not keep patients coming back constantly for more drugs and treatments, spending more money at the doctor's office, the natural modalities are neither promoted nor explored by the mainstream allopathic medical doctors and medical industrial complex. The Kemetic (Ancient Egyptian) treatments such as vegetarianism, fasting, meditation, herbs and refraining from consuming liquors would be rejected in the corrupted culture and it's for-profit meat and alcohol beverage industries. The following Ancient Egyptian proverbs give a taste of the culture of natural heath through balance and purity in service to humanity.

"The source of illness is the food you ingest; to purge the dreadful
UKHEDU
which lurks in your bowels, for three consecutive days each month purge yourself."

"Her name is Health: she is the daughter of Exercise, who begot her on Temperance. The rose blushes on her cheeks, the sweetness of the morning breathes from her lips; joy, tempered with innocence and modesty, sparkles in her eyes and from the cheerfulness of her heart she sings as she walks."

Maat Philosophy Versus Fascism and the Police State

"If you would live in harmony with yourself and the Earth you must follow the laws of the Earth. For your body is of the Earth; lest it lead your SOUL to the path of disease, death and reincarnation. The Neters of the divine will desert you, and those of evil will destroy your body and your spirit."

-Ancient Egyptian Wisdom on Health[28]

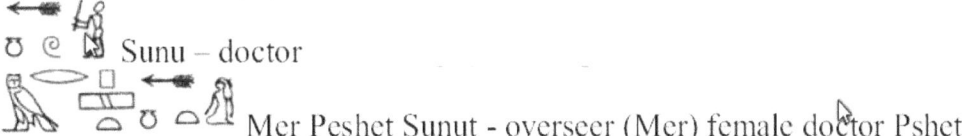

Sunu – doctor

Mer Peshet Sunut - overseer (Mer) female doctor Pshet

The Ancient Egyptian doctors served the community and were attached to the temples and their colleges where they were trained. Service to the community was not predicated upon money, therefore human beings would not be turned away and allowed to suffer or die due to inability to pay and no one would be allowed to go bankrupt or have their home foreclosed due to inability to pay a medical bill, as is allowed to occur routinely in the culture of the USA.

> (12) You will endure on earth when you do justice;
> Calm those who weep, don't oppress the widow who is grieving,
> Don't **drive out** a man from the property of his father;
>
> -Teachings to MeriKaRa

---

[28] see the book *Kemetic Diet* by Muata Ashby

Secrecy and The Loss of Constitutional Guarantees of Freedom of the Press and the Establishment of Citizens Spying on Citizens, and the American Stasi

AmeriSnitch[29]

"Community residents will be provided with information which will enable them to recognize signs of potential terrorist activity, and to know how to report that activity, making these residents a critical element in the detection, prevention, and disruption of terrorism."

Following in the footsteps of his predecessor, president Bush, who instituted "Operation TIPS", president Obama has continued and expanded the practice of recruiting citizen informants, thereby opening the door to fomenting wider suspicions, and fear among ordinary citizens and residents of the USA and as a means to introduce police into the lives of citizens. This also increases the likelihood of more police arrests, police brutality, as well as more police reinforcement and control of the population through intimidation and information gathering that can be used later (retroactively/forensically), all contributing to an atmosphere of fear and subservience to the police.

---

[29] http://progressive.org/node/1572

The Obama Administration and the Press[30]

The Stasi[31] or secret police of East Germany was considered as a prime example of a police force that ran one of the most powerful police states in Europe. One of their tactics was to coerce ordinary citizens to spy on each other and this way everyone was so paranoid that they did not know who they could trust in the society, even including their family or friends. After decrying the secrecy and excesses of the previous president, president Barak Obama claimed that he would create the most transparent administration in years. By the year 2013 it was clear that the opposite was true. Obama has attempted to prosecute more journalists than any other president in history, for revealing activities that he wants to maintain secret, which have later been found to be immoral, unethical or illegal. On the other hand, the Obama administration has leaked information favorable to its agenda. This hypocrisy and duplicity, consistent and in some ways surpassing his predecessors, demonstrates the nature of the government

---

[30] http://www.cpj.org/reports/2013/10/obama-and-the-press-us-leaks-surveillance-post-911.php
[31] *A Dictionary of World History*, Market House Books, Oxford University Press, 2000.

that has been engendered under Obama; one of secrecy, and collusion with corporations. The unprecedented report by the Committee to Protect Journalists, for the first time was directed at the USA due to the abuses of power and blatant attempts to suppress reporting on any activities of the government. Most sensitive of those activities have been those of the National Security Agency (NSA), which the revelations of whistleblower, Edward Snowden, have demonstrated to be illegal, unconstitutional and fascistic, being that as a spy agency, they have not been only spying on enemies to prevent attacks but also on ally governments as well as foreign corporations and then passing on their corporate espionage data to domestic and multinational USA corporations so that they may gain an advantage over the competition.

ASSESSMENT OF WHERE WE ARE NOW

So from an economic standpoint there are many possible triggers that can set off a renewed and worse economic downfall much worse than the market crash in 2008, including:

- *income inequality*
- *Malfeasance in Wall Street related to derivatives schemes and real estate scams*
- *Excessive personal, corporate and national debt due to constant deficit spending, subsidies and bailouts to corporations and loss of confidence in the bond market*
- *Depreciation of the US Dollar through debt, bailouts and malfeasance at the Federal Reserve*
- *Healthcare costs and poor delivery of services*
- *Loss of demand in the economy because of low wages and most income going to the top 10% of the population.*
- *Bond market failure due to loss of confidence in the US Dollar and or the US Economy,*
- *Loss of status of the US Dollar as the world reserve currency*

SUMMARY NOTE #1: The US Economy is collapsing due to a criminal banking system and bond market that steals wealth from the population and transfers it to the banks and the wealthy investors and owners of the banks. Added to this fundamental fraud is malfeasance and corruption related to mortgages and loans. The question is how slow or fast will the collapse occur and how to avoid getting caught up in the disaster. What are the reasons for the collapse of the US economy?

SUMMARY NOTE #2: The US Economy can collapse due to loss of confidence by world investors in a few ways. Most governments sell bonds to investors to fund their operations. The US Government treasury department sells bonds to investors through the Federal Reserve Bank, an institution that did not exist until 1913 and is merely a "middle man", a bank that was inserted into the process to collect interest on the bonds that would otherwise go to the Treasury (In other words, to the general population) and instead the benefit goes to the banks, which are not necessary but rather are a drain on the system for no reason other than rich wall street banks got politicians to make a law saying that they could be in the middle of the process to collect the interest. This artificial drain on the economy eventually sucks the marrow (wealth) out of the bones (structure) of the economy and leaves a jelly-fish like weak structure, a hollowed out economy that is weak and prone to collapse in which the middle class and the poor suffer most while the wealthy have already absconded with the wealth of the nation. In other words, the population becomes financially poor and then the repayments of the bonds comes into question especially if the capture by the rich of the government [crony capitalism/corporatism/fascism] prevents the government from making laws that will tax the rich in a fair way to repay the bonds.

SUMMARY NOTE #3: If those investors do not want to risk investing in those bonds the country cannot fund its government. The government can lose the confidence of investors by <u>printing too much money</u> (from money printing out of thin air and bailouts) which dilutes the value of the currency people are paid back when the bond is due. This is a kind of slow default which the US Government has been doing and is only possible because the USA has the status of world reserve currency, but even that has limits. As a response to this problem of slow default that could become a fast collapse of the bond market and with it a collapse of currencies[32], so holders of USA Bonds have been buying less bonds and more hard assets including precious metals, real estate, natural resources around the world since if the currencies collapse, the hard assets will be revalued in whatever system of currency is devised for after the collapse. In this way, holders of currencies and bonds will stand the risk of devaluation while holders of assets will have less risk.

SUMMARY NOTE #4: Since the 2008 economic crash and now with fear of the USA government slow or fast default on bond repayment, less investors bought US Bonds and that means that the value goes down due to loss of confidence. If it goes down to a certain extent it will collapse, so to avoid a collapse the Federal Reserve Bank stepped in to buy US Bonds and sustain the market, which is like you making a loan to yourself but you just create the money for the loan by just saying you have it and writing a check from an account with $.0 balance in it but the money just magically appears in to pay your bills or buy whatever you want. When the FED writes a check to pay for bonds, out of thin air, that is a loan to the US government that must be paid back with interest, so the FED creates money by creating debt, again, there is no reason to have a banking system like this with a middle man that collects interest on debt. The US Government can bring the money into existence and pay itself without the need for a middle man (banks). So there was also no need for the FED; and this is how things were before 1913. So for 100 years since 1913 the value of the dollar has declined and that is the wealth of the USA economy, the wealth of its population-multi-trillions of dollars to the power elite and impoverishment of the population over the last 100 years. Now the FED is buying most of the bonds which sustains the economy, because investors have not returned in sufficient numbers for the FED to stop. The continued buying by the FED increases the national debt and at the same time reduces the value of the US Dollar. Therefore, at some point the devaluation will reach such an extend as to cause investors to lose confidence in the US Dollar. When that happens nothing the FED could do would stop the crash of the bond market and with it the US economy. The FED also gives free money to banks to keep them from defaulting over the derivative schemes and real estate loan frauds committed by the Wall Street banks which led to the 2008 crash of the economy and still have not been resolved and actually still render the banks insolvent, even after the initial bailouts and continued free money called "Quantitative Easing". All of this bailout activity of the FED is being put on tax payers, the same consumers that can barely afford to pay their bills and sustain the consumer economy.

SUMMARY NOTE #5: The US Economy can collapse due to <u>loss of demand</u> in the economy because consumers do not make sufficient in wages or other income to support the economy as most of the income has been redirected to the rich and powerful segment of

---

[32] all currencies are related to the US Dollar through the Bretton Woods Agreement but some have been trying to go independent

the population [plutocracy]. Since the early 1980's wages have remained flat and people were accessing loans especially from inflated real estate second mortgages which after 2008 are no longer available. The USA was in the past responsible for 25% of world consumption but due to all of these issues that number is going down. This means that people would not be able to afford to buy foreign products. Investors would not want to allow the USA to keep its status as world reserve currency because 1-the USA no longer provides a good consumer market for the foreigners to sell their products to the USA consumers, the bond investors would fear that the bonds they bought will not be paid back since there would be diminishing consumer activity (economy not growing)[33] to pay them back.

SUMMARY NOTE #6: The US Economy can collapse because the policy of low interest rates[34] and the program called QE or Quantitative Easing which is a euphemism for bailout of the stock market, banks and bond market, cannot stop. When earlier this year (2013) the FED hinted at sopping, the support (slow bailout) of the markets, the bond market began to implode until the chairman of the FED, Mr. Bernanke said he would not stop. Most people are not aware that after the FED announcement, two of the biggest US bond holders, China and Japan, began aggressively selling their bond holdings so as not to get caught holding a sinking asset (US bonds) and this alone would have served as a warning to the US Government and the FED. If the selling had continued it would had precipitated a bond market collapse and with it the collapse of the USA economy. This support of the markets by the FED, with money created out of thin air, is only possible because of the size of the US economy, the integration it has with the world economy, the fact that investors around the world are for now preferring to look the other way and because of the world reserve currency status (other countries cannot print money and loan it to themselves) is diluting the value of the US Dollar and is not helping to fix the economy because there is no investor willing to take over the role of the FED as investors were previously since the US economy has not improved. The FED cannot stop the support for financial reasons but it cannot go on forever-for monetary/economic reasons. So if the FED stops the support it would precipitate a collapse of the bond market and if it continues (which it will have to do) the markets will be sustained longer but eventually will not be sustained due to loss of confidence by bond holders in the value of the US Dollar which is being devalued to buy more bonds. Investors would move away from the US markets since investors would not want to invest in a country that is dysfunctional and has declining consumer power, malfeasance in its financial sector and diminishing value in its currency. This would cause interest rates to rise and costs to go up to sustain the debt and for consumers to buy products. This latter scenario is the slow default and slow collapse scenario being attempted and being aided by foreign governments and banks.

---

[33] the only way t pay back loans in a banking system that creates money through debt is to have an expanding economy. Expanding means expansion in production and consumption. The USA produces less and is consuming less so is becoming less attractive to investors from an investment risk perspective which should mean that its bonds will cost more and that will be the death-knell to the status of the USA economy as the largest and most secure investment market.

[34] favors the wealthy and speculators in the economy and robs retail investors and savers with bank savings accounts the opportunity to gain income through saving and getting decent interest on their savings and money market accounts.

China calls for dollar to be replaced as global reserve currency[35]

SUMMARY NOTE #7: *World investors allowed the USA to have their currency to be used as the world reserve currency because the USA had the biggest, safest economy and high consumption as well as a currency that held value relative to gold, silver and thus other currencies. Today the US Dollar is off the gold standard and the Chinese economy is poised to overtake the US economy. Additionally, the US consumer is incapable of sustaining the past level of consumption due to low income and the USA banks are insolvent due to malfeasance and greed. For these reasons and others, many countries are setting up alternatives to using the US Dollar and US bond investment. The status of the US Dollar as the world reserve currency is eroding as we speak. To the extent that it is lost, to that extent the domestic US economy will suffer. If the status of the US Dollar as the world reserve currency were lost[36] the consequences would mean dramatic changes for the USA economy and no longer will the USA be able to buy goods from around the world and pay for them with magical dollars created through*

---

[35] http://www.latimes.com/business/la-fi-shutdown-china-20131015,0,260996.story
[36] *currently the US Dollar is used in 60% of world transactions*

Maat Philosophy Versus Fascism and the Police State

the magical banking system (Federal Reserve). As the usage of the US Dollar around the world continues to decline and eventually goes below 50% of world usage -due to loss of confidence in the bond market), the demand in the economy, or the dilution of the value through reckless money printing and or bailouts, etc. then the underpinnings of the USA economy and world influence will continue to fall and eventually collapse and the price of assets will rise not slowly as now but will accelerate dramatically, reaching catastrophic levels, even as those who have US Dollars will buy up assets frantically to avoid losing the value of the plunging US Dollar, further causing poverty and destitution among those who do not have large quantities of US Dollars (Middle Class and the poor). If the USA loses the status of the world reserve currency that will be the end of the capacity to sustain the consumer economy and the American Empire with its army and navy stationed around the world enforcing USA policies and hegemonic politics. However, this change may be seen by some as an opportunity to use that military to attempt to try to impose its rule as done in Iraq, Afghanistan, Africa, the South Pacific and so many other places, which could lead to war for the purpose of trying to maintain hold of the empire. Officials in the USA government and bond holders are hoping for a slow decline as opposed to a fast decline since the slow one is seen as more manageable by means of the soft and or hard police state, and the fast one could lead to riots, widespread social strife, economic collapse, wars and even revolution. Yet, one way or the other, either the fast decline or the slow decline, leads to the impoverishment of the US population and the default on USA bonds and with these the decline of the USA as a world power and empire. In other words, the power elite will seek to keep their ill gotten gains and let the country collapse rather than give back their gains, close the FED and operate the economy in a form as it existed prior to 1913.

Maat Philosophy Versus Fascism and the Police State

China's State Press Calls for 'Building a de-Americanized World'[37]

*SUMMARY NOTE #8: The US Economy can collapse due to investor fear that the US Government cannot support its economy and pay back the bonds because of the continued dysfunctionality and brinkmanship in politics whereby extremists continue to threaten to shut down government if they don't get their way makes investors believe that that might happen. This very issue has prompted China, one of the biggest US Bond holders, to call for a move away from the USA dollar which the B.R.I.C. countries (**B**razil, **R**ussia, **I**ndia and **C**hina,) are working to make happen. If the USA loses its status then this will lead to a collapse of the Bond market and the value of the US Dollar, which would be devastating for ordinary consumers but good for those who own assets denominated in US Dollars since those will go up in value but only in terms of US Dollars. Everything would cost more and this could lead to hyperinflation. If this decline occurs rapidly, this would lead to widespread poverty in the USA and the dire scenario of social unrest, protests and the hard police state and perhaps martial law. If this decline happens slowly as is being attempted, then like the proverbial boiling frog,*

---

[37] http://www.businessweek.com/articles/2013-10-14/chinas-state-press-calls-for-building-a-de-americanized-world

the US population will gradually normalize to a great depression-like reality of poverty and neo-serfdom. China has been purchasing massive amounts of gold to back its currency with something other than nothing as the US Dollar, which has been merely a "fiat"[38] currency ever since the US went off the gold standard in 1971. China is preparing to float its currency on the open market. When that occurs they will be ready to have their currency compete with the US Dollar for the status of premiere world reserve currency or at least shared status, which would diminish the US Dollar's role in the world and its value as outlined earlier.

SUMMARY NOTE #9: *When the US bond market and currency collapse accelerates what will happen to the economy? One scenario: In the short run, the immediate aftermath, the same thing that happened in 2008 but only worse, the stock market crash (including gold and silver) and collapsing real estate values, bankruptcies, higher unemployment, etc. This will be a initial deflationary period lasting for days, weeks or months. Then the dollars that bondholders have been holding and selling off along with the dollars that US consumers paid to other countries for goods (more than 8 trillion) will be used in a scramble to buy tangible assets meaning that foreigners will want to get rid of dollars and since other countries will not want them they will come to the USA to buy up real estate, businesses, the stock market and anything else that is tangible. That will raise the prices of consumer goods and tangible assets and since the local USA population will not be able to afford them anymore they will be destitute, unemployed and angry.*

FINAL NOTE: *there have been some suggestions that the obvious malfeasance of the banking system and the tilt of taxation in favor of the rich is a concerted plan to dethrone the USA as the #1 economy, as a means to topple it as the preeminent world economy. If this were true the other consequences are that world consumption and waste would be reduced and the power of the US government to make war around the world would be reduced. These could be seen as positive factors as the USA has been the purveyor of the most wars and destabilizations of other governments around the world.*

POSSIBLE ACTIONS IN RESPONSE TO THE CURRENT NEGATIVE ECONOMIC CONDITIONS

In response to these social, political and economic issues and since no one knows when the collapse may occur, because there are many factors and manipulations by central banks and governments around the world involved, some defensive actions should be taken to one's capacity in order to protect one's life and assets regardless of if the events related here were to happen or not. All should take certain precautions so that they may be able to avoid the worst effects of these probable events. The malfeasance of government leaders, on Wall Street and the USA banking system led to the crash and the continuing malfeasance and illegalities are currently leading to a greater crash and likely collapse of the economy. However, as if those risks listed above, any of which could lead to or trigger a catastrophic downfall, were not enough, the demographic change of baby boomers retiring is causing the country to enter

---

[38] A currency by government decree and not backed by anything substation. Since it has little backing it (like gold or silver), a fiat currency must have the confidence of the people who use it.

into a long-term cycle of low economic activity and higher dependency (less people producing and more people dependent) which facilitates the downfall of the economy and the social order. These issues are reasons alone to take serious actions to protect your finances such as reducing debt, purchasing tangible assets, like some gold and or foreign real estate, converting some us dollars into other currencies.[39] More serious action is to move to a region out of the big cities where life is "more" sustainable with "more" safety and food sources away from poor and angry masses. A more severe and I believe warranted action, if possible, is to leave the country or at least ready a plan to leave the USA to another country, at least temporarily, where those issues of economic collapse, the hard police state and the possible social, political and economic upheavals would be less likely or less impactful.

NEW WORLDWIDE ENVIRONMENTAL THREAT

As if the above were not enough, and in themselves cause enough for the serious considerations discussed here, a new issue has arisen that threatens the environment in a most disastrous way and will continue to threaten the world environment over the next several years (at least 4 decades). The nuclear plants at Fukushima Japan were struck in 2011 by an earthquake and tsunami which caused extensive damage. They seemed to be stabilized but the Japanese and USA governments have been lying for 2 years, after the initial disaster, which killed thousands of people and contaminated many thousands of others with nuclear radiation. They have been hiding the true level of damage and ongoing release of radiation into the environment. There is a real potential that the Pacific Ocean will be completely contaminated for hundreds of years if not thousands and there is also a possibility that the continuing disaster may not be able to be contained and the air environment is being contaminated with low level radiation as we speak. If the damaged buildings of the Fukushima nuclear power plant completely collapse or if there is a severe accident while there are ongoing efforts, trying to contain the damage, or if another major earthquake strikes the site before the nuclear fuel is removed or secured, then a more dire situation will likely occur in which the nuclear reactions will be out of control and not only will most of Japan become uninhabitable, including Tokyo, a city of over 40 million inhabitants (larger than New York and Chicago -combined), causing a severe shock to the world economy, but the entire northern hemisphere of the world will be severely contaminated with radiation, making everything north of the equator unfit for human (especially children) habitation.

---

[39] See *Malfeasance and Immorality* by Muata Ashby for more specific actoins.

Tokyo, Japan

If such a dire scenario were to come to fruition, in this case the better solution would not be just to leave the USA but to move to a country in the southern hemisphere of the world, south of the equator, as, even though connected, the air masses of the world mostly stay in their hemispheres and consequently the contamination would occur over time but would be less in the south. For this reason the northern hemisphere has always been more polluted than the south, due to the larger population and large scale industrialization and wars in Asia, Europe and North America.

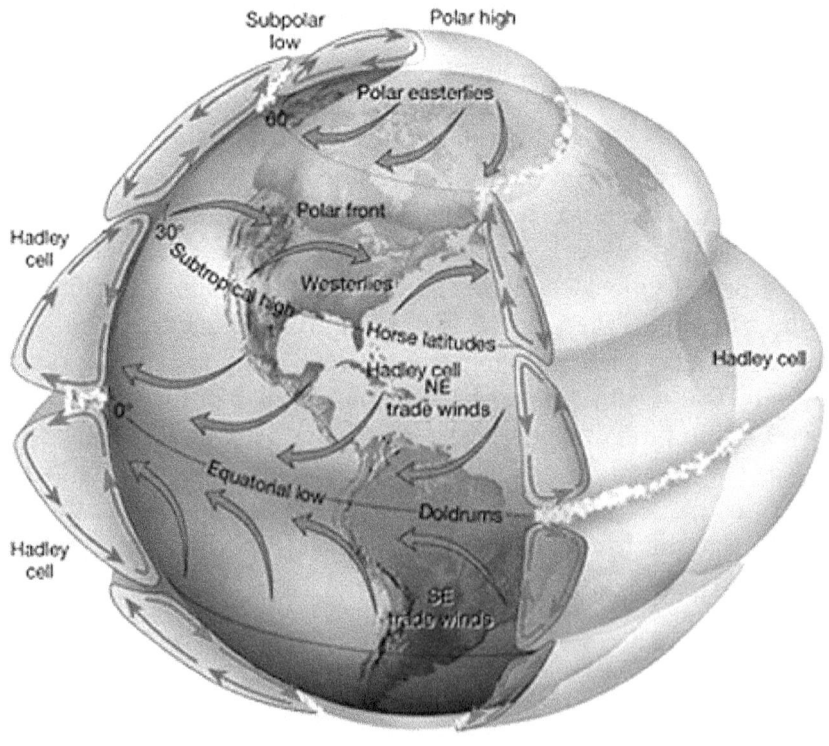

Illustration of the world wind patterns showing how the air masses of the northern and southern hemispheres move and how they meet at the equator.

Even without considering the Fukushima disaster, the Southern Hemisphere is normally significantly less polluted than the Northern Hemisphere because of lower overall population densities (a total of 10 to 12% of the human population), lower levels of industrialization, and smaller land masses. (Air currents run mostly west–east, so pollution does not easily spread north or south.)[40]/[41] A study at MIT demonstrated that an estimated 200,000 people die every year, in the USA alone (which is located in the northern hemisphere), as a result of regular pollution just in the USA. That statistic does not include radiation from the Fukushima power plant disaster. This leaves South America and Africa south of the equator and places such as southern Australia as possible sites for relocation in response to this issue.[42]

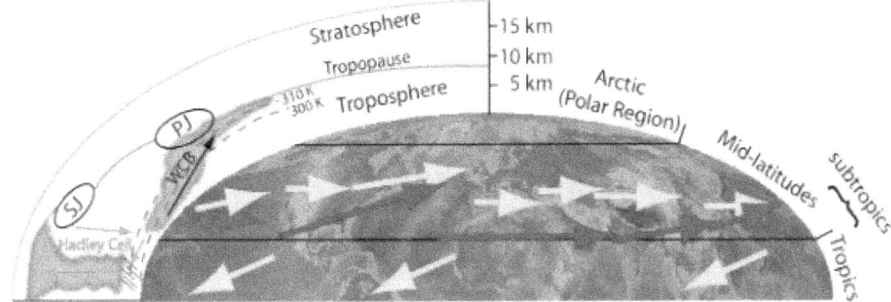

Figure 2.1. Schematic diagram showing some of the main features of the atmosphere related to the transport of air pollutants. The vertical cross section shows the average location of the tropopause (the boundary between the troposphere and stratosphere) and the polar (PJ) and subtropical (SJ) jet streams during winter. Vertical transport during winter is dominated by deep convective clouds in the tropics (the upward branch of the Hadley cell) and warm conveyor belts (WCBs) created by cyclones in the mid-latitudes. The average location of the jet stream is shown across the entire Northern Hemisphere for winter (magenta arrows) and summer (yellow arrows); locations of the tropical easterlies are also shown (light blue arrows). Also shown are the winter locations of the 300 K and 310 K potential temperature surfaces (red).

Schematic diagram showing some of the main features of the atmosphere related to the transport of air pollutants (northern Hemisphere).[43]

---

[40] https://en.wikipedia.org/wiki/Southern_Hemisphere
[41] Continental sources, transoceanic transport, and interhemispheric exchange of carbon monoxide over the Pacific http://acmg.seas.harvard.edu/publications/staudt2000/staudt2000.html
[42] **Reports of Fukushima ongoing disaster On Youtube:**
Arnold Gundersen Radiation Leaking Into Ocean Will Never Be Stopped Cost half a trillion dollar!
Atomic Chain Reaction Possible at Fukushima Unit 4 Clean Up!
Dr. Christopher Busby ~ The Coming Fukushima Global Disaster
Fukushima Ground Turning to QUICKSAND, Buildings May Topple update 8 13 13
fukushima out of control august 2013
fukushima radiation dispersal area part 1
fukushima radiation dipersal area part 2
Has the Fukushima China Syndrome begun
Record Radiation Levels At Fukushima Nuclear Plant
[43] http://www.unece.org/fileadmin/DAM/env/lrtap/Publications/11-22136-Part-D.pdf

Study: Air pollution causes 200,000 early deaths each year in the U.S.[44]

Indeed, if the Fukushima disaster worsens and the nuclear fuel rods break or come into contact or are not continuously cooled this would start a nuclear reaction that would release radiation amounts that would change the world as we now know it, not just environmentally wise but economically, socially and politically as well as medically.

---

[44] http://web.mit.edu/newsoffice/2013/study-air-pollution-causes-200000-early-deaths-each-year-in-the-us-0829.html

The Fukushima I Nuclear Power Plant after the 2011 Tōhoku earthquake and tsunami. Three of the reactors at Fukushima Daiichi overheated, causing meltdowns that eventually led to explosions, which released large amounts of radioactive material into the air.[45]

Of particular concern is reactor #4 because it has a pool of water several stories up in the air that contains nuclear fuel. The building was damaged due to an earthquake, leaving it and much of the country 29 inches lower than where it was previously; The tsunami also caused damage but the efforts to stop the underground water flow entering the site and flowing out and contamination of the ocean and the efforts to cool the other reactors with water as well as the effect of typhoon storms has caused the site to become saturated with water and the building to list on its side. So if the fuel is not successfully removed and if the building collapses, that could start an uncontrolled nuclear reaction that could contaminate the entire world but the northern hemisphere of the world, the area north of the equator, would be contaminated first and most severely.

---

[45] Martin Fackler (June 1, 2011). "Report Finds Japan Underestimated Tsunami Danger". *New York Times*.

Maat Philosophy Versus Fascism and the Police State

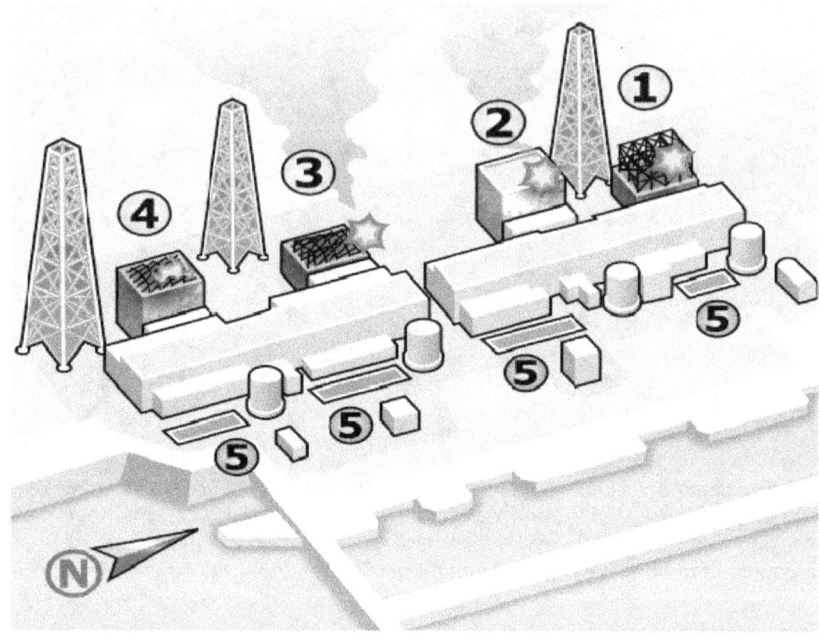

☢ Illustration of post-accident state of 1–4 reactors, all but 2 display obvious damage to secondary containment

The issues discussed in this volume may seem hard to believe and face or difficult to understand, or hard to grasp, or too dire or unbelievable, however, we can recall that the 2008 crash was unbelievable and a surprise to most economists and financial analysts just as the events at Fukushima were not imagined by the nuclear physicists. Now, the possible disasters discussed here are being seriously considered by creditable professionals, scientists, engineers and professors in the sciences and it behooves all to do the same now, consider these issues presently and not later. The potential disaster is real and the best course of action is to do your own research to verify the issues and then decide if you want to take action in response to them. It is prudent, at least, to prepare for any eventuality. One prudent suggestion is that you look into these matters and protect your finances and livelihood as soon as possible. The best plan of action would be in creating a common group plan, with family, friends or likeminded individuals to cooperate in order to pool resources and have a backup plan of action to cope with the possible situations that may arise. Save that, then the next best thing is to create and individual plan. No one knows for sure when such eventualities might occur but it is prudent to assess their likelihood and be prepared for any such eventualities which can occur at any time. The footnotes contain resources to start researching these issues. Finally, Helen Caldicott, MD.,[46] a prominent researcher of the problems of nuclear power and the dire

---

[46] http://www.helencaldicott.com/about/
https://www.youtube.com/watch?v=Hk0xHuhDP-0&noredirect=1

situation humanity faces due to the Fukushima disaster has stated publically that if the situation at Fukushima deteriorates as described earlier, she will be evacuating her family from the USA. This author has spoken to another nuclear scientist in Canada who said that when the disaster first occurred he had his family packed and ready to go at a moment's notice and will leave the northern hemisphere if the situation becomes critical.

« Video shows dark smoke from Fukushima Daiichi blowing over Japan on Mar. 15, 2011 after explosion at Reactor No. 3

Japan Gov't Study: Fukushima contamination in ocean reached Alaska in under a month (MAP) »

Caldicott: If Spent Fuel Pool No. 4 collapses I am evacuating my family from Boston (VIDEO)

Title: Dr. Helen Caldicott: What We Learned From Fukushima
Source: PirateTV Seattle Date: April 2, 2012[47]

Caldicott... received her medical degree in 1961 from the University of Adelaide Medical School. In 1977 she joined the staff of the Children's Hospital Medical Center in Boston, and taught pediatrics at the Harvard Medical School from 1977 to 1978. [...]

---

[47] http://enenews.com/caldicott-if-spent-fuel-pool-no-4-collapses-i-am-evacuating-my-family-from-boston-to-southern-hemisphere-video
https://archive.org/details/scm-30754-drhelencaldicottwhatwelearnedf

Maat Philosophy Versus Fascism and the Police State

During her time in the United States from 1977 to 1986, Caldicott was involved with Physicians for Social Responsibility (founded originally in 1961), an organization of 23,000 doctors committed to educating others on the dangers of nuclear energy. She also **worked** abroad **to establish** similar groups [...] One such international group (**International Physicians for the Prevention of Nuclear War**) was **awarded the Nobel Peace Prize** in 1985 [...]

David Suzuki has issued a scary warning about Japan's Fukushima nuclear plant,[48] saying that if it falls in a future earthquake, it's "bye bye Japan" and the entire west coast of North America should be evacuated.

The "Nature of Things" host made the comments in a talk posted to YouTube after he joined Dr. David Schindler for "Letting in the Light," a symposium on water ecology held at the University of Alberta on Oct. 30 and 31.

An excerpt of the talk shows Suzuki outlining a frightening scenario that would result from the destruction of the nuclear plant.

"Fukushima is the most terrifying situation I can imagine," he said.

---

[48] http://www.huffingtonpost.ca/2013/11/04/david-suzuki-fukushima-warning_n_4213061.html
http://www.youtube.com/watch?v=iTqzqoKMLEg&noredirect=1

Maat Philosophy Versus Fascism and the Police State

"Three out of the four plants were destroyed in the earthquake and in the tsunami. The fourth one has been so badly damaged that the fear is, if there's another earthquake of a seven or above that, that building will go and then all hell breaks loose.

"And the probability of a seven or above earthquake in the next three years is over 95 per cent."

-David Susuki

David Takayoshi Suzuki, CC OBC (born March 24, 1936) is a Japanese Canadian academic, science broadcaster and environmental activist. Suzuki earned a PhD in zoology from the University of Chicago in 1961, and was a professor in the genetics department at the University of British Columbia from 1963 until his retirement in 2001. Since the mid-1970s, Suzuki has been known for his TV and radio series and books about nature and the environment. He is best known as host of the popular and long-running CBC Television science magazine, *The Nature of Things*, seen in over forty nations. He is also well known for criticizing governments for their lack of action to protect the environment.[49]

---

[49] http://en.wikipedia.org/wiki/David_Suzuki

Chapter 1: Introduction to Maat Philosophy

Before proceeding we will go through a brief introduction to Maat philosophy so as to have a starting basis for the discussion. Then as we look at fascism and the police state we will see how the teachings of Maat look at fascism and police state policies.

Who is Maat? Maat as a Secular and Non-Secular Philosophy

Mythologically, MAAT is an Ancient Egyptian Goddess of justice, order and truth and the daughter of the God *Ra, the Creator,* and she was with him on His celestial barque when he first emerged from the primeval waters along with His company of gods and goddesses. She is the prototype of the Greek goddess of divine order, law and custom, *Themis.* She is also known as the *eye of Ra, lady of heaven, queen of the earth, mistress of the Netherworld and the lady of the gods and goddesses.* MAAT also has a dual form or *MAATI.* In her *capacity* of God(dess), MAAT is *Shez MAAT* which means *ceaseless-ness and regularity* of the course of the sun (i.e. the universe). In the form of MAATI, she represents the South and the North which symbolize Upper and Lower Egypt as well as the Higher and Lower Self. MAAT is the personification of justice and righteousness upon which God has created the universe and MAAT is also the essence of God and creation. Therefore, it is MAAT who judges the soul when it arrives in the judgment hall of MAAT. The heart of the deceased is judged against the feather of Maat to determine how virtuous it is. Sometimes MAAT herself becomes the scales upon which the heart of the initiate is judged. MAAT judges the heart (unconscious mind) of the initiate in an attempt to determine to what extent the heart has lived in accordance with MAAT or truth, correctness, reality, genuineness, uprightness, righteousness, justice, steadfastness and the unalterable nature of creation.

The Ancient Egyptian Goddess MAAT, holds a papyrus reed scepter. Papyrus is the ancient medium for writing upon which the teachings of wisdom are recorded. She is the symbolic embodiment of world order, justice, righteousness, correctness, harmony and peace. She is also known by her headdress composed of a feather of truth. Her name is synonymous with mother since the syllable *"ma"* is a universal hekau or mantram signifying mother in many countries of the world. For example, mother in English, madre in Spanish, mata in Hindi all convey the same meaning. All of these arise from the root *Ma.* Thus, she is also known as *Ma* or *Maa* or the universal mother, the cosmic mother. She is a form of the Goddess Isis, *Aset,* who represents wisdom and spiritual awakening.

This detail scene, from the Papyrus of Hunefer (ca. 1275 BCE), shows the scribe Hunefer's heart being weighed on the scale of Maat against the feather of truth, by the jackal-headed Anubis. The ibis-headed Thoth, scribe of the gods, records the result. If his heart equals exactly the weight of the feather, Hunefer is allowed to pass into the afterlife. If not, he is eaten by the waiting chimeric devouring creature Ammit composed of the deadly crocodile, lion, and hippopotamus. Vignettes such as these were a common illustration in Egyptian books of the dead.

When Ra emerged in his Barque for the first time and creation came into being, he was standing on the pedestal of Maat. Thus the Creator, Ra, lives by Maat and has established Creation on Maat. Who is Maat? Maat represents the very order which constitutes creation. Therefore, it is said that Ra created the universe by putting Maat in the place of chaos. So creation itself is Maat. Creation without order is chaos. Maat is a profound teaching in reference to the nature of creation and the manner in which human conduct should be cultivated. It refers to a deep understanding of Divinity and the manner in which virtuous qualities can be developed in the human heart so as to come closer to the Divine.

Maat is a philosophy, a spiritual symbol as well as a cosmic energy or force which pervades the entire universe. She is the symbolic embodiment of world order, justice, righteousness, correctness, harmony and peace. She is also known by her headdress composed of a feather of truth. She is a form of the Goddess Isis, who represents wisdom and spiritual awakening through balance and equanimity.

In ancient Egypt, the judges and all those connected with the judicial system were initiated into the teachings of MAAT. Thus, those who would be in the position to discharge the laws and regulations of society were well trained in the ethical and spiritual-mystical values of life (introduced in this volume), fairness, justice and the responsibility to serve society in order to promote harmony in society and the possibility for spiritual development in an atmosphere of freedom and peace. For only when there is justice and fairness in society can there be an abiding harmony and peace. Harmony and peace are necessary for the pursuit of true happiness and inner fulfillment in life.

Along with her associates, the divinities *Shai*, *Rennenet* and *Meskhenet*, Maat encompass the teachings of Karma and Reincarnation or the destiny of every individual based on past actions, thoughts and feelings (aryu). Thus, they have an important role to play in the Judgment scene of the Ancient Egyptian Book of Coming Forth By Day. Understanding their principles leads the aspirant to become free of the cycle of reincarnation and human suffering and to discover supreme bliss and immortality.

MAAT signifies *that which is straight*. Two of the symbols of MAAT are the ostrich feather (𓆄) and the pedestal (𓊵) upon which God stands. The Supreme Being, in the form of the God *Ptah*, is often depicted standing on the pedestal.

MAAT is the daughter of Ra, the high God, thus in a hymn to Ra we find:
The land of Manu (the West) *receives thee with satisfaction, and the goddess MAAT embraces thee both at morn and at eve... the*

god Djehuty and the goddess MAAT have written down thy daily course for thee every day...

Another Hymn in the Papyrus of Qenna provides deeper insight into MAAT.

Qenna says:
> *I have come to thee, O Lord of the Gods, Temu-Heru-khuti, whom MAAT directeth... Amen-Ra rests upon MAAT... Ra lives by MAAT... Osiris carries along the earth in His train by MAAT...*

MAAT is the daughter of *Ra*, and she was with him on His celestial barque when he first emerged from the primeval waters along with His Company of gods and goddesses. She is also known as the *eye of Ra, lady of heaven, queen of the earth, mistress of the Netherworld and the lady of the gods and goddesses*. MAAT also has a dual form or *MAATI*. In her *capacity* of God, MAAT is *Shez MAAT* which means *ceaseless-ness and regularity* of the course of the sun (i.e. the universe). In the form of MAATI, she represents the South and the North which symbolize Upper and Lower Egypt as well as the Higher and Lower Self. MAAT is the personification of justice and righteousness upon which God has created the universe and MAAT is also the essence of God and creation. Therefore, it is MAAT who judges the soul when it arrives in the judgment hall of MAAT. Sometimes MAAT herself becomes the scales upon which the heart of the initiate is judged. MAAT judges the heart (unconscious mind) of the initiate in an attempt to determine to what extent the heart has lived in accordance with MAAT or truth, correctness, reality, genuineness, uprightness, righteousness, justice, steadfastness and the unalterable nature of creation.

WHAT IS TRUE VIRTUE?

Maat represents living by principles of virtue, order and truth. That virtue is contained in the hieroglyphic writing, *medtu neter* and is to be practiced in life. The injunctions of Maat are primarily contained in the Ancient Egyptian Book of Coming Forth By Day, the Ancient Egyptian Wisdom Texts and Ancient Egyptian Proverbial Wisdom. Maat has two important aspects, one is secular, relating to the order and virtue of society; and the other is noon-secular, relating to order and harmony with spiritual life leading to spiritual enlightenment.. In order to understand what true virtue is and all of the elements that drive a human being and cause him or her to be the way he or she is, we must begin by understanding the teachings of Meskhenet and uhemankh (karma and reincarnation). The human being is not simply a mind and body which will someday cease to exist. In fact, every human being's mind and body are in reality emanations or expressions of their eternal soul. The mind and body are referred to as the ego-personality, and it is this ego-personality which is temporal and mortal. The soul is immortal and perfect while the ego-personality is subject to error, confusion and the consequences of these. The soul that is caught up in the relative reality of the ego-personality will suffer along with it. The soul that has discovered its higher nature will be free of that suffering and the consequences of worldly error and death. This is called *nehast* or *Enlightenment*. Living in accordance with Maat Philosophy is a foundation and framework for a life that leads to spiritual enlightenment. If a human being is aware of the deeper soul-reality, this state of being is known as the state of *Enlightenment*. However, if a human being does not have knowledge and experience of their Higher Self, then they exist in a condition of ignorance which will lead to sinful behavior, pain and sorrow in life.

The ego-personality is subject to the forces of time and space and will suffer the consequences of its actions. This is the basis for the teaching of Karma. When the ego-personality dies, the soul moves on. If the human being has discovered his/her Higher Self (purified the heart (mind and body)), then the soul moves forward to unite with the supreme Self (God). If the ego in a person is fettered by ignorance, then the soul moves in an astral plane until it finds another ego-personality about to be born again in the world of time and space so that it may have an opportunity to have experiences that will lead it to discover its higher nature. This is the basis for the teaching of reincarnation.

> *"He delivers whom he pleases, even from the Duat (netherworld)."*
> *"He saves a man or woman from what is*
> *His lot at the dictates of their heart."*

The utterances above are directly referring to what the Ancient Egyptians called *aryu, presided over by Meskhenet* and a concept similar to what the East Indians call "karma." Many people believe that karma is equal to fate or destiny; however, this interpretation could not be further from the original understanding of the ancient Sages. The etymology of the word, karma, comes from the Sanskrit "karman" which means deed or action. In Yoga philosophy, karma also refers to one's actions and these same actions lead to certain experiences and consequences. In ancient Egyptian philosophy, the word Meskhenet comes from the goddess who goes by the same name. She presides over the birth circumstances and life experiences of every individual. She is the one who carries out the decree which has been ordained by Djehuty after the judgment of the heart in the hall of MAAT. It is Djehuty who records the deeds (actions) or karmas of every individual and then decrees what the Shai and Rennenet which are fitting for that particular individual. Then with the help of Shai and Rennenet, Meskhenet causes the individual to experience the proper circumstances in a future birth or on higher planes of existence, based on their previous deeds and the sum total of their wisdom gained through many lifetimes of experiences of many deeds.

The ancient Egyptian hieroglyphic symbol of the heart is a heart shaped vase, ☥. A vase is a container which may be used for water, beer, wine, milk, etc. Likewise, the human heart is seen as a vessel which contains thoughts, feelings, desires and unconscious memories. In mystical terms, the heart is a metaphor of the human mind including the conscious, subconscious and unconscious levels. The mind is the reservoir of all of your ideas, convictions and feelings. Therefore, just as these factors direct the path of your life, so too they are the elements which are judged in the Hall of Maati by the two Maati goddesses, Aset (Isis) and Nebethet (Nephthys), along with Osiris. The heart then, contains the sum total of your experiences, actions and aspirations, your conscience or karma, and these are judged in the balance against the feather of Maat.

The Ancient Egyptian word "Ari" means "actions". It is akin to the Indian philosophy called Karma. Karma should be thought of as the total effect of a person's actions and conduct during the successive phases of His/her existence. But how does this effect operate? How do the past actions affect the present and the future? Your experiences from the present life or from previous lifetimes cause unconscious impressions which stay with the Soul even after death. These unconscious impressions are what constitute the emerging thoughts, desires, and aspirations of every individual. These impressions are not exactly like memories; however, they work like impressions of memories. For example, if you had a fear experience in a previous lifetime or the childhood of your present lifetime, you may not remember the event that caused the fear, but you may experience certain phobias when you come into contact with certain objects or certain people. These feelings are caused by the unconscious impressions which are coming up to the surface of the conscious mind. It is this conglomerate of unconscious impressions which are "judged" in the Hall of MAAT and which determine where the soul will go to next in the spiritual journey toward evolution or devolution, also known as the cycle of birth and death or reincarnation, as well as the experiences of heaven or hell. The following segment from the ancient Egyptian "Instruction to Mer-ka-Ra" explains this point.

> *"You know that they are not merciful on the day when they judge the miserable one..... Do not count on the passage of the years; they consider a lifetime as but an hour. After death man remains in existence and His acts accumulate beside him. Life in the other world is eternal, but he who arrives without sin before the Judge*

of the Dead, he will be there as a Neter[50] and he will walk freely as do the masters of eternity."

The reference above to "His acts accumulate beside him" alludes to the unconscious impressions which are formed as a result of one's actions while still alive. These impressions can be either positive or negative. Positive impressions are developed through positive actions by living a life of righteousness (MAAT) and virtue. This implies living according to the precepts of mystical wisdom or being a follower of Horus (*Shemsu Hor*) and Isis. These actions draw one closer to harmony and peace, thus paving the way to discovering the Self within. The negative impressions are developed through sinful actions. They are related to mental agitation, disharmony and restlessness. This implies acts based on anger, fear, desire, greed, depression, gloom, etc. These actions draw one into the outer world of human desires. They distract the mind and do not allow the intellect and heart wisdom (*Saa*) to function. Thus, existence at this level is closer to an animal, being based on animal instincts and desires of the body (selfishness), rather than to a spiritually mature human being, being based on reason, selflessness, compassion, etc.

(Purification of the heart)

How then is it possible to eradicate negative karmic impressions and to develop positive ones? The answer lies in your understanding of the wisdom teachings and your practice of them. When you study the teachings and live according to them, that is, living a life of ethical conscience, balance and harmony with nature and human affairs, the mind undergoes a transformation at all levels. This transformation is the "purification of heart" so often spoken about throughout the *Egyptian Book of Coming Forth By Day*. It signifies an eradication of negative impressions, which renders the mind pure and subtle. When the mind is rendered subtle, then spiritual realization is possible. This discipline of purifying the heart by living according to the teachings is known as the Yoga of Action or MAAT.

The philosophy of MAAT is a profound teaching which encompasses the fabric of creation as well as a highly effective system of spiritual discipline. In creation stories, God (Neter Neteru, Supreme Being) is said to have established creation upon MAAT. Consequently it follows that MAAT is the orderly flow of energy which maintains the universe. Further, MAAT is the regularity which governs the massive planetary and solar systems as well as the growth of a blade of grass and a human cell. This natural process represents the flow of creation

---

[50] A divinity

wherein there is constant movement and a balancing of opposites (up-down, hot-cold, here-there, you-me, etc.).

Most people act out of the different psychological, physiological and or environmental forces which are affecting then and coursing through them at the time. These actions may be based on recollections of past events and feelings and or present thoughts and feelings, such as: hunger, lust, fear, hatred, anger, elation, etc. The ignorant, unethical and egoistic people have little or no control over these because they have not understood that their true essence is in reality separate from their thoughts and emotions. They have *identified* with their thoughts and therefore are led to the consequences of those thoughts and the deeds they engender. You, as an informed reader, having developed a higher level of spiritual sensitivity, are now aware that you have a choice in the thoughts you think and the actions you perform. You can choose whether to act in ways that are in harmony with MAAT or those that are disharmonious. You have now studied the words of wisdom and must now look beyond the level of egoistic and ignorant relation to the world and to humanity to a higher order of respect for and in harmony with the order of Creation which is a foundation for self-improvement and mastery as well as human progress.

In ordinary human life, those who have not achieved the state of Enlightenment (the masses in society at large) perceive nature as a conglomeration of forces which are unpredictable and in need of control. However, as spiritual sensitivity matures, the aspirant realizes that what once appeared to be chaotic is in reality the Divine Plan of the Supreme Being in the process of unfolding. When this state of consciousness is attained, the aspirant realizes that there is an underlying order in nature which can only be perceived with spiritual eyes born of ethical conscience.

The various injunctions of MAAT are for promoting the development of ethical conscience in individual human beings and for the purpose of keeping order in society among ordinary people, people without psychological maturity and, or spiritual sensitivity, meaning that they lack an awareness of spiritual principles and moral - ethical development. Also, the teachings of Maat provide insight into the order of creation and a pathway or spiritual discipline, which when followed, will lead the aspirant to come into harmony with the cosmic order. When the individual attunes his or her own sense of order and balance with the cosmic order, a spontaneous harmony occurs between the individual and the cosmos. Thus, the principles of MAAT, rather than being a blind set of moral rules which we must strive to follow for their own sake, actually are discovered to have a deeper underlying source and become a part of one's inner character. From there, the ethically conscious person becomes a pillar of society and a guide for humanity.

This means that through the deeper understanding of cosmic order and by the practice of living in harmony with that order, the individual will lead him or herself to mental and spiritual peace and harmony. It is this peace and harmony which allows the lake of the mind to become a clear mirror in which the individual soul is able to realize its oneness with the Universal Soul.

THE SOURCE OF ETHICS IN MAAT PHILOSOPHY

(A)

From a philosophical perspective why should we consider Maat philosophy as correct and worthy to be followed and practiced and concluding that the objectivist, sociopathic philosophy is incorrect, anti-human and not worthy to be followed? The Ancient Egyptian Creation myth states that Maat sits in the bow of the boat of Ra which emerged from the primeval unformed waters. (image A) When the boat sails on the ocean it causes a wake and that wake is infused with Maat that is order and form. That order and form constitute Creation. The principle that forces eventual dissolution of that order is called Apep. Apep is a divinity, pictured as a massive serpent that metaphorically fights against the boat of Ra and tries to stop its movements sustaining Creation (image B), that has been ordered by Maat. Therefore, Creation is predicated upon order and that means that everything in Creation that exists with form and or is alive, exists in that form because of Maat, that is to say, the order in Creation that allows those forms and living beings to exist as such.

(B)

With the understanding of the aforesaid wisdom of Maat and Apep, what is orderly is desirable and true; what is in harmony with order and truth in life is also desirable but also beneficial because those ideals and actions produce quality, longevity and prosperity as well as peace and enlightenment for the individual and for society. Therefore, the thoughts, actions, ideals and policies that are in harmony with that natural order (Maat infused in Creation) are beneficial for life and for the capacity to promote peace in the world as well as to discover the meaning of life. In terms of economics and social order what is most beneficial and orderly is group cooperation and not, objectivism, libertarianism or abnormal individualism and reliance on personal responsibility, while relieving society (including those most able and wealthy in the society) of responsibility for the other individuals in society (self-centered egoism that clouds the intellect and ethical conscience). Indeed, socialism is closer to the concept of Ancient Egyptian economics though it should not be confused with the same. Capitalism, market economy, libertarian government and "laissez-faire" economics facilitate selfishness, narcissism, sociopathy and criminality and are therefore contradictory to good order and ethical conscience as well as the rule of law.

MAAT AS THE SPIRITUAL PATH OF RIGHTEOUS ACTION

MAAT is similar to the Chinese concept of the *Tao* or *"The Way"* of nature. This *"Way"* of nature, from the *Tao-te-Ching*, the main text of Taoism, represents the harmony of human and Divine (universal) consciousness. Also, MAAT may be likened with the Indian idea of *Dharma* or the ethical values of life and the teachings related to *Karma Yoga,* the yogic spiritual discipline which emphasizes selfless service and the attitude that actions are being performed by God who is working through you, in the form of Maat, instead of your personal ego-self. God is working through you to serve humanity, which is also essentially God. Similarly, the practice of living by Maat means acting in a way that is in harmony with the nature of the body and the nature of the world and by extension, all Creation. In so doing that harmony opens the door to the vast wisdom and connection to the world and the universe, leading to unification with it and in so doing also with God who is manifesting as nature and its orderly processes.

Above: Ra, the father of Maat, traverses in his boat and she sits in the bow of the boat making order so that the boat may sail on orderly waters instead of chaotic waters. This symbolizes the need to have order before spirituality can unfold.

Below: (A and D) The Maati goddesses.
(B) Maat standing
(C) Maat sitting with eyes closed

In Maat philosophy one is admonished to keep company with the wise. This is known as *khnumt nefer* or good association. Good association allows the virtuous qualities of Maat to develop in the human personality. The Buddhist aspirant is admonished to take refuge in the *Buddha* (one's innate *Buddha Consciousness*), the *Dharma*, and the *Sanga* (company of enlightened personalities). In Hindu-Vedanta philosophy the concept is called *satsanga*. The following statement from chapter 9 of the Bhagavad Gita shows how Lord Krishna admonished his followers to seek sanctuary in him.

> 32. O Arjuna, those who take refuge in Me whether men born in a lowly class, or women, or Vaishyas, or Shudras, even they are

Maat Philosophy Versus Fascism and the Police State

sure to attain the highest goal.

Jesus also exhorted his followers to bring him their troubles "and He will give them rest". Dharma is understood as the spiritual discipline based on righteousness, order and truth which sustains the universe. In the same way, the ancient Egyptian Initiate was to lean upon MAAT in order to purify his or her heart so as to uncover the virtuous character which leads to Divine awareness. From the Temple of Isis in Ancient Egypt we find the same admonishment, to seek out and stay near the Goddess.

> "The end and aim of all these toils and labors is the attainment of the knowledge of the First and Chief Being (11), who alone is the object of the understanding of the mind; and this knowledge the goddess invites us to seek after, as being near and dwelling continually (12) with her."
>
> - Teachings from the Ancient Egyptian Temple of Isis

The idea of taking refuge in the divinity, is primarily accomplished by taking recourse to devotion to the Divine and diligence in the practice of ethical conscience as related in the mythic teaching of the divinity. This is the common thread of the aforementioned religions and it is the foundation of Maat philosophy. It is important here to gain a deeper understanding of what is meant by *action*. In primeval times, before creation, the primordial ocean existed in complete peace and rest. When that ocean was agitated with the first thought by God, the first *act* was performed, which gave rise to the opposites of creation and all forms of duality. This duality allows human beings to have different visions of life but in reality the duality is two sides of the same single reality. Through the subsequent *acts of mind* or *efforts of divine thought,* creation unfolded in the form of the various gods and goddesses who form the Ancient Egyptian "companies of Gods and Goddesses" and at the same time they also manifest as the multiplicity of forms in Creation. They represent the qualities of nature (hot-cold, wet-dry, etc.) in the form of pairs of opposites. When the first primeval thought emerged from the primeval ocean of pure potentiality, immediately there was something other than the single primordial essence. Now there is a being who is looking and perceiving the rest of the primordial essence. This is the origin of duality in the world of time and space and the triad of human consciousness. Instead of there being one entity, there appear to be two, self and other. The perception instruments of the personality, the mind and senses, is the third factor which comprises the triad. Therefore, while you consider yourself to be an individual, you are in reality one element in a triad which all together comprises the content of your human experiences. There is a perceiver (the real you), that which is being perceived (the object) and the act of perception itself (through the mind and senses).

With this first primordial act, God set into motion events which operate according to regular and ceaseless motion or action (movement of the boat of Ra with Maat). This is the foundation upon which the universe is created and it emerges from the mind of God. Therefore, if one is able to think and act according to the way in which God thinks and acts, then there will be oneness with God. Human beings are like sparks of divine consciousness, and as such, are endowed with free will to act in any given way. This free will, when dictated by the egoism of the individual mind, causes individual human beings to feel separate from God. This delusion of the mind leads it to develop ideas related to its own feelings and desires. These egoistic feelings and desires lead to the performance of egoistic acts in an effort to satisfy those perceived needs and desires. This pursuit of fulfillment of desires in the relative world of the mind and senses leads the soul to experience pain, sorrow and frustration, because the fulfillment of desires can never be 100% satisfied in an ever changing unpredictable and fleeting world. Because of that underlying factor of human existence, the incapacity to fulfill egoistic desires, frustration leads to endlessly pursuing more futile actions in search of fulfillment.

The fleeting feelings which most people have associated with happiness and passion are only ephemeral glimpses of the true happiness and peace which can be experienced if the source of true fulfillment within were to be discovered. MAAT shows a way out of the pain and sorrow of human existence and leads you to discover Osiris within you, the source of eternal bliss and supreme peace. If you choose to act according to your own will without ethical conscience (egoism), then you will be in contradiction with MAAT. This means that you are contradicting your own conscience, creating negative impressions which will become lodged in the heart (unconscious mind) and will cause continuous mental agitation while you are alive and hellish experiences for yourself after death. The negative impressions rise up at given times in the form of uncontrolled desires, cravings, unrest, and the other forms of self-torment with which human life abounds.

It is important to understand that when the soul is attuned to a physical body, mind and senses, the experiences occur through these. Thus, the experiences of pleasure and pain are regulated by how much the body, mind and senses can take. If there is too much pain the body faints. When there is too much pleasure the mind and senses become weakened and the personality swoons into unconsciousness or sleep. If there is too much pleasure, there develops elation and the soul is carried away with the illusion of pleasure, which creates a longing and craving for more and more in an endless search for fulfillment.

However, after death, there is no safety valve as it were. Under these conditions the soul will have the possibility of experiencing boundless amounts of pleasure or pain according to its karmic basis. This is what is called heaven and hell, respectively. Therefore, if you have lived a balanced life (MAAT), then you will not have the possibility of experiencing heaven or hell. Rather, you will retain presence of mind and will not fall into the delusion of ignorance. Therefore, the rewards of developing a balanced mind during life continue after death. This mental equanimity allows you to see the difference between the truth and the illusions of the mind and senses, in life as well as in death.

Thus, if you choose to act in accordance with MAAT, you will be in a position to transcend the egoistic illusions of the mind and thereby become free from the vicious cycle of actions which keep the mind tied to its illusory feelings and desires. When the mind is freed from the "vicious cycle", the soul's bondage to the world of time and space is dissolved because it is not being controlled by the mind but has become the controller of the mind. When the practice of MAAT is perfected, the mind becomes calm. When this occurs, the ocean of consciousness which was buffeted by the stormy winds of thoughts, anxieties, worries and desires, becomes calm. This calmness allows the soul to cease its identification with the thoughts of the mind and to behold its true nature as a separate entity from the mind, senses, feelings and thoughts of the ego-self. The soul is now free to expand its vision beyond the constrictive pettiness of human desires and mental agitation, in order to behold the expansion of the inner Self.

Actions are the basis upon which the Cosmic Plan of creation unfolds for individuals as well as for societies. In human life, it is the present action which leads to the results that follow at some point in the future, in this life or in another lifetime. Therefore, if you are in a prosperous situation today or an adverse one, it is because of actions you performed and or experienced in the past and the sum total of your soul memory thoughts and feelings about those. Thus, both situations, good or bad, should be endured with a sense of personal responsibility and equanimity of mind (MAAT). From a transcendental point of view, the Soul looks at all situations equally. This is because the Soul knows itself to be immortal, eternal, and untouched by the events of human existence which it has witnessed for countless lifetimes. It is the ego, which is transient, which looks on life situations as pressing and real and therefore either tries to hold onto situations which it considers to be "good" or to get away from or eradicate situations which it considers to be "bad". This endless back and forth agitates the mind and is the source of all delusions of life and the conflicts and sufferings those delusions lead to. All situations, whether they are considered to be good or bad by the ego, will eventually pass on, so we should try to view them as clouds in the sky, which inevitably pass on, no matter how terrible or how wonderful they may seem to be. When life is lived in this manner, the mind develops a stream of peace which rises above elation and depression, prosperity and adversity. By looking at situations with equal vision and doing your best regardless of the circumstances, you are able to discover an unalterable balance within yourself. This is MAAT, the underlying order and truth behind the apparent chaos and disorder in the phenomenal world. In doing this, you are able to attune your mind to the cosmic mind of the innermost Self which exists at that transcendental level of peace all the time.

This means that if you are, indeed the Universal Self, one with God, deep down, and if you have come to your current situation in life of bondage to the world of time and space due to your own state of mental ignorance, then it follows that if you undertake certain disciplines of knowledge (studying the teachings) and daily practice (following the teachings), those same actions will lead you to liberation from the state of bondage. Ignorance of your true Self is the root cause of your bondage to the karmic cycle of life-death-reincarnation-life-death-reincarnation, etc.

Actions must be performed by everyone. Even breathing is an action. Therefore, nobody can escape actions. No one can say: "I will go far away from civilization and escape all actions and then my actions will not lead me to a state of ignorance about my true Self". This form of thinking is a fallacy because, as just discussed, breathing, eating, drinking, sleeping, sitting, and walking are all actions. The process of liberation requires more than just removing yourself from the field of physical actions; what is necessary is to discover what you are beyond the actions you are experiencing. . You could go to a quiet cave, temple or church and you would still be plagued by the unruly thoughts of the mind which cause distraction from the Self. Thoughts are subtle forms of actions. Therefore, an action performed in thought can be equally significant and cause as much karmic entanglement as an action performed with the body. An action first originates in the mental field (astral plane) of consciousness which is stirred by desires rising from the unconscious mind. This agitation prompts the mind toward thoughts and actions in an attempt to fulfill the desires of the unconscious, but those actions and thoughts create more desires and more future agitation. This is the state of bondage which is experienced by most people and it continues for lifetimes without end. This cycle continues until there is a discovery that desires cannot be fulfilled in this manner. Therefore, the root of desire, ignorance, must be eradicated in order to end the desires of the mind and achieve true peace and balance.

You need to develop subtlety of intellect and profound insight into the nature of the universe and of your innermost Self. The best way to achieve this goal is to practice a blending of wisdom and action in your personal spiritual discipline in order to harmonize your mental and physical qualities.

In this process, you must understand that the ancient Sages have given guidelines for which thoughts and actions are in line with the scales of MAAT, and which actions and thoughts are not. The 42 precepts of MAAT constitute the foundation of the Egyptian Book of Coming Forth By Day, however, throughout the book, many injunctions are given. Their purpose is to cleanse the heart of the aspirant.

Maat Philosophy Versus Fascism and the Police State

"The wise person who acts with MAAT is free of falsehood and disorder."
-Ancient Egyptian Proverb

The practice of MAAT signifies *wisdom in action*. This is to say that the teachings are to be practiced in ordinary day to day situations, and when the deeper implications of this practice are understood, one will be led to purity in action and thought.

Though the soul is ultimately responsible for is condition in human existence that does not mean that that should be accepted as the ultimate fate. Through the practice of Maat a person's condition can and should be improved. From a societal perspective, there too, a society needs to practice ethical conscience as a group in order to have a positive group outcome. So in a group that does not practice ethical conscience, those conscious and ethical individual in the society may suffer along with the general society, by being associated with that society, even if they themselves are ethical personalities.

MAAT AS A LEGAL BASIS FOR LAWS AND LAW ENFORCEMENT[51]

Over the years I have lectured on the great ancient African philosophy known as *Maat,* the principle of righteousness, truth, justice, order and harmony. It was in Ancient Egypt that this beatific vision for society was developed to a very high degree. It found expression through the spiritual researches of the ancient Egyptian sages and became the cornerstone upon which the entire civilization depended, beginning with the *Per-aah,* or Pharaoh. The Per-aah's main duty was to see that the country was ordered by Maat, lest society be destroyed by the evil of greed, corruption and lawlessness. This aspect of Ancient Egyptian culture is what allowed the creation of a well ordered society that persisted for so many thousands of years. The Per-aah (Pharaoh), guided by the council of priests and priestesses, delegated the management of the laws of the country to the Vizier, who oversaw the judges and law enforcement officials of the country. Unlike the modern western system of justice, in Ancient Egypt there was no notion of an adversarial system as conceived in modern times where a trial consists of one side trying to prove guilt and the other trying to prove innocence even if that means hiding the truth.. That is, there was an understanding that all parties should desire after truth and all advocates (lawyers) would be required to speak truth.

The legal system of ancient Egypt was managed by the judges who were priests and priestesses of the goddess Maat and were expected to uphold very high standards of ethics in their treatment of accusers and the accused and the judgments rendered as well as in their own personal lives, lest they lose the confidence of the populace and also even worse, the spiritual merit and be given over to the demoniac forces after death, all due to their own unrighteousness. Laws were based on A- the teachings of the sages, B- decrees by the Per-aah as well as C- on previous court cases, which were recorded and kept in archives (previous case law/precedent).

Thus, Maat was not just a legal system but a philosophical way of life which promoted righteous dealing amongst human beings in order to promote social harmony and in turn this social harmony could then allow the entire society to turn

---

[51] The principles of Maat are known popularly as the *Forty-two laws of Maat*. However, the study of Maat Philosophy is an extensive in depth endeavor. **The 42 Principles of Maat and the Philosophy of Righteous Action.** The recording lectures based on the book are available Secondly, the book **Introduction to Maat Philosophy**, provides an overview of Maat Philosophy and its application in society as well as its importance in spiritual life. Thirdly, you may be interested in reviewing my book **Egyptian Proverbs**, which contains the essential precepts of Kemetic (Ancient Egyptian) Maat Philosophy. Other books of interest are the **Healing the Criminal Heart Book I and Book II.** These books were written specifically for inmates at correctional institutions, introducing them to Maat Philosophy and the means to transform their lives through righteous living in accordance to the ancient spiritual principles.

towards spiritual pursuits. All members of society were expected to live by Maat, including especially the Per-aah and the Vizier. This factor is what allowed ancient Egyptian society to create such magnanimous monuments which still attest to their devotion to the Divine.

Grounded in spiritual principles, Maat Philosophy of Africa is in every way comparable to the *Dharma* of the Hindus and Buddhists. It can be taught in an ecumenical religious format or in a secular format. It is based on the teachings of the Ancient Egyptian sages such as Sage Ptahotep, Sage Ani, Sage Amenemope, Sage Kaqemna and many others.

Aside from the precepts listed in the **Pert M Heru** or Ancient Egyptian Book of Coming Forth By Day, and the writings of the Sages (Known as the Wisdom Texts), containing precepts and expositions on righteous living, the laws were not codified in Ancient Egypt in the same way as in modern culture. This is because the law was something to be applied in principle and spirit in everyday life as opposed to following a strict regulation for the court and law enforcement system alone. Maat was seen as an integral aspect of life and it was to be practiced not just in the court room but in all areas of life. However, in the late period of Ancient Egyptian history when the Persians temporarily conquered the country, a law code was written based on the preexisting statutes of Ancient Egypt. Emperor Darius commanded that the laws be written. This writing was set down in Aramaic,[52] and Demotic (late ancient Egyptian script).

It is appropriate to include here that ancient Greek ethics and spiritual culture was also an outgrowth of Kemetic culture and religion and this all served as a basis for Western culture.[53] Thus, the study and application of the timeless principles of Maat Philosophy has wide ranging implications for society, law enforcement officials, the clergy and for individuals who want to evolve spiritually. It can benefit society as a whole, the African community in general and individual practitioners in their specific spiritual pursuits, for, spiritual evolution cannot occur in unrighteous personalities and societies whose basis is unrighteousness, greed, and unfairness. Such societies will promote discontent and frustration in people, obstructing their spiritual lives. According to the Ancient Egyptian teachings (see the book *Egyptian Proverbs*) this type of society will ultimately experience unrest, disintegration and collapse.

"When opulence and extravagance are a necessity instead of righteousness and

truth, society will be governed by greed and injustice."

−Ancient Egyptian Proverb

---

[52] (the original language of parts of the Old Testament. After the Babylonian captivity, it was the common written and spoken language of the Middle East until replaced by Arabic.)
[53] (see the books: *Egyptian Yoga Volume I* and *From Egypt To Greece*).

Chapter 2: Introduction to Fascism

Now that you have an idea of what Maat Philosophy is about, you will be better able to see how divergent democracy and fascism are from it. In order to understand what a police state is, it is necessary also to understand the reason for its existence. If you have read the book *Collapse of Civilization and the Death of American Empire,* you are well on your way to understanding the history and issues around the policies of not just the empire setup by one country, the USA, but also a policy developed and instituted by what may be referred to as a worldwide "power elite" that control world finances through the USA Banks, government and military.

Who are the *power elite*? The term *power elite* include the aristocracy, oligarchy, moneyed interests segment of a population, also referred to as "the 1%. They are a worldwide group that controls most of the wealth of the world and the *commanding heights of the economy.* In the book, the authors of *Commanding Heights*[54] attempt to trace the rise of free markets during the last century, as well as the process of globalization. The book attributes the origin of the phrase "commanding heights" to a speech by Vladimir Lenin referring to the control of perceived key segments of a national economy.[55] The Power Elite are the owners of the 40-50 largest transnational companies including the major world banks: Barclays, Goldman Sachs, JPMorgan Chase & Co, Vanguard Group, UBS, Deutsche Bank, Bank of New York Mellon Corp, Morgan Stanley, Bank of America Corp, and Société Générale, whose board of directors, the same people, rotate amongst the boards of those companies. So those companies are not different but are actually owned and controlled by the same group of people. This is the same reason why South Africa was allowed to go from an apartheid system of government to a system of democracy. The power elite of South Africa, who were and are the white minority population, knew that it does not matter who is the elected government official; what matters more is who controls the key segments of a national economy. Among the most important key segments of a

---

[54] *The Commanding Heights : The Battle for the World Economy* by Daniel Yergin and Joseph Stanislaw (Apr 2, 2002)
[55] http://www.dlc.org/ndol_ci.cfm?contentid=1570&kaid=125&subid=162 Review of Commanding Heights by the Fred Seigel of the Democratic Leadership Council.
http://www.amazon.com/Commanding-Heights-Battle-World-Economy/dp/product-description/068483569X Excerpt from Commanding Heights.

national economy are the area of banking/finance, mainstream media, the issuance of currency and debt, interest rates, campaign donations, courts and market economy regulation.

The power of the power elite stems from setting themselves up as creditors to world economies and commerce as the descendants of the old British and European powers. In the case of the USA empire, after world war two the USA emerged as the strongest country and set itself up with the world reserve currency. This capacity, the factor of having the US dollar in position of world reserve currency, along with the capacity already setup previously, of creating money out of thin air through the debt fractional banking system, allowed the USA to expand as an ever self-multiplying hydra, whose tentacles extend through world economies and governments and which acts to undermined and control them covertly, through financial manipulations using the world bank and international monetary fund or with the USA military, as a blunt spearhead to intimidate other countries into opening their markets and resources for USA corporations to plunder; this process ends up leaving the indigenous population to suffer while the 1% of the country in question prospers from being in collusion with the 1% of the controlling country. This may be considered as an evolution of the concept of neo-colonialism wherein the colonial power governed the colony (occupied country or territory) with the help of local collaborators and wealthy individuals. Now, instead of a colony ruled by armies and navies the territory or country is ruled through the banking system and shackling the economy through debt. The new overlords are the controllers of the banks and their enforcers are those in charge of the police state.

Before going forward it is important to understand that the following study of Maat Philosophy versus Fascism and the Police State should not be taken to mean that the worldwide power elite are a monolithic group that agrees on every single thing or that they are not affected by groups who are not part of the power elite. This study does contend that the power elite are THE driving force on major issues in human life on earth and they collude by having common goals, even if, sometimes they may compete amongst each other for power. Examples of such competitions were the USA revolutionary war, the USA civil war, world wars 1 and two, the Korean war, the Viet Nam war, the wars against Iraq, Syria etc. Another kind of example of conflict is when corporations fight each other for resources, corporate espionage, or when one executive is convicted of a crime; it is not because of the power of the people of an independent court system, but rather because one member or members of the power elite (one faction) wanted and had the power to force the conviction or the killing or the stripping the power of the other previous member of the power elite. Some examples of differences of opinion are over socio-economic policy, will there be renewable energy or polluting industries based on fossil fuels? Etc. So there can be disagreements and there can even be wars instigated by those disagreements. Of course, the wars are fought with members of the masses (pawns) pitted against the poor or duped, powerless peoples (pawns) of the other side. Rarely do members of the power elite die in armed conflicts. However, there is a driving force among the members of the power elite globally, to usurp, gain and maintain control over, commodify worldwide resources, invalidate local laws, usurp individual liberties and wealth; all actions are directed for the benefit of that tiny minority, the power elite, while impoverishing and weakening the worldwide masses, who are seen as objects to be manipulated, to serve the main purposes of the power elite: power, wealth and control of the economy and politics. **Social studies and economics researchers have found that capitalism promotes unemployment, poverty, crime and the disparity between classes; therefore, it is a conflict producing way of social order. Below is an example of the present day competition between the North American power elite (USA and Canada) and the power elite of the European Union.**

> *Here's the important point.* Among industrial democracies, there are two kinds of political-economic policies emerging in the contemporary world: (1) The Anglo-American model, which creates lots of jobs, many with lousy wages, with huge pools of poverty at the bottom and huge pools of wealth at the top; and (2) the continental European model (for lack of a better term), which creates fewer jobs but better ones and relies on powerful states to redistribute sufficient benefits to people and groups to preserve social peace. The disadvantages of the European model are well known: powerful governments, large bureaucracies, higher taxes, and sometimes an inclination for authoritarian "solutions" in hard times. The disadvantages of the Anglo-American model are the very real social costs of vast inequality, such as a large and growing economically and politically marginalized segment of the population characterized by high levels of anxiety and despair; predatory criminality and gang activity in cities; and homegrown terrorists (like the militias of the 1990s).
> In the end, vast and increasing levels of inequality have a coercive effect on American social and community life. This happens because high levels of inequality undermine the basis for cooperation in a free society. As many analysts have pointed out, a world with lower inequality is one we would choose without knowing what our eventual place was in it (Galbraith 1998). High levels of inequality make the future certain, undermine the belief that we are all part of a common society, and allow significant segments of the population to opt out of public activities that they would support if their future was unclear and it was possible that (at some future time) they would need those services. In short, rising U.S. inequality is more than just an economic problem. It is a political and cultural one as well..[56]

---

[56] Exploring Social Change by Harper and Leicht pp 63-64

GOVERNMENT BASED ON FASCISM

Fascism should more appropriately be called Corporatism because it is a merger of state and corporate power.[57]
-Benito Mussolini

Fascism is the power of those who are the wealthiest persons in the society who also own or control large corporations to wield that power over government leaders and directly control or influence them and thereby rule over government policy, social initiatives, the court system and the media, without interference from the majority of the population. In essence, a fascist /corporatist leader has dominion over the state's ability to make laws, the media's ability to support the agenda of the politicians and the law enforcement capacity to enforce the laws and agenda set by the fascists. What has the current system of government devolved into in the USA and Europe? Many people in those countries think they have *democracy* (or rule by the majority of the people). Again, the words of Mussolini are instructive.

Democracy is beautiful in theory; in practice it is a fallacy.[58]
-Benito Mussolini

The evolution of "democracy", even if it starts out as well intentioned, eventually leads to a situation in which a power elite joins and colludes to control those who are elected and to set a public and social agenda that is in their favor, following their vision of reality and thereby they gradually gain control of any government (democratic, communist, socialist, etc.) that is based on worldly values and ideals. Ideas such as the "Pursuit of Happiness" as a social goal, as practiced in the USA culture, are worldly values for they do not recognize that happiness cannot be found in material possessions. Maat Philosophy does recognize this all important issue. The absence of this recognition allows people (including the power elite) to be deluded into the idea that happiness can be found through becoming rich or controlling politicians so as to amass power or creating think tanks, and secretive advocacy organizations such as the Heritage Foundation, the Chamber of Commerce and ALEC, to strategize how to get laws passed that are in favor of policies that enrich corporations regardless of the harm to the world ecology or to individual human beings or even the capacity of government to function for the benefit of all people. The next step is to then put paid and trained representatives on talk shows, as supposed "experts", to constantly advocate for those ideas that benefit the fascist /corporatist agenda, which is easy since the mass media are actually companies that can be bought and thereby controlled directly by ordering

---

[57] http://www.brainyquote.com/quotes/authors/b/benito_mussolini.html#pvZy7msipqqLVeGt.99
[58] http://www.brainyquote.com/quotes/authors/b/benito_mussolini.html#Cdi57HIMKCjmIe5d.99

its employees to advocate certain ideas or denigrate or ignore others or indirectly by selecting those who will work in the media and who will not; or decide who gets the loudest mouthpiece since, as explained elsewhere. It is important to understand that the neo fascists have discovered that it is not desirable to suppress all speech as in the classic police state but rather, it is more desirable to actually not completely suppress free speech so that people can think they actually have rights even though that right serves no practical purpose other than facilitating the self delusion that one can advocate for oneself or protest, even though since the power of dissent (alternative ideas in media or even protests in the streets) is diluted because does not have a mass capacity (does not have access to mass media or funds to support its own think tanks) it is ineffectual and irrelevant to its purpose but useful to the fascist because the fascist can point to that and say there is democracy and freedom in the country. Even if it were compelling, public protests can be easily put down by the fascist enforcers, the police, since these are paid by and the heads of those police organizations are selected or appointed by the fascists (even if people vote for judges and police commissioners they are only voting for people who have been financially supported indirectly (indirect selection) or directly selected by the power elite (fascists), put up as candidates and not directly by the masses. This control by the power elite through corporations and the government leaders and employees and judiciary, and the impotence of everyone else is the description, definition and objective of fascism. In this context, fascism and corporatocracy/corporatism are one in the same.

GOVERNMENT BASED ON MAAT PHILOSOPHY

> When opulence and extravagance are a necessity instead of righteousness and truth, society will be governed by greed and injustice."
> −Ancient Egyptian Proverb

The Maat Philosophy underpinnings of Ancient Egyptian government are diametrically opposed to the foundations of the fascist/corporatist ideals. Firstly, the Maatian ideal is against wealth and income imbalance and for the fair distribution of resources.

Secondly, Maat Philosophy includes the wisdom of the illusoriness of searching for happiness in an ever changing and fleeting world wherein ignorant people are pursuing happiness through actions, possessions, fame, fortune, power, etc. This means they do not understand the futility of their pursuits and the ultimate frustration they are leading themselves to but due to their aryu they are compelled to follow that path. That path also leads to a personality that is unhappy and that unhappiness can be manipulated into anger and hatred against whatever the perceived cause of the unhappiness might be or might have been pointed to by the media employees of the power elite. Hate-mongers such as those on right wing talk radio, know how to expertly whip up hatred especially in white men,[59] who feel entitled to a position of high standing in the society, to feel anger against minorities, women and the poor. These can then be easily manipulated by politicians to support rightwing agendas and social policies even if those policies are against the best interest of those same angry people.

Maat philosophy recognizes that extreme imbalances in income and wealth accumulation foment resentments and also distorted intellects. Those who are in a state of want cannot serve properly in matters of the dispensation of justice or fairness for they cannot see clearly due to their state of deprivation which causes inordinate desire to such a degree that the feeling capacity and the intellectual capacity are atrophied in favor of actions and desires of the ego, selfishness, short sightedness instead of wisdom, compassion, understanding and caring for others. This condition can even progress to lawbreaking in the pursuit of fulfilling the real or perceived objects of desire, be they physical or intangible (happiness, power, etc.). So what would good government look like if Maat Philosophy was the foundation of human social, political and legal interactions?

Maat philosophy was the basis of Ancient Egyptian society and government as well as the heart of Ancient Egyptian myth and spirituality. Maat philosophy has two wings or aspects; one relates to secular life and the other to spiritual/mystic life. The first is dedicated to creating an atmosphere of peace and balance so that the second may be pursued effectively and without undue stress. The Ancient Kamitans (Egyptians) based their government and business concerns on spiritual values and therefore, enjoyed an orderly society which included equality between the sexes, and a legal system based on universal spiritual laws. The *Ancient Egyptian Government and Economic Systems* are a tribute to their history, culture and legacy. As historical insights unfold, it becomes clearer that modern culture has derived its basis from Ancient Egypt, though the credit is not often given, nor the integrity of the practices maintained in the new religions. This is another important reason to study Ancient Egyptian Philosophy, to discover the principles which allowed their civilization to prosper over a period of thousands of years in order to bring our systems of government, religion and social structures to a harmony with ourselves, humanity and with nature.

> The governance of (district) one is in the hands of ten men, a magistrate is appointed who will levy [...] the amount of all taxes. The priest is provided with a farm, and men work for you like a single gang. How is it that disaffection does not occur? (Because) you will not suffer from a Nile which fails to come, and the revenues of the Delta are in your hand.
> -Teachings to MeriKaRa

---

[59] http://sb.cc.stonybrook.edu/happenings/facultystaff/sociologist-michael-kimmels-book-featured-in-new-york-times/

Maat Philosophy holds that the proper distribution of resources and allowing members of society the opportunity to work and thrive in their areas of endeavor will lead to prosperity and personal fulfillment of individuals since, under such a social system, they can meet the necessities of life and also pursue their spiritual goals, to discover the meaning of life even before death. Since before the time of the Pyramid Texts (c. 5,000 B.C.E.), it was known that peace and order on a society wide scale can be achieved through righteousness, order and truth. This is the system of governance that was put into effect and which allowed the Ancient Egyptian society to persist for thousands of years without destroying the environment or destroying itself, as other empires have done throughout history (Greek, Roman, Byzantine, Ottoman, etc. and as the USA (American Empire) is doing to itself and the world right now.

THE ECONOMIC OBJECTIVE OF CAPITALISM AND THE OBJECTIVE OF FASCISM: THE WEALTH DISPARITY AND INCOME INEQUALITY

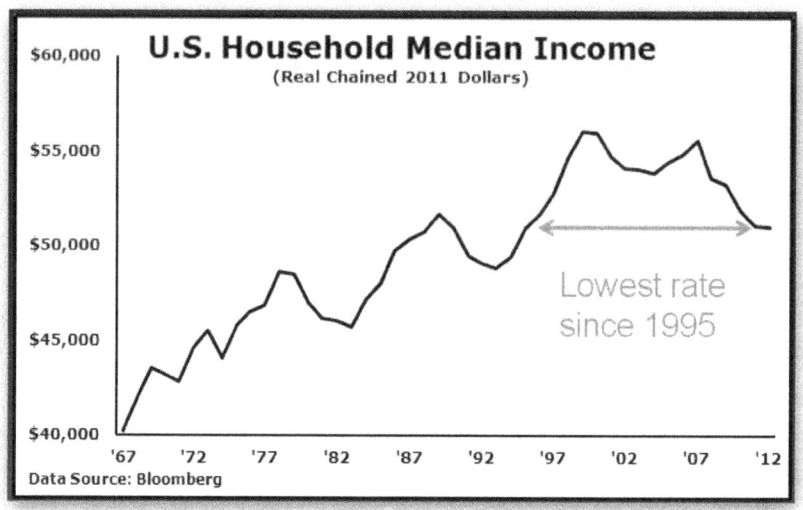

The chart above shows that median income is at the same level as in 1995. So the median income of the population, which makes up 70% of the economy is flat to down and therefore the general economy cannot grow and is moving downward.

Now that we have established an introduction to Maat philosophy principles and an introduction to fascism and the power elite we will turn back to the modern culture and begin to look at areas where ethical principles are lacking or are nonexistent and what effects that has on the society. Then we will return to Maat philosophy at the end of the chapter for a final review of the themes of the chapter.

Firstly, pure capitalism does not and cannot exist, therefore when most people talk about or refer to having a capitalist system they are incorrect because if capitalism were allowed to run completely unchecked, unregulated, eventually there would be one corporation, one rich person, owning everything, as in the famous monopoly game; and everyone else would be a serf as in the old feudal system or like the population in the old European kingdoms who were actually subjects and property of the monarch. Capitalism was a system of economics that replaced the old economic system but achieved the same goal, and more spectacularly, to impoverish the masses and allow a plutocracy to exist, amassing most of the wealth and power but instead of having an overtly unjust system with a king as a figurehead, now the masses are fooled into believing they have a choice about their rulers and thus the pressure towards revolutionary feelings and thoughts can be diffused even before it takes shape, for people may become upset by injustices in society but what are they to do since they live in a free society with free speech and freedom to select their leaders? Many people do not want to think about these issues and prefer to rely on ignorance and fanatical nationalistic patriotism believing in ideas such as: "The problem is not some power elite working in the background but must be the politics, or the politicians, but anyway we still have the best country in the world, USA! #1!, USA! #1!, USA! #1!" This is an example of the widespread social delusion that allows the corruption and power of the power elite to persist for such a population is rendered docile, ignorant and weak, incapable voting in its own interest, incapable of civil disobedience and let alone revolution.

What we have now is not capitalism but a system of fascist collusion between government and corporate power that has developed into a worldwide banking empire in which nations, populations, natural resources as well as governments, court systems and corporate entities are controlled financially. Fascism allows Crony Capitalism to exist as a foundation for inordinate and unjust wealth accumulation by a minority of the society, the power elite. Crony Capitalism is maintained and strengthened when persons in government, who make the laws, collude with the wealthy and those in business to create laws that maintain them in power and wealth while maintaining everyone else weak and impoverished. One stark example of that fascism is evident in the recently revealed spying by the USA NSA agency. Supposedly their mission is to spy to discover terrorist plots against the USA but they were spying on foreign heads of state and passing on their information to USA corporations so they could use that information to their benefit in negotiations, or knowing what trends were coming along to invest in the right places and not lose money, etc.

NSA leaks: Years of spying on Mexico govt. gave US investment benefits[60]

What was the thinking that went into the creation of the constitution and government of the USA? Since pure capitalism cannot exist since it would lead to concentration of power in one despot or would lead to a revolution, then it was thought beneficial to place limits on the power any person can have by imposing limitations of government power even as the power remains with the wealthy elite; therefore the debate is over which person or group within the power elite will have the power at any given time and the debate is not whether or not anyone other than the power elite will ever be in a position of power. That same government was supposed to curb the excesses of capitalism and make it work for

---

[60] http://rt.com/news/nsa-leaks-mexico-government-458/

more of the population. The wealthy however, have gained control of those who operate government and the legal system so as to control and make sure that the balance is always tilted towards the rich and powerful; this is fascism. Fascism is the natural evolution of corruption by the plutocrats wherein capitalism evolves into crony capitalism and crony capitalism is merely a modern term for fascism, a term that few in government or even the press like to use for its evocative images of the German, Italian and Spanish governments in the 1930's and during world war two.

> Definition of 'Crony Capitalism'[61]
> A description of capitalist society as being based on the close relationships between businessmen and the state. Instead of success being determined by a free market and the rule of law, the success of a business is dependent on the favoritism that is shown to it by the ruling government in the form of tax breaks, government grants and other incentives.[62]
> NOTE: Other terms that are synonymous with "fascism" are: crony capitalism, corporatocracy, corporatism, kleptocracy, captive state/state capture.

Beyond crony capitalism, the more important point is that crony capitalism is merely a tool for wealth accumulation and wealth transfer from the masses to the minority power elite; We do not have capitalism as such but rather an imperial financial plutocracy that has no borders and no remorse about plundering cities, communities or countries, regardless of the pain and suffering it may cause. When corrupt forms of government, unethical government, mature, they reach a level where commerce is rigged for the benefit of the wealthy and powerful causing markets to become distorted and prone to crashes and collapse. In this historical period there have been many crashes, which are an endemic flaw[63] in a capitalist based system of government and economics. Yet it is maintained and dissent against it is suppressed, so as to maintain the power and wealth structure of the society. This purpose is of course the ideal of the fascist. In Ancient Egypt, under Maat philosophy, the ideal of government and economics was to produce Maat or balance and order as well as peace in society as well as a foundation for human beings to discover their higher nature. This high ideal of maat is not best carried forward in an atmosphere of resentment between social groups based on gender or income. War (conflicts between nation states) is not a conducive environment and neither is a workplace where workers are despotically ruled by managers and corporate leaders who have only their own interests in mind and do not care about the welfare of workers or the welfare of the country. Rather, their primary concern is about profits even if that pursuit produces pain and suffering, unemployment, destruction of the environment or even if it risks the very existence of life on earth, their own or that of their family or even their own progeny.

---

[61] http://www.investopedia.com/terms/c/cronycapitalism.asp
[62] Like subsidies, and preventing competition
[63] http://www.pbs.org/newshour/bb/business/july-dec08/crisishearing_10-23.html
http://theflawmovie.com/synopsis.html

The fascist is not interested in democracy or competition. So, the main purpose of controlling politics and the economy is to secure information about economic trends and to insure conditions that will lead to increasing wealth and less competition or uncertainty. The USA government has been at work all around the world trying to suppress real democracy unless it is "USA style democracy", i.e. crony capitalism/fascism, which allows USA corporations to have free reign over the resources and people (slave labor and consumerism) of other countries, for which they are willing to compensate the power elite of the country in question. In Haiti, after the legitimate elections, the U.S.A. support for the opposition led to a *coup* that was supported by the U.S.A. under the Republican president, George H. Bush (Bush Sr.). After the *coup,* the U.S.A., under President Clinton, a member of the Democratic Party, supported the military junta that ruled the country and even authorized the U.S.A. oil companies to deal with them. After the people suffered under the rule of the junta, Clinton sent in troops and more people died. The democratically elected president, Aristide, was restored to the government, but only if he agreed to include the policies of his opponent who lost the 1990 election, the opponent who was in favor of U.S.A. corporate policies. (Neo-liberalism) Haiti's economy failed and people suffered more violence and disruption until on February 29, 2004, the governments of France and the United States exiled president Aristide by forcing him to leave the country and stay in Africa. This removal and exiling of a democratically elected president was strongly protested by several governments in the Caribbean but those protests had no effect. This episode was only the latest display of U.S.A. policy that Noam Chomsky referred to as *"another illustration of the near passionate hatred of democracy,* (by the American rulers) *which is consistent and is indeed recognized."*[64]

The fascist has two main political goals, to suppress democratic expression (stop more people voting) and controlling the political process in order to set the agenda and thus the economy for their own benefit. In this area, a man by the name of Paul Weyrich stands out as the face of modern conservatism (rancorous, vitriolic and despotic politics), and religious conservatism/fascism (Christian theocracy)[65]. The strategy was simple, to increase polarization in the electorate, suppress voting by the general public and raising the voting level of his minority constituency (right wing, religious conservative, politically conservative minded persons). Then the task was to get conservatives elected into state and national legislatures, governorships and judgeships as well as, through them, secretly coordinate the laws passed in state and national legislatures with bills created and written by and in favor of corporations and their owners.

---

[64] http://en.wikipedia.org/wiki/Aristide
[65] In reality the theocracy is not to impose Christian laws or values but instead is a front to manipulate Christians into supporting the agenda of ALEC which is in reality a corporatist agenda and not a religious agenda.

Maat Philosophy Versus Fascism and the Police State

"Now many of our Christians have what I call the "goo goo" syndrome. Good Government. They want everybody to vote. I don't want everybody to vote. Elections are not won by a majority of people. They never have been from the beginning of our country, and they are not now. As a matter of fact, our leverage in the elections quite candidly goes up as the voting populace goes down."[66]

-Paul Weyrich Founder of ALEC

This work of subverting democracy and packing legislatures and courts with political puppets, paid for and supported congress men and women, judges and presidents, to do the bidding of the corporations was carried forth through an organization called ALEC, with the consent of both political parties. What is ALEC and what corporate funders are backing it? In other words, who is the power elite behind this process?

The American Legislative Exchange Council (ALEC) was founded in 1973 by Paul Weyrich, who helped build a nationwide right-wing political infrastructure following the reelection of Richard Nixon. In the same year, he helped establish the Heritage Foundation, now one of the most prominent right-wing policy institutes in the country. One year later, Weyrich founded the Committee for the Survival of a Free Congress, the predecessor of the Free Congress Foundation. In 1979, he co-founded and coined the Moral Majority with Jerry Falwell, and in 1981 he helped establish the ultraconservative Council on National Policy.

ALEC's major funders include Exxon Mobil, the Scaife family (Allegheny Foundation and the Scaife Family Foundation), the Coors family (Castle Rock Foundation), Charles Koch (Charles G. Koch Charitable Foundation and the Claude R. Lambe Charitable Foundation), the Bradley family (The Lynde and Harry Bradley Foundation) and the Olin family (John M. Olin Foundation). These organizations consistently finance right-wing think tanks and political groups.

Members of ALEC's board represent major corporations such as Altria, AT&T, GlaxoSmithKline, Johnson & Johnson, Koch Industries, Kraft, PhRMA, Wal-Mart, Peabody Energy, and State Farm. Such corporations represent just a fraction of ALEC's approximately three hundred corporate partners. According to the American Association for Justice, over eighty percent of ALEC's finances come from corporate contributions.[67]

NOTE: for the full listing of the funders (power elite), board members, and the legislatures (congress men and women) governors, judges ALEC has under its control go to the following link.
https://en.wikipedia.org/wiki/List_of_members_of_the_American_Legislative_Exchange_Council

---

[66] http://www.sourcewatch.org/index.php?title=Interesting_ALEC_Quotes
[67] ALEC: The Voice of Corporate Special Interests In State Legislatures

The fascist is not interested in promoting income equality but rather the reverse. From the early 1980's, and to the present, a move, by the power elite, was accelerated in the USA and England, to remove trade barriers and tariffs so that corporations could offshore[68] manufacturing jobs to countries with lower wages. This led to a situation of wages, in the USA, that have remained stagnant while the income of the top 2% of the population, the wealthiest segment, has increased manifold. The economists Dr. Ravi Bhatra[69] and Dr. Richard Wolff[70] have pointed out that since the USA economy is sustained by mass consumer spending which constitutes 70% of the economy, that the economy is not sustainable under conditions of lowered or stagnating wages.[71] What sustained the economy between the early 1980's and the crash of the economy in 2008 was the factor of increasing debt whereby wages were not increased but loans to the general public were increased; this led to unprecedented public debt. The lower interest rates and low cost money produced by the Federal Reserve Bank of the USA led to a stock market bubble referred to as the "dot com bubble" and crash in 1999-2000 and next to a real estate bubble in 2003-2007, which was exacerbated by the Wall Street mortgage frauds that finally failed in 2008 and produced a stock market crash.

---

[68] close factories in the country and move them to countries that have lower wages for their workers.
[69] http://www.ravibatra.com/
[70] http://rdwolff.com/
[71] *THE MYTH OF FREE TRADE: THE POORING OF AMERICA BY RAVI BATRA*
CAPITALISM HITS THE FAN: THE GLOBAL ECONOMIC MELTDOWN AND WHAT TO DO ABOUT IT BY RICHARD D. WOLFF

Maat Philosophy Versus Fascism and the Police State

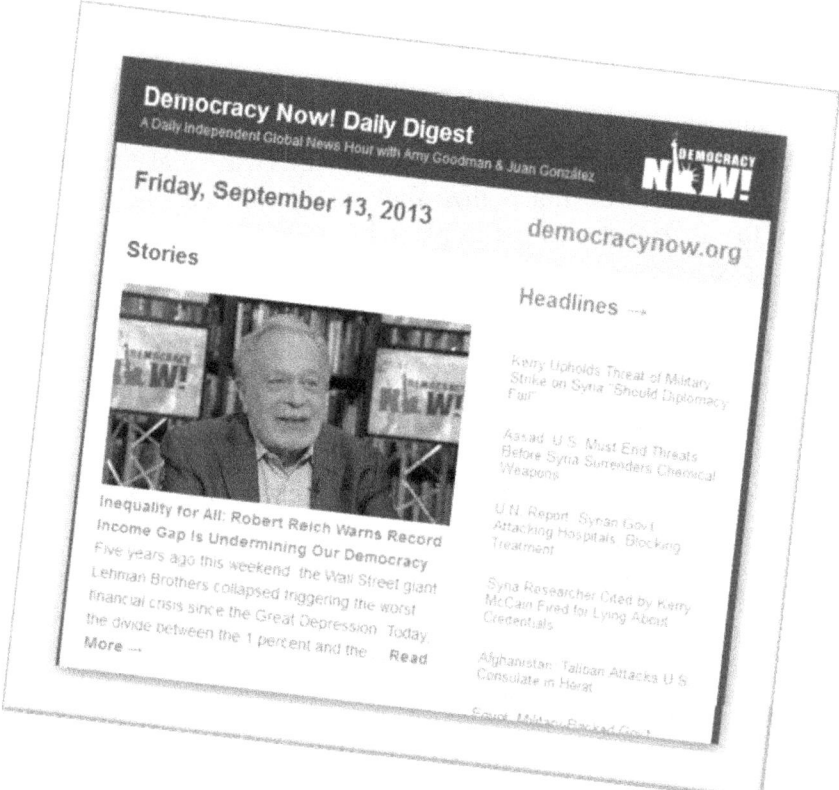

Inequality for All: Robert Reich Warns Record Income Gap Is Undermining Our Democracy[72]

From the standpoint of Maat Philosophy, the actions of the USA government and its culture of people who support it in mistreating, discriminating against, segregating or enslaving part of the population or in attacking other countries for their resources, the allowance of bankers to defraud the whole world, causing financial crisis and untold deaths and sufferings worldwide, bombing women and children, kidnapping, torture, destruction of the environment, toppling governments, extra-judicial killings of USA citizens and non-citizens, abductions, arrests without due process under the law, warrantless searches, supporting murderous dictators, etc., that all presidents and elected leaders and corporate leaders have engaged in, and which religious leaders have sanctioned (by not speaking against corruption and immorality in government (especially that of the presidents and the congress)) constitutes not democracy but despotic fascism (collusion of corporate and government leaders for the benefit of corporations and the wealthy by autocratic and violent rule of the wealthy minority). Most people are mesmerized by politics, during election time, and the prospect of getting their person elected to do their bidding; this is especially true of the position of President. That person is idolized as a hero who will set things right and redress the excesses of their predecessor or fulfill the vision of the

---

[72] http://www.democracynow.org/2013/9/13/inequality_for_all_robert_reich_warns

supporters (be that positive or negative). Meanwhile, even if the person was elected by a constituency that desired a turning away from perceived law-breaking or undemocratic policies of the predecessor, the concentration of power and the abuses of power continue and increase with the new president while the followers rationalize, apologize or otherwise make excuses for their candidate. The masses do not realize that presidents "preside" over the power structure of the state that was put in place by the ruling class and are not agents of change or keepers of ethical conscience. Such personalities, even if they meant well, are coerced by the army of lobbyists and moneyed interests who could plunge the economy into a downward cycle if their demands are not heeded. So presidents and congresspersons also cannot manifest ethical conscience beyond that which is allowed by the degraded (mesmerized) culture (composed of the ignorant, duped and psychologically impaired by propaganda, entertainments and drugs (prescription or otherwise) masses who vote for candidates based on fear, greed, ignorance, the rhetoric of the demagogic leaders, etc.) and allowed by the power elite that control the commanding heights of the economy, mass media and public opinion to support the same politicians and placed them before the masses as "choices" for their choosing. So there is no real democracy but rather a selection by the power elite as they are the financial supporters of candidates of their choosing, from which the masses are allowed to pick which one is most appealing; appealing, that is, in terms of style and personality but not in terms of substantive or fundamental progressive, or ethical government or economic policies. So presidents can be leaders and or innovators in terms of social issues or other inconsequential aspects of public life such as in matters of gay marriage or civil rights but not, for example, in areas such as income inequality or changing from a carbon based economy to a green economy, areas that would be fundamental to the social, political and economic power structure of the power elite. Specifically, no fundamental change from the current format, that favors the power elite, would be proposed or allowed in the areas of the USA, European, Japanese economic systems, including the political system, banking system, system of corporate law, education and health systems, etc., as these are thoroughly corrupted by the profit motive.

Aside from the operational corruptions of how the varied industries are setup to favor the power elite, the economic wealth of the country as a whole has been captured by the underlying debt based and interest bearing money creation system involving the Federal Reserve and fractional banking/inflationary system that causes the masses to be perpetually under the pressure of debt and inflation which, over the last 100 years, has allowed the power elite to extract wealth from the masses and maintain them in a state of perpetual debt and consequently a subservient position to the state institutions, who are composed of: the creditors (same power elite) behind banks, corporations, etc. that own most of the wealth and property in the economy and who control wages and allow disparities between men and women and between ethnic majorities and minorities.

BAIL-OUTS AND BAIL-INS

The bailouts of the world banks that were done by the US congress, president and Federal Reserve bank, in 2008-2009 without the consent of the people and in their name, pledging them to pay those debts, is a primary example of fascism/crony capitalism. Since that time, the Federal Reserve also bailed-out banks and corporations around the world to the tune of over 20 trillion dollars. All the actions that were taken were without the consent of the people but with public funds or commitments to pay and the pledge was for the benefit of those corporations and banks and not for the people who are being forced to pay for it.

In 2010 an investment broker, MF Global,[73] in collusion with JPMorgan Chase confiscated client funds and no one was punished or jailed. In early 2013 a new strategy was implemented, of using not just pledging future public funds to bailout corporations but using existing bank accounts.

---

[73] http://www.forbes.com/sites/realspin/2013/03/22/mf-global-and-the-cypriot-banking-crisis-troubling-similarities/

In Cyprus, a banking crisis led to what is now referred to as *bail-in*.[74] Now a precedent has been set, and laws have been placed on the books in Europe, Canada, the USA and other countries to confiscate bank accounts and or pension funds to bail-out corporations. The first ethical violation was not allowing crony companies to go bankrupt or take funds to bail them out from those who drained them of the funds and those whose malfeasance led the corporation to bankruptcy, the CEOs, the stockholders and bondholders. Another proper source of funds would be to raise taxes on the wealthy that have benefitted in an unprecedented way by the unethical favoritism of tax rates on the wealthy over the last two to three decades and has made them fabulously rich while impoverishing the rest of the population. Those who have been benefitted unjustly should bear the brunt of any bailouts or bailins.

---

[74] http://www.reuters.com/article/2013/07/28/cyprus-bank-idUSL6N0FY09020130728

Bailouts that are unapproved by the public are immoral and unethical and illegal; now the bailins[75] are an outright and boldface example of fascism (Crony Bankster scam for stealing-redistribution of wealth from the general population to the wealthy and corporations) and theft of the population by the wealthy and politically powerful.

---

[75] http://www.forbes.com/sites/nathanlewis/2013/05/03/the-cyprus-bank-bail-in-is-another-crony-bankster-scam/

It behooves all to understand that the banking systems are completely corrupt and that any funds kept in them are subject to confiscation. Laws are being setup now and made ready worldwide, to do what was accomplished in Cyprus[76]. Therefore, immediate action should be taken to remove those funds, and convert to hard assets by acquiring assets such as real estate and gold and silver internationally and whatever smaller amount of funds is maintained in cash should be maintained in foreign currency and in worldwide accounts in small, sound banks. Crypto-currencies may be another way to protect funds.

THE FATALLY FLAWED ECONOMIC SYSTEM: CRONY CAPITALISM (FASCISM)

The policies outlined above have the effect of keeping the masses of the population (lower 90% of the population) in a perpetual state of, what Alan Greenspan, the former chairmen of the USA Central Bank [Federal Reserve], an institution setup by congress with the supposed mandate to look out for the welfare of the entire population, referred to as "insecurity", even though that mandate is nowhere written in the Federal Reserve Law that originally setup the FED.

> "…as Alan Greenspan frankly told the Wall Street Journal in 1989, his job as
> Fed chairman was to maintain a certain minimum level of "worker insecurity"

---

[76] http://www.globalresearch.ca/cyprus-style-wealth-confiscation-is-now-starting-to-happen-all-over-the-globe/5351565

so there wouldn't be "wage inflation" – income increases among the middle class."

and

... front page Jan. 27, 1997, the newspaper that represents the voice of what it calls the "investor class" [The Wall Street Journal] pointed out how former Federal Reserve chairman Alan Greenspan saw one of his main responsibilities as maintaining a high enough level of worker insecurity that employees wouldn't demand pay raises or benefit increases: "Workers' fear of losing their jobs restrains them from seeking the pay raises that usually crop up when employers have trouble finding people to hire. Even if the economy didn't slow down as he expected, he told Fed colleagues... he saw little danger of a sudden upturn in wages and prices. 'Because workers are more worried about their own job security and their marketability if forced to change jobs, they are apparently accepting smaller increases in their compensation at any given level of labor-market tightness,' Mr. Greenspan told Congress at that time."

So Greenspan was basically working against the stated purpose of the Fed, which is to provide "maximum employment" where he was saying he thought "worker insecurity" was a good thing. Greenspan was not acting alone – he had presidents (starting with Reagan and including Clinton, Greenspan's "favorite Republican president") and congress who obviously went along with this, otherwise he would have been replaced.

But why is no one talking about "maximum employment" as part of the Fed's mandate??? And one of its obvious failures?

-*Threshold* Thom Hartmann

Federal Reserve Board Building

The Federal Reserve bank system of the USA supposedly has a mandate to promote "maximum employment", which would be a benefit for 100% of the population. However, in the 100 years of its existence (created in 1913) it has demonstrated that in reality it is a front for world banks and their owners (power elite) through which they control and manipulate the currency supply, markets and maintain wages low, maintain cash on hand for wars to impose vulture capitalism and globalization [opening up foreign markets to USA corporations and plunder their resources[77] by force] on weaker countries under the pretext of "protecting the interests of democracy" or "our way of life", euphemisms for propagating and perpetuating a neoliberal[78] business and political agenda, to provide the wealthy with unhindered access to the markets and natural resources of other countries. The FED also provides the wealthy banks and institutions controlled by the world power elite with free or low cost capital for investment, an advantage given to no one else. The FED also applies inflation to the economy and thereby reduces the value of the currency in favor of the wealthy and to the detriment of everyone else. Greenspan, hailed as leading exponent of "free markets", later, when questioned about the 2008 economic crash that he allowed and helped to occur, admitted his ideology of economics, which is essentially "Libertarian" government and "laissez-faire"[79]/[80] (unrestricted, unregulated, without legal protections) commerce, was "flawed".

> REP. HENRY WAXMAN: You had the authority to prevent irresponsible lending practices that led to the subprime mortgage crisis. You were advised to do so by many others. And now our whole economy is paying its price.
>
> Do you feel that your ideology pushed you to make decisions that you wish you had not made?
>
> ALAN GREENSPAN: Well, remember that what an ideology is, is a conceptual framework with the way people deal with reality. Everyone has one. You have to -- to exist, you need an ideology. The question is whether it is accurate or not.

---

[77] including cheap labor
[78] The term neoliberal is now used mainly by those who are critical of legislative market reforms such as free trade, deregulation, privatization, and reducing government control of the economy. [Taylor C. Boas and Jordan Gans-Morse, Neoliberalism: From New Liberal Philosophy to Anti-Liberal Slogan, Studies in Comparative International Development (SCID), Volume 44, Number 2, 137–161]
[79] **Laissez-faire** (lɛseɪˈfɛər-/,) (or sometimes laisser-faire) is an economic environment in which transactions between private parties are free from government restrictions, tariffs, and subsidies, with only enough regulations to protect property rights.Gaspard, Toufick. *A Political Economy of Lebanon 1948-2002: The Limits of Laissez-faire*. Boston: Brill, 2004. Print
[80] The phrase *laissez-faire* is French and literally means "let [them] do", but it broadly implies "let it be," "let them do as they will," or "leave it alone". Scholars generally believe a *laissez-faire* state or a completely free market has never existed. Buder, Stanley. 2009. *Capitalizing on Change: A Social History of American Business* Pg. 13. ISBN 978-0-8078-3231-8.
Hessen, Robert. ""A fully free economy, true laissez-faire, never has existed...", Robert Hessen, senior research fellow at Stanford University's Hoover Institution". Econlib.org. Retrieved 2013-07-30.

And what I'm saying to you is, yes, I found a flaw. I don't know how significant or permanent it is, but I've been very distressed by that fact.[81]

Firstly, notice that Greenspan, who was considered as the "high priest" of Wall Street and greatest steward of the economy, speaks of his guiding principles as an ideology, not as science or proven concept or well accepted practice or economic theory approved by university peer reviewed studies. He was operating and managing the economy based on his ideology, in other words, his imagination based on a theory about how the economy and commerce should work. Another way of putting it is, he was operating, not with a fact-based ideology but rather under a delusion that businesses and corporations did not need to be regulated because they would act in their own best interest and not let the economy crash leading even to their own bankruptcy. Despite all evidence to the contrary, crackpots like Greenspan have been allowed to promulgate their ideology and since they have enough funds to spread their message for and wide, they begin to rationalize and believe in their own imaginative concepts

---

[81] http://www.pbs.org/newshour/bb/business/july-dec08/crisishearing_10-23.html
http://theflawmovie.com/synopsis.html

even when there is plain evidence to prove the contrary. He is not alone. Millions of people have an ideology about what life is, what religion is, what politics is or should be. This way of life leads to contradictions, frustrations, conflict and even wars. This deluded way of life is a contravention to the foundation of Maat Philosophy which has, among its main principles, the virtue of following truth, regardless of if it contradicts your desires to have things work some other way. This "flaw" Greenspan spoke of and the admission that his understanding of economics is based on an ideology and not based on proven economic principles, is a severe indictment of the economic system, from one of its foremost proponents, should have been a wakeup call to all who want to see a just and correct form of economics being used that works for all or at least most of the population instead of exclusively for the elite alone that causes economic bubbles and periodic crashes over the past 100 years. These revelations should have allowed everyone affected to realize that Greenspan's ideas of economics have not just a flaw but a "fatal flaw" and should be therefore, abandoned. Greenspan openly admitted that his philosophy (which is held by those [power elite] who control the economy and government) was "flawed" and that his actions were complicit in the economic crash of 2008. Yet, the same system of economics persists to this day, without any fundamental change, even after its inadequacies have been repeatedly demonstrated through various crashes, causing more imbalances and economic distortions that eventually lead to economic disaster. Why will there be no fundamental changes? The answer because it serves the interests of the power elite and it will continue unless there is a mass uprising in the population to force the congress, president and supreme court to make the fundamental changes and uphold the established laws or unless there is a massive collapse of the economy that will force a reevaluation. However, even if that were to occur, if a "democratic" system were reestablished, the same power elite will eventually (over decades) again deteriorate the politics and economics through bribery (campaign contributions), as they have done before. So a more comprehensive answer would be to rewrite the constitution with special provisions that would force a fair distribution of resources and force government officials to uphold the laws and apply them to all equally. It is important also to understand that just changing laws without changing from a culture of pleasure-seeking, corporate greed, mindless entertainments, faith based religion, faith-based economics Greenspan's ideology, (Reaganomics, trickledown economics, neo-liberalism, etc.) and unethical standards in business, any law will eventually be subverted and violated to such a degree as to reproduce the current situation. So there needs to be a simultaneous change of the heart and a change of ethics in leadership from the present greed based, sociopathic corporate and government leadership to a leadership of the wise and ethically conscious members of society.

CONCLUSIONS

Maat Philosophy Versus Fascism and the Police State

Maat philosophy exhorts order, ethical conscience, benevolence and peace. The policies, institutions and actions of western culture, in particular the USA, Europe and Japan, constitute an antithesis to best practices and ethical culture suggested by Maatian wisdom. Consequently, the people of those cultures suffer the indignities of financial slavery, wars, impoverishment and political impotence, while thinking they have any input into the policies of government. The masses are powerless because they too are deluded by the ignorance about the possibility of life based on the wisdom of harmonious living, living by truth instead of ideologies and instead seeking to discover the true purpose of life as well as the means to attain true happiness in life. That ignorance weakens them and makes them susceptible to those who have no compunction about manipulating them and tyrannically ruling over them. All of those actions, by the power elite, that are based on the greed and unethical models of economics, are in complete and utter contravention with the tenets of MAAT, not only because they are morally reprehensible but because they are unsustainable. Maat dictates that what is sustainable is the good and only balance, justice and truth can be sustainable in the long run and this is why Ancient Egyptian society survived without economic or ecological crises over thousands of years. One cannot find any of the 42 main principles of Maat that have not been repeatedly and continuously broken by the USA government officials and or corporate leaders including lying, murder, fraud and all manner of malfeasance including neglect of the elderly and children, allowing hunger, homelessness and saddling students with debt, denying healthcare and decent wages that allow opportunity for human and social positive development. All of these issues are covered by the Maatian injunctions which are enshrined in the Pert-M-Heru texts.

Below: A compilation of the 42 main Precepts of Maat (with their variant readings) for ethical conscience in human interpersonal, government, and economic interactions.

(1) "I have not done iniquity." <u>Variant: Acting with falsehood.</u>
(2) "I have not robbed with violence."
(3) "I have not done violence (To anyone or anything)." <u>Variant: Rapacious (Taking by force; plundering.)</u>
(4) "I have not committed theft." <u>Variant: Coveted.</u>
(5) "I have not murdered man or woman." <u>Variant: Or ordered someone else to commit murder.</u>
(6) "I have not defrauded offerings." <u>Variant: or destroyed food supplies or increased or decreased the measures to profit.</u>
(7) "I have not acted deceitfully." <u>Variant: With crookedness.</u>
(8) "I have not robbed the things that belong to God."
(9) "I have told no lies."
(10) "I have not snatched away food."

(11) "I have not uttered evil words." <u>Variant: Or allowed myself to become sullen, to sulk or become depressed.</u>
(12) "I have attacked no one."
(13) "I have not slaughtered the cattle that are set apart for the Gods." <u>Variant: The Sacred bull – (Apes)</u>
(14) "I have not eaten my heart" (overcome with anguish and distraught). <u>Variant: Committed perjury.</u>
(15) "I have not laid waste the ploughed lands."
(16) "I have not been an eavesdropper or pried into matters to make mischief." <u>Variant: Spy.</u>
(17) "I have not spoken against anyone." <u>Variant: Babbled, gossiped.</u>
(18) "I have not allowed myself to become angry without cause."
(19) "I have not committed adultery." <u>Variant: And homosexuality.</u>
(20) "I have not committed any sin against my own purity."
(21) "I have not violated sacred times and seasons."
(22) "I have not done that which is abominable."
(23) "I have not uttered fiery words. I have not been a man or woman of anger."
(24) "I have not stopped my ears against the words of right and wrong (Maat)."
(25) "I have not stirred up strife (disturbance)." "I have not caused terror." "I have not struck fear into any man."
(26) "I have not caused any one to weep." <u>Variant: Hoodwinked.</u>
(27) "I have not lusted or committed fornication nor have I lain with others of my same sex." <u>Variant: or sex with a boy.</u>
(28) "I have not avenged myself." <u>Variant: Resentment.</u>
(29) "I have not worked grief, I have not abused anyone." <u>Variant: Quarrelsome nature.</u>
(30) "I have not acted insolently or with violence."
(31) "I have not judged hastily." <u>Variant: or been impatient.</u>
(32) "I have not transgressed or angered God."
(33) "I have not multiplied my speech overmuch (talk too much).
(34) "I have not done harm or evil." <u>Variant: Thought evil.</u>
(35) "I have not worked treason or curses on the King."
(36) "I have never befouled the water." <u>Variant: held back the water from flowing in its season.</u>
(37) "I have not spoken scornfully." <u>Variant: Or yelled unnecessarily or raised my voice.</u>
(38) "I have not cursed The God."
(39) "I have not behaved with arrogance." <u>Variant: Boastful.</u>
(40) "I have not been overwhelmingly proud or sought for distinctions for myself (Selfishness)."
(41) "I have never magnified my condition beyond what was fitting or increased my wealth, except with such things as are (justly) mine own possessions by means of Maat." <u>Variant: I have not disputed over possessions except when</u>

they concern my own rightful possessions. Variant: I have not desired more than what is rightfully mine.
(42) "I have never thought evil (blasphemed) or slighted The God in my native town."

Chapter 3: The Modern Police State

As for a police state, the USA already is in a police state that is every year becoming more oppressive. Specifically, the USA is experiencing what may be referred to as a "soft police state". A soft police state is a form of government in which people have acquiesced to being spied on in every area of society and to being physically intimidated by the police, who act as enforcers of the current government and economic system in service of those who wield the power over government and the economy. In the soft police state the population acquiesces to the domination by the elite of the society but they do so willingly and even seeing it as a beneficial condition, either due to fear and desiring protection from other countries or from poverty. Another motivation can be greed; since they see and admire the wealth and power of the power elite the population may support the system in hopes of one day becoming a member of that power elite.

Under the soft police state, force in the form of police violence, threats or arrest and incarceration, is only needed for those who violate the social order in such a way that it disturbs the program of the power elite (how government and the economy are setup) or for those on the fringe who speak out against it with real capacity to fundamentally change the conditions in politics or economics. For those people there is reserved the treatment of illegal character assassination through the media, indefinite detention, audits, police brutality and extrajudicial killing which also serve to intimidate the rest of the society. The tactics just listed occur in an environment where the media works to "soften" the news by only mentioning abuse occurrences by giving them light treatment and moving on to other news or even promoting the need for such actions, by the police or government, and or advocating the position taken by government/police officials and not the position of the aggrieved citizen. The police state also occurs while frivolous entertainments, legal and illegal drugs and the illusion of democracy[82] are promoted widely and are also profit centers for big industries. When people think of a police state they think of police on every corner asking for identification papers or beating or abusing people publicly and constantly. This description might be termed "classical police state". In the classical sense a police state is defined as:

police state
    noun

---

[82] [the public is allowed to have elections of persons selected by the power elite [the political, wealthy {billionaires} and corporate elite] of the society)]

Maat Philosophy Versus Fascism and the Police State

a nation in which the police, especially a secret police, summarily suppresses any social, economic, or political act that conflicts with governmental policy.
Origin:
1860–65
Dictionary.com Unabridged
Based on the Random House Dictionary, © Random House, Inc. 2013.

police state

a state or country in which a repressive government maintains control through the police
World English Dictionary
Collins English Dictionary - Complete & Unabridged 10th Edition

A police state is a state in which the government exercises rigid and repressive controls over the social, economic, and political life of the population. A police state typically exhibits elements of totalitarianism and social control, and there is usually little or no distinction between the law and the exercise of political power by the executive.

The inhabitants of a police state experience restrictions on their mobility, and on their freedom to express or communicate political or other views, which are subject to police monitoring or enforcement. Political control may be exerted by means of a secret police force which operates outside the boundaries normally imposed by a constitutional state.[83]

-Wikipedia

The police state par excellence is recognized to by the cold war era "*stasi*" of East Germany.

Seal of the Ministry of State Security of the GDR
(The secret police of East Germany.)

---

[83] *A Dictionary of World History*, Market House Books, Oxford University Press, 2000.

Maat Philosophy Versus Fascism and the Police State

> The **Ministry for State Security** (German: *Ministerium für Staatssicherheit*, MfS), commonly known as the **Stasi** (IPA: [ˈʃtaːziː]) (abbreviation German: *Staatssicherheit*, literally State Security), was the official state security service of the German Democratic Republic or GDR, colloquially known as East Germany. It has been described as one of the most effective and repressive intelligence and secret police agencies in the world. [84]The Stasi was headquartered in East Berlin, with an extensive complex in Berlin-Lichtenberg and several smaller facilities throughout the city. The Stasi motto was "*Schild und Schwert der Partei*" (Shield and Sword of the Party), that is the ruling Socialist Unity Party of Germany (SED). Several Stasi officials were prosecuted for their crimes after 1990.

The definition above, of "Police State" may be thought of as a classical form based on a pre-internet, pre-digital time in history. The old idea was to have extensive physical (paper) files on all members of the society and also have a large segment of the population informing on the rest so as to keep everyone afraid of saying or doing things by not knowing who was an informant (even in one's own family), for fear of being extra-judicially and without notice, arrested and imprison, incommunicado, tortured or worse, never to see one's family again, or even being "mysteriously" disappeared, or killed. The *Stasi* kept extensive files on all members of the society.[85] Nowadays, with the capacity to collect all communications, what need would the NSA need with armies of informants or vast physical files since they have accessed all telephone, internet communications, financial transactions, and travel plans by tapping into the records of corporations that handle travel, telephone and the internet? What do they need with informants and voluminous paper files if they have access to extensive online dossiers on all citizens including their DNA (programs have been uncovered showing that the governments of varied states are now collecting the DNA of newborns and as for adults, they are collecting during hospital stays and routine checkups and also by using the pretexts of incarceration or even arrest or detention for the simplest infractions or even without proof of probable cause, guilt or conviction).

Many people thought that the Soviet Union was the ultimate fascist regime, but as Noam Chomsky, the renowned professor of MIT, put it, the U.S.A. is much more powerful because they do not need guns to keep people in line, they just use narcissistic propaganda about how wonderful and good Americans are and fear propaganda about how bad the world is while dangling the ideal of attaining the "American Dream" just out of reach of most people. Chomsky referred to

---

[84] Chambers, Madeline,No remorse from Stasi as Berlin marks fall of Wall, *Reuters*, 4 Nov 2009.
Angela Merkel 'turned down' job from Stasi, *The Daily Telegraph*, 14 November 2012.
Connolly, Kate,'Puzzlers' reassemble shredded Stasi files, bit by bit, *The Los Angeles Times*, 1 November 2009.
Calio, Jim, The Stasi Prison Ghosts, *The Huffington Post*, 18 November 2009.
Rosenberg, Steve, Computers to solve Stasi puzzle, BBC, 25 May 2007.
New Study Finds More Stasi Spooks, *Der Spiegel*, 11 March 2008
[85] Most of te spying commissioned by the USA government is contracted to corporations –another example of a fascist alliance.

this process of social control (manipulation through deception and propaganda) as "Manufacturing Consent." The same concept was explained in detailed graphic form by the Nazi commander and, Hermann Goering, during world war two. The Nazi regime in Germany used these tactics expertly to control and coerce the population into militarizing and supporting genocide as well as the quest for world conquest which the masses were convinced [consent was manufactured] would be for their glory but which in reality would be for the benefit of the power elite of Germany.

> "Why of course the people don't want war. . . . That is understood. But, after all, it is the leaders of the country who determine the policy, and it's always a simple matter to drag the people along whether it's a democracy, a fascist dictatorship, a parliament or a communist dictatorship . . . the people can always be brought to the bidding of the leaders. . . . All you have to do is tell them they are being attacked, and denounce the pacifists for lack of patriotism, and exposing the country to greater danger.
>
> --Hermann Goering, Nazi Reichsmarshal and Luftwaffe chief at Nuremberg trials, 1945[86]

How often have we witnessed the same kinds of calls from Republicans or other right wing groups calling members of the Democratic Party or those who are war protesters, unpatriotic? How many times did president Bush say that the USA was under threat of imminent attack only to find out later that it was a lie and there was never any threat? In the pre-digital age the Soviet Union and East Germany kept people under control through mass intimidation and repression of independent thought or dissent and restrictions of assembly and group meeting. In the USA and western countries there are now in vast networks of information gathering technologies to monitor individuals and groups. Additionally, there are also extensive entertainments in the form of Hollywood productions from the few interesting and thought provoking, enlightening, caring presentations to the more abundant inane, absurd and mind numbing reality shows, sports, violent cop and war movies complemented by the availability of tranquilizers in the form of prescription drugs and consequently half of the population is medicated or self-medicating with prescription drugs or recreational drugs (including alcohol) which render the personality sedated, compliant and dull.

---

[86] **Hermann Wilhelm Göring** (or **Goering**;; 12 January 1893 – 15 October 1946), was a German politician, military leader, and leading member of the Nazi Party (NSDAP). After helping Adolf Hitler take power in 1933, he became the second-most powerful man in Germany. He founded the Gestapo in 1933. Göring was appointed commander-in-chief of the Luftwaffe (air force) in 1935, a position he held until the final days of World War II. By 1940 he was at the peak of his power and influence; as minister in charge of the Four Year Plan, he was responsible for much of the functioning of the German economy in the build-up to World War II. Adolf Hitler promoted him to the rank of Reichsmarschall, a rank senior to all other Wehrmacht commanders, and in 1941 Hitler designated him as his successor and deputy in all his offices. http://en.wikipedia.org/wiki/Hermann_Goering

Maat Philosophy Versus Fascism and the Police State

The people who are in control of government do not apply its own laws to all citizens since the elite and wealthy, oligarchy, do not go to jail for infractions that are orders of magnitude greater than the lowly street criminal who goes to jail for life.

Here are some facts based on information gathered over the past 40 years about the increased militarization, extrajudicial killings and police brutality in the USA. Like the proverbial boiling frog that does not realize he is boiling until it's too late because of the slow rate at which the heat has been turned up, so too the population of the modern police state has had the pressure of police militarization turned up on them, so slowly and imperceptibly that they have become acclimated to it. When incidents of police misconduct occur they are often excused as rogue officers or mistakes for which fines are paid but hardly is there ever an apology or a review leading to changes in tactics or procedures. For their part, the populace has become lulled into a sense that the brutality is necessary to keep them safe or that they are powerless to do anything about the police. The following reports are not anecdotal, but rather increasingly prevalent throughout the country.

Overkill: The Rise of Paramilitary Police Raids in America[87]

Another feature of increased paramilitary policing is the decrease of neighborhood policing. The police do not know the people they are policing and

---

[87] http://www.cato.org/publications/white-paper/overkill-rise-paramilitary-police-raids-america

their first reaction is to shoot to kill especially if they are confronted with an armed or unarmed person of color (African American, Latino, Asian, Native American).

> "We've known for a while now that American neighborhoods are increasingly being policed by cops armed with the weapons and tactics of war," said Kara Dansky, senior counsel at the ACLU's Center for Justice, which is coordinating the investigation. "The aim of this investigation is to find out just how pervasive this is, and to what extent federal funding is incentivizing this trend."[88]

ACLU Launches Nationwide Police Militarization Investigation[89]

---

[88] http://www.huffingtonpost.com/2013/03/06/aclu-police-militarization-swat_n_2813334.html
[89] http://www.huffingtonpost.com/2013/03/06/aclu-police-militarization-swat_n_2813334.html

Maat Philosophy Versus Fascism and the Police State

SWAT Team Usage Has Increased By 1500 Percent[90]

The following headlines are representative of many reports demonstrating an alarming increase of savage beatings of adults, who were not committing any crime or who were questioning police tactics, is evident but also there is an emergence of children being brutally beaten by police; not just those supposedly up to no good, but quiet or even sleeping children, has been detected.

---

[90] http://beforeitsnews.com/alternative/2013/08/swat-team-usage-has-increased-by-1500-percent-2749324.html

Woman Savagely Beaten By Police After They Spot Her Filming Them Beating A Suspect[91]

Texas man was beaten by the police, nearly drowned after being busted for sleeping in his own car without permit[92]

---

[91] http://www.addictinginfo.org/2013/05/12/woman-savagely-beaten-by-police-after-they-spot-her-filming-them-beating-a-suspect/

Maat Philosophy Versus Fascism and the Police State

Diabetic High School Girl Beaten by Police Officer and Arrested -- For Falling Asleep in Class[93]

---

[92] http://www.sott.net/article/266873-Texas-man-was-beaten-by-the-police-nearly-drowned-after-being-busted-for-sleeping-in-his-own-car-without-permit
[93] http://www.alternet.org/news-amp-politics/diabetic-high-school-girl-beaten-police-officer-and-arrested-falling-asleep-class

Maat Philosophy Versus Fascism and the Police State

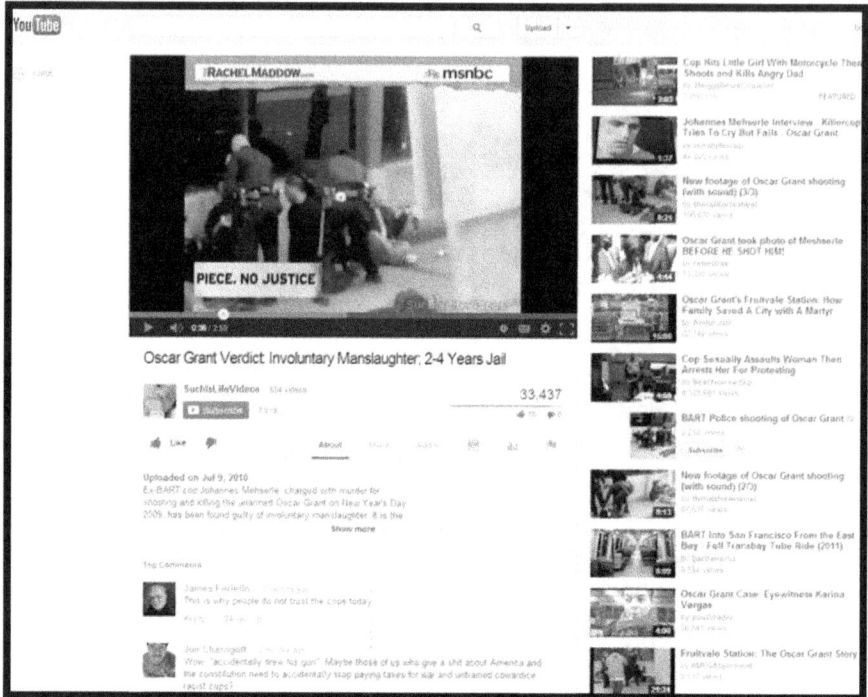

Uploaded on Jul 9, 2010[94]
Ex-BART cop Johannes Mehserle, charged with murder for shooting and killing the unarmed Oscar Grant on New Year's Day 2009, has been found guilty of involuntary manslaughter. It is the least serious of the three charges against him and comes with a sentence of 2-4 years, though he can now petition for probation alone.

The point is that the police nationwide seem to have made a calculated effort to increase the frequency and profile of beatings and extrajudicial killings (also referred to as "summary execution"), to intimidate the population. This purpose can be surmised by the decrease in crime in the last three decades. Since crime has been decreasing in the USA the increased violence projected by the police generally, has no justification except to intimidate the population preemptively, with the expectation of increased violence due to some expected cause, like economic instability. In other words, the projection of violence by the police may be considered as an effect of fear being experienced by those who control the police as to what may happen if such social unrest were to occur. The projection of violence thus serves the purpose of "training"/"grooming" the population so that they may become used to and compliant with the dictates of those in control of the police. The expressions of undue violence against a population may be termed: police brutality"[95] This issue does not mean that all

---

[94] http://www.youtube.com/watch?v=Wb35riCXs18
[95] Police brutality is the abuse of authority by the unwarranted infliction of excessive force by personnel involved in various aspects of law enforcement while in performance of their official duties. The term is also applied to abuses by corrections personnel in municipal, state and federal penal facilities including military prisons.

police officers are perpetrators of police brutality but that the effect of policing amounts to social intimidation. Therefore, those who work in or support such an unethical or immoral police department, even if they are not the primary perpetrators of violence or threat of violence, are also responsible for the misconduct and its results. While in the media the events may be portrayed as isolated incidents or incidents that occur in particular areas, statistically, a pattern may appear that demonstrates that these issues constitute a systemic problem, a structural problem that actually affects all members of the society that are targeted; in this case the target is not necessarily racial but based on income and wealth, which determines whether or not the person is in the insulated group: power elite. The idea is to intimidate the population not by constant pressure or threat of violence but through intermittent and seemingly random (variable) violence or threat of violence. Though it may seem counterintuitive, a variable threat of violence (violence may or may not be directed toward a given person versus another) can be more effective than the constant threat of violence because the variable threat of violence allows intermittent periods of stress release whereby people can live within a fiscally targeted, even though the statistical evidence demonstrates they are being targeted as a group.

Thomas Shipp and Abram Smith, lynched in Marion, Indiana on August 7, 1930

The same thing occurred with the targeting of black people for lynching. A minority of the population was lynched but the population as a whole was terrorized by the prospect of being lynched at any given time and for any given reason. In the same way, the regular presentations of possible threats from terrorism, or street crime, even though incidences are rare in comparison to the size of the population, causes people to acquiesce to being strip and cavity searched on a public road just as people accept unreasonable or seemingly nonsensical searches at airports, for example.

Incidence of police brutality in the United States[96]

While the prevalence of police brutality in the United States is not comprehensively documented, statistics on the use of physical force by law enforcement are available. For example, an extensive U.S. Department of Justice report on police use of force released in 2001 indicated that in 1999, "approximately 422,000 people 16 years old and older were estimated to have had contact with police in which force or the threat of force was used."[97]

Statistics on police brutality are much less available. The few statistics that exist include a 2006 Department of Justice report, which showed that out of 26,556 citizen complaints about excessive use of police force among large U.S. agencies (representing 5% of agencies and 59% of officers) in 2002, about 2000 were found to have merit.[98]

Other studies have shown that most police brutality goes unreported. In 1982, the federal government funded a "Police Services Study" in which over 12,000 randomly selected citizens were interviewed in three metropolitan areas. The study found that 13 percent of those surveyed claimed to have been victims of police brutality the previous year. Yet only 30 percent of those who acknowledged such brutality filed formal complaints.[99] A 1998 Human Rights Watch report stated that in all 14 precincts which it examined, the process of filing a complaint was "unnecessarily difficult and often intimidating."[100]

Police brutality can be associated with racial profiling. Differences in race, religion, politics, or socioeconomic status sometimes exist between police and the citizenry. Some police officers may view the population (or a particular subset thereof) as generally deserving punishment. Portions of the population may perceive the police to be oppressors. In addition, there is a perception that victims of police brutality often belong to relatively powerless groups, such as minorities, the young, and the poor.[101]

Recent Amnesty International and Human Rights Watch reports confirm that prison guard brutality is common in the U.S. A 2006 Human Rights Watch report revealed that five state prison systems permit the use of aggressive, unmuzzled dogs on prisoners as part of cell removal procedures.[102]

---

[96] http://everything.explained.at/Police_brutality/
[97] Web site: Contacts between Police and the Public: Findings from the 1999 National Survey. Bureau of Justice Statistics. 2001-03-21.
[98] Web site: Citizen Complaints about Police Use of Force. Bureau of Justice Statistics. Matthew Hickman. 2006-06-26.
[99] Web site: Fighting Police Abuse: A Community Action Manual. American Civil Liberties Union. 1997-12-01.
[100] Web site: Shielded from Justice: Police Brutality and Accountability in the United States. Human Rights Watch. June. 1998.
[101] Book: Powers, Mary D.. Winters, Paul A.. Policing the Police. 1995. Greenhaven Press. San Diego. 1-56510-262-2. 56–60. Civilian Oversight Is Necessary to Prevent Police Brutality.
[102] Web site: Cruel and Degrading: The Use of Dogs for Cell Extractions in U.S. Prisons. Human Rights Watch. 2006.

Abu Ghraib torture and prisoner abuse[103]

A man is intimidated, or threatened, by at least two dogs.

From late 2003 to early 2004, during the War in Iraq, military police personnel of the United States Army and the Central Intelligence Agency[104] committed human rights violations against prisoners held in the Abu Ghraib prison.
They physically and sexually abused, tortured,[105] raped,[106] sodomized,[107] and killed[108] p risoners.

It came to public attention in early 2004, beginning with Department of Defense announcements. As revealed in the *Taguba Report* (2004), an initial criminal investigation by the United States Army Criminal Investigation Command had already been underway, in which soldiers of the 320th Military Police Battalion had been

---

[103] http://en.wikipedia.org/wiki/Abu_Ghraib_torture_and_prisoner_abuse
[104] Greenwald, Glenn. "Other government agencies". Salon.com. Retrieved April 3, 2012.
[105] A-a b Hersh, Seymour M. (May 17, 2004). "Chain of Command". The New Yorker. Retrieved September 13, 2011. "NBC News later quoted U.S. military officials as saying that the unreleased photographs showed American soldiers "severely beating an Iraqi prisoner nearly to death, having sex with a female Iraqi prisoner, and 'acting inappropriately with a dead body.' The officials said there also was a videotape, apparently shot by U.S. personnel, showing Iraqi guards raping young boys.""
B-Jump up to: a b Benjamin, Mark (May 30, 2008). "Taguba denies he's seen abuse photos suppressed by Obama: The general told a U.K. paper about images he saw investigating Abu Ghraib – not photos Obama wants kept secret.". Salon.com. Archived from the original on June 11, 2009. Retrieved June 6, 2009. "The paper quoted Taguba as saying, "These pictures show torture, abuse, rape and every indecency." [...] The actual quote in the Telegraph was accurate, Taguba said – but he was referring to the hundreds of images he reviewed as an investigator of the abuse at Abu Ghraib prison in Iraq"
C- Jump up to: a b Hersh, Seymour Myron (June 25, 2007). "The general's report: how Antonio Taguba, who investigated the Abu Ghraib scandal, became one of its casualties.". The New Yorker. Retrieved June 17, 2007. "Taguba said that he saw "a video of a male American soldier in uniform sodomizing a female detainee"."
[106] A-a b Hersh, Seymour M. (May 17, 2004). (see above), B-Jump up to: a b Benjamin, Mark (May 30, 2008).(see above)
[107] C-Jump up to: a b Hersh, Seymour Myron (June 25, 2007). (see above)
[108] Walsh, Joan; Michael Scherer, Mark Benjamin, Page Rockwell, Jeanne Carstensen, Mark Follman, Page Rockwell, Tracy Clark-Flory (March 14, 2006). "Other government agencies". *The Abu Ghraib files* (salon.com). Archived from the original on February 12, 2008. Retrieved February 24, 2008. "The Armed Forces Institute of Pathology later ruled al-Jamadi's death a homicide, caused by "blunt force injuries to the torso complicated by compromised respiration.""

charged under the Uniform Code of Military Justice with prisoner abuse. In April 2004, articles describing the abuse, including pictures showing military personnel appearing to abuse prisoners, came to wide public attention when a *60 Minutes II* news report (April 28) and an article by Seymour M. Hersh in *The New Yorker* magazine (posted online on April 30 and published days later in the May 10 issue) reported the story.[109]

Lynndie England holding a leash attached to a prisoner, known to the guards as "Gus", who is lying on the floor

On May 7, 2004, International Committee of the Red Cross Operations Director Pierre Krähenbühl stated that the ICRC's inspection visits to Coalition detention centers in Iraq did "not allow us to conclude that what we were dealing with ... were isolated acts of individual members of coalition forces. What we have described is a pattern and a broad system." He went on to say that some of the incidents they had observed were "tantamount to torture".[110]

U.S. and UK armed forces are jointly trained in so-called *resistance to interrogation (R2I)* techniques. These R2I techniques are taught ostensibly to help soldiers cope with or resist torture by the enemy. On May 8, 2004, *The Guardian* reported that, according to a former British special forces officer, the acts committed by the Abu Ghraib Prison military personnel resemble the techniques used in R2I training.[111] Also related are pride-and-ego down techniques to make captives more willing to cooperate.[112]

The same report states that:

The U.S. commander in charge of military jails in Iraq, Major General Geoffrey Miller, has confirmed that a battery of 50-odd special "coercive techniques" can be used against enemy detainees. The general, who previously ran the prison camp at

---

[109] "Annals of National Security: Torture at Abu Ghraib", *The New Yorker*
[110] "Red Cross saw 'widespread abuse'". *BBC News*. May 8, 2004.
[111] Leigh, David (May 8, 2004). "UK forces taught torture methods". *The Guardian* (London).
[112] "U.S. losing 'hearts, minds,' despite sensitivity training". WorldNetDaily. April 2, 2004. Retrieved April 3, 2012.

Maat Philosophy Versus Fascism and the Police State

Guantanamo Bay, said his main role was to extract as much intelligence as possible.
—*The Guardian*

The point being made here now is that the USA prison system, as part of law enforcement, condones and advocates torture and abuse of prisoners. This culture of torture and abuse extends therefore, to the prison system, the police system and also to the military. The following demonstrates that the abusive and anti human rights practices extended to the treatment of Iraqi prisoners. The idea is the same, to intimidate through violence or the threat of violence to demand obedience. Including the use of dogs, it was demonstrated that the techniques used in Abu Ghraib were in use in domestic USA prisons.

> Punish firmly and chastise soundly, then repression of crime becomes an example. But punishment except for crime will turn the complainer into an enemy.
> -Ancient Egyptian Maatian Proverb

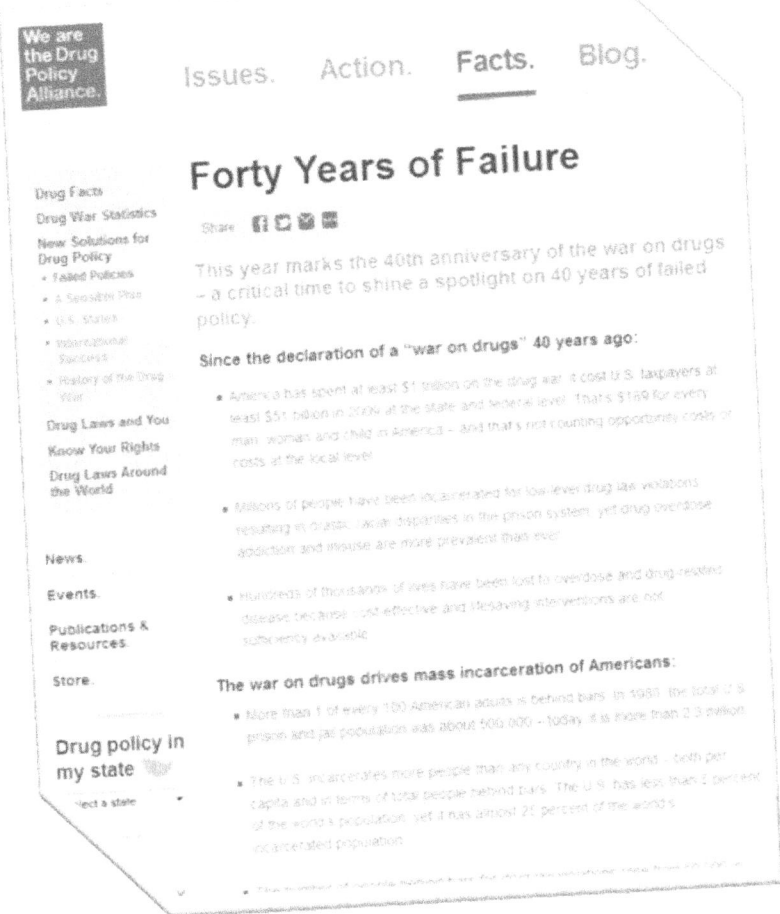

Maat Philosophy Versus Fascism and the Police State

Forty Years of Failure[113]

Even though the USA is the country with the highest number of incarcerated persons in the world it is also one of the most lawless when it comes to punishment of white collar crimes. For financial crimes and the like there is impunity and as such "repression of crime" does not become an example in western culture. Instead the encouragement of crime is the example, the opposite of Maatian philosophical wisdom; so it is clear to see why the current state of culture has developed as it has. Part of the reason is the insidious and seemingly irrational policy of incarcerating drug abusers. Drug abusers are mostly non-violent though rating drug addicts often makes the problem worse and turns them into hardened criminals by the time they get out. Otherwise, it has the effect of damaging their ability to earn and have a career as well as be a productive and positive member of society. Another issue demonstrating the unjust application of the law is the finding of disproportionate incarceration of black men. It is not known that part of the impetus behind harsh and mandatory prison sentences is the push by corporations directly or indirectly, through business advocacy groups such as ALEC or the US Chamber of Commerce, to fill the beds of their corporate run jails. This profit motive, injected into the penal system, has even led to overcrowding prisons and to bribery of judges and legislative officials. The "war on drugs", besides being a failure at stopping the influx of illegal drugs into the country, has had the effect of creating an excuse to incarcerate and fill corporate jails and put people in the penal system which harms their social mobility and capacity to participate in the political process since their ability to vote is often curtailed or cancelled. They become dependent on and fall victim to the state and thus controlled by it.

The overcrowding condition in modern day jails[114] is reminiscent of the slave ships[115] that brought Africans to the Americas as slaves. The inhumanity of prison overcrowding and the inhumanity of Slavery are stark realities of a capitalist system that causes crime and poverty and despair that lead people to crime, drug abuse and self-destruction. There is a common thread between the mistreatment of Africans, Native Americans and the prison/slavery population. It is the purposeful and callous disregard for human life, dignity and caring; a lack of empathy and understanding of human relationship. It is a result of atrophied intellects and hearts that have come to care only about their own desires, rendering the world as a place of conflict between classes, countries and between humanity and nature, the final of these which humanity will eventually lose.

---

[113] http://www.drugpolicy.org/new-solutions-drug-policy/forty-years-failure
[114] http://www.salon.com/2013/10/25/prison_overcrowding_a_boon_for_the_for_profit_industry/
[115] https://en.wikipedia.org/wiki/Slave_ship

Maat Philosophy Versus Fascism and the Police State

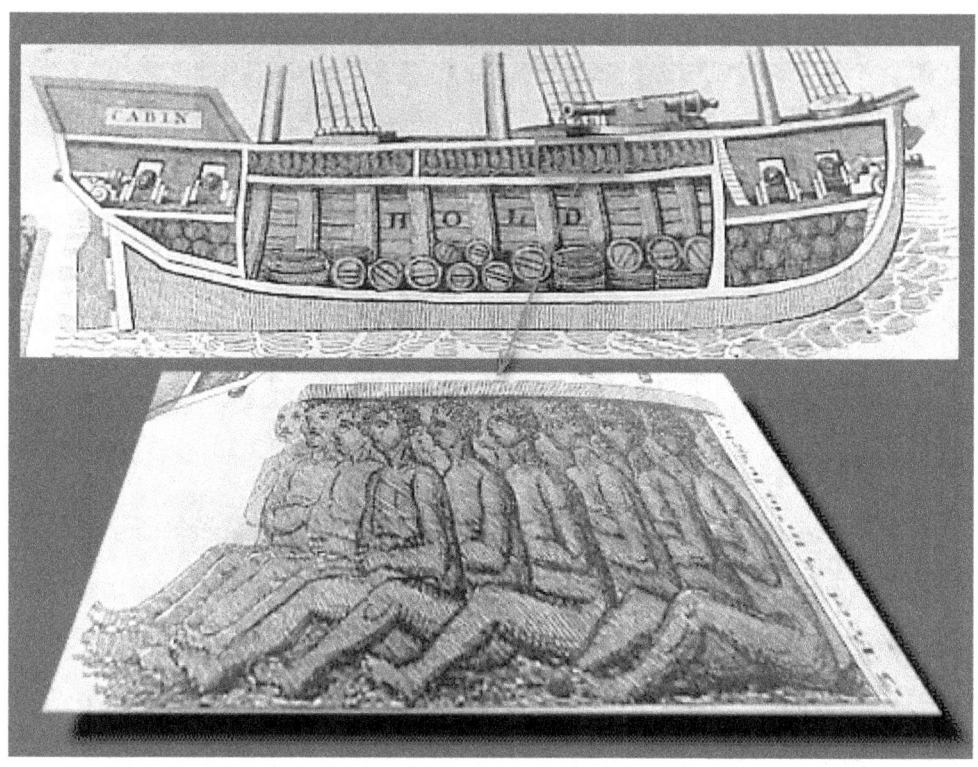

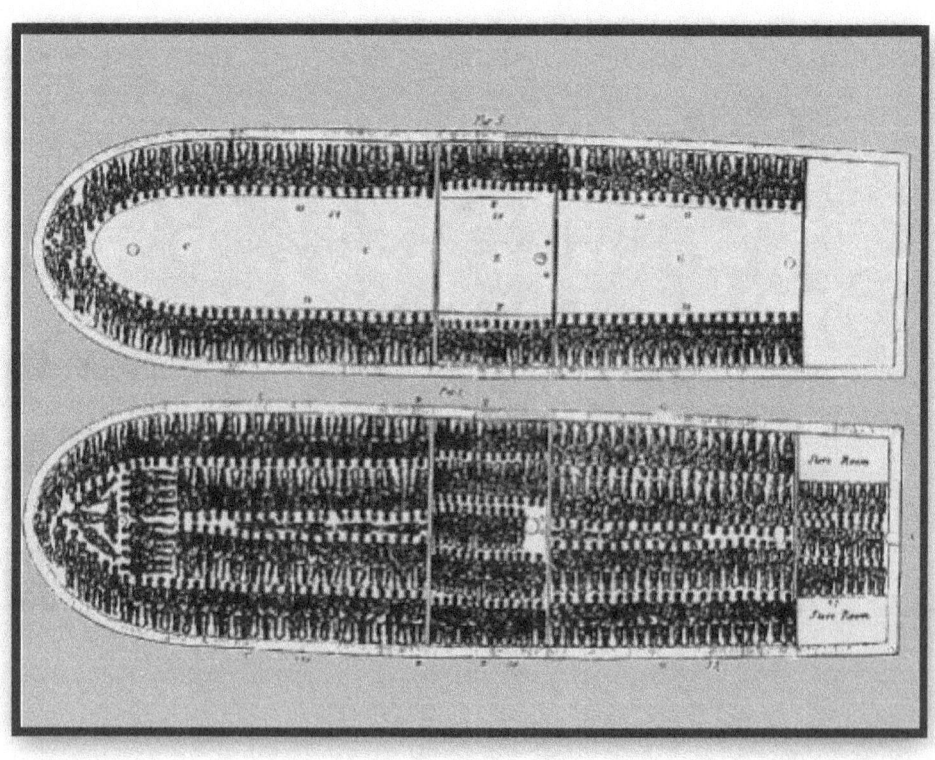

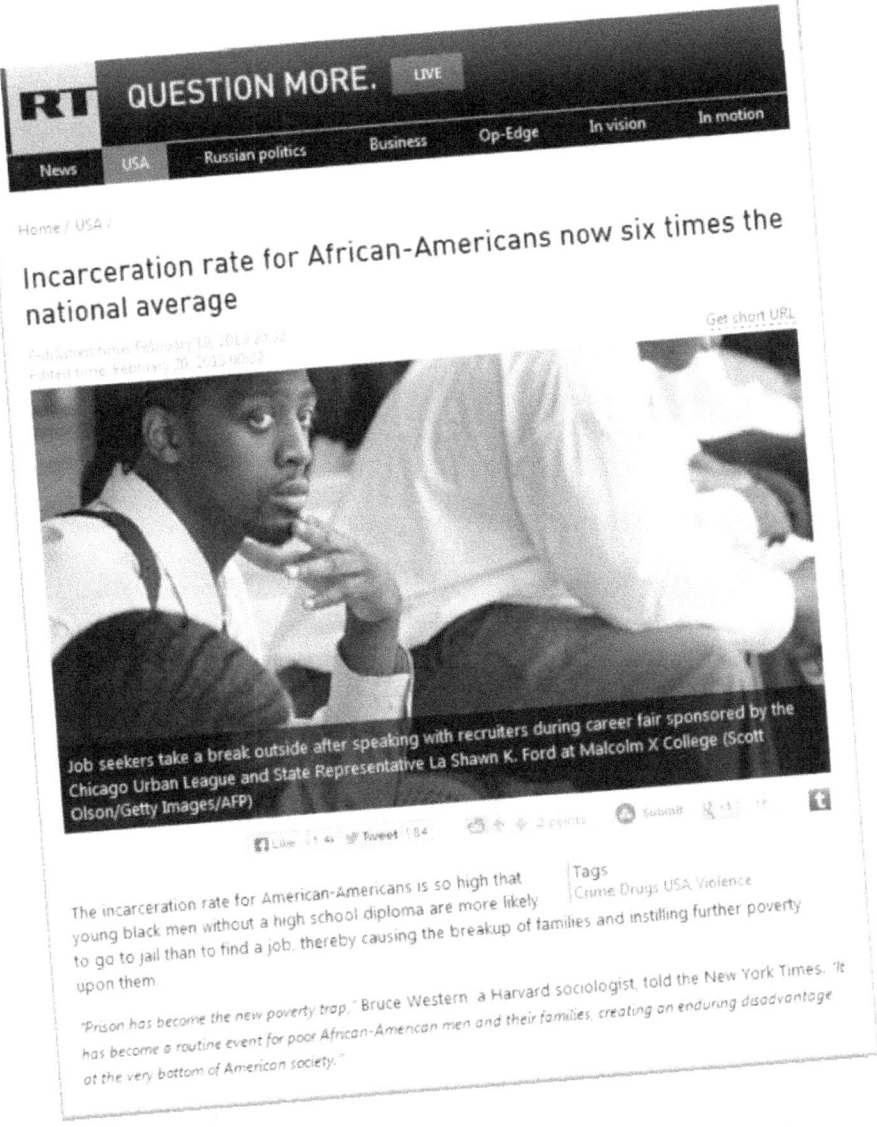

Incarceration rate for African-Americans now six times the national average[116]

Here are two examples of the violation of the Maatian injunction as regards punishing for a real crime. Consequently, to the extent that the population is not on drugs (over 50% of the USA population is on prescription, non-prescription, alcohol or other drug usage), especially the younger segment of the population, is beginning to feel increasingly angry and abandoned by the society, which will lead to social unrest and unnecessary human suffering. The injustices of society do have a disproportionately negative effect on the poor in general and an even more disproportionate effect on ethnic minorities.

---

[116] http://rt.com/usa/incarceration-african-black-prison-606/

Maat Philosophy Versus Fascism and the Police State

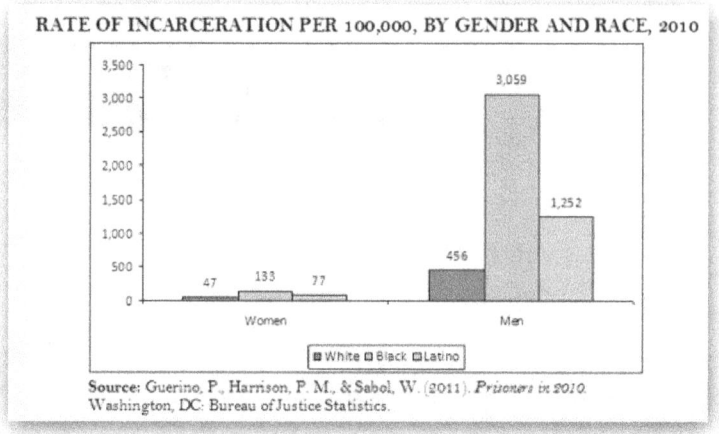

RACIAL DISPARITY[117]

> More than 60% of the people in prison are now racial and ethnic minorities. For Black males in their thirties, 1 in every 10 is in prison or jail on any given day. These trends have been intensified by the disproportionate impact of the "war on drugs," in which two-thirds of all persons in prison for drug offenses are people of color.

The disproportionate incarceration rate of African American men has been noted by many civic organizations and yet the injustice has found no legislators to resolve it. Compounding this issue is the finding that racist criteria are being applied institutionally to disproportionately give minorities and people of color longer and harsher sentences than "white" people. So, in addition to the unjust jailing of people for political or corporate reasons, there is also the compounding issue of the lingering problem of racism that continues to plague the USA and western culture in general.

The war on drugs is the new Jim Crow:[118]

- While African Americans comprise only 13 percent of the U.S. population and 13 percent of drug users, they make up 38 percent of those arrested for drug law violations and 59 percent of those convicted of drug law violations.

- Relative to population, African-Americans are 10.1 times more likely than whites to be sent to prison for drug offenses.

---

[117] http://www.sentencingproject.org/template/page.cfm?id=122
[118] http://www.drugpolicy.org/new-solutions-drug-policy/forty-years-failure

Maat Philosophy Versus Fascism and the Police State

It is important to consider that the practice of slavery in the United States of America did not end with the civil war. Many people erroneously believe that the institution of slavery was abolished by president Abraham Lincoln. However, in fact, the practice of slavery was not removed from the USA Constitution but was instead protected in the constitution in such a way that the poorest and least politically powerful members of the population could be re-enslaved in the prison system. The practice of slavery was ratified in the 13th amendment to the US Constitution. Ironically, it was signed by President Abraham Lincoln in February of 1865, who has come to be known as the president who freed the slaves.

AMENDMENT XIII

Passed by Congress January 31, 1865. Ratified December 6, 1865.

Note: A portion of Article IV, section 2, of the Constitution was superseded by the 13th amendment.

Section 1.
Neither slavery nor involuntary servitude, except as a punishment for crime whereof the party shall have been duly convicted, shall exist within the United States, or any place subject to their jurisdiction.

Section 2.
Congress shall have power to enforce this article by appropriate legislation.

Convicts Leased to Harvest Timber, around 1915, Florida

Federal Prison Industries (UNICOR or FPI) is a wholly owned United States government corporation created in 1934 that uses penal labor from the Federal Bureau of Prisons (BOP) to produce goods and services. FPI is restricted to selling its products and services to federal government agencies and has no access to the commercial market[119] The reader may be thinking that this arrangement of corporations using prison labor as slaves is something of the past, from the year 1915 or 1855 but it is going on right now.

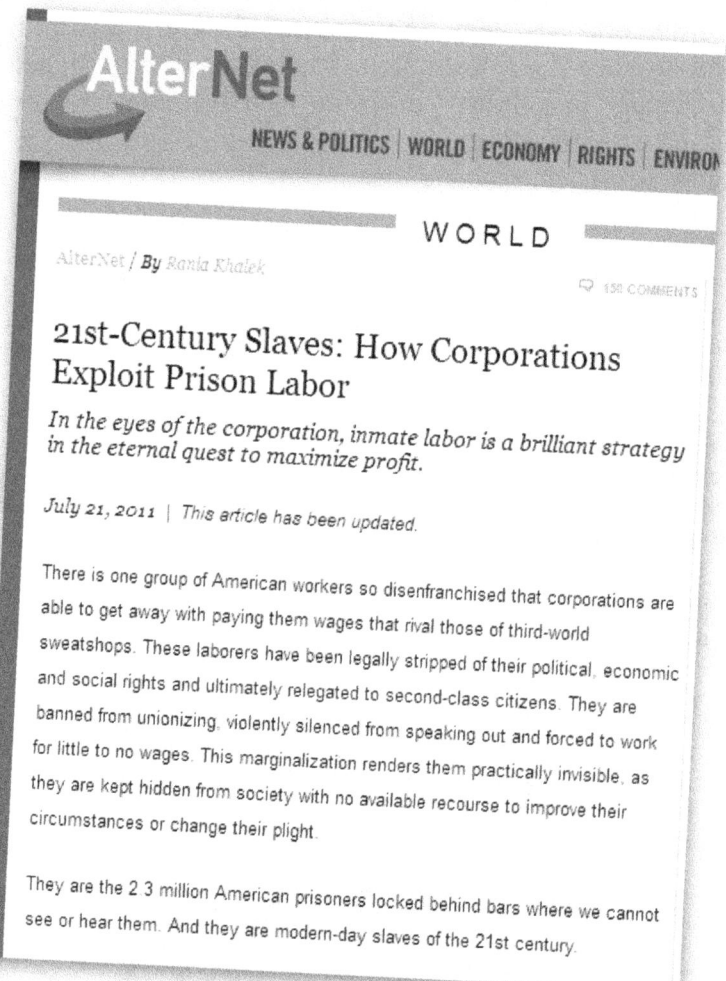

21st-Century Slaves: How Corporations Exploit Prison Labor[120]

China also exploits its workers in a similar manner as the USA. Any criminal or malcontent or political dissident or unemployed person might find him/her self working for major corporations and thereby increasing profits even more than if

---

[119] McCollum, William (1996). *Federal Prison Industries, Inc: Hearing Before the Committee on the Judiciary, U.S. House of Representatives*. DIANE Publishing. p. 1. ISBN 978-0-7567-0060-7
[120] http://www.alternet.org/story/151732/21st-century_slaves%3A_how_corporations_exploit_prison_labor

working for a corporation as a free Chinese person. Still, in the USA, prison labor can be as exploitative as the Chinese forced labor camps and can have the same effects, taking jobs away from the USA population and impoverishing the population thereby.

American prison labor means longer unemployment lines[121]

The more prison labor there is, the less people are needed in the free labor market and the less those who are working as free laborers are paid for their labor. Therefore, the disgraceful and immoral scourge of humanity, the practice of slavery, continues and thus invalidates the position of the USA as a moral or

---

[121] http://www.foxnews.com/us/2012/09/16/american-prison-labor-means-longer-unemployment-lines/

exceptional country where the rule of law and human dignity are real ideals, actual practiced features of its government, society and economic ideals Rather, the USA is exceptional in terms of the heights of government and corporate duplicity, immorality and lack of ethics. The USA culture is also exceptional in terms of the vaingloriously avaricious and vicious manner in which its leadership has been able to control its population and impoverish it for hundreds of years while inspiring in the population the idea that they are privileged for the opportunity to be impoverished, stressed, used as cannon fodder for wars, and duped into following the ever enticing but also ever elusive clique of the country's narcissistic oligarchy (small group that composes the power elite [plutocrats]).

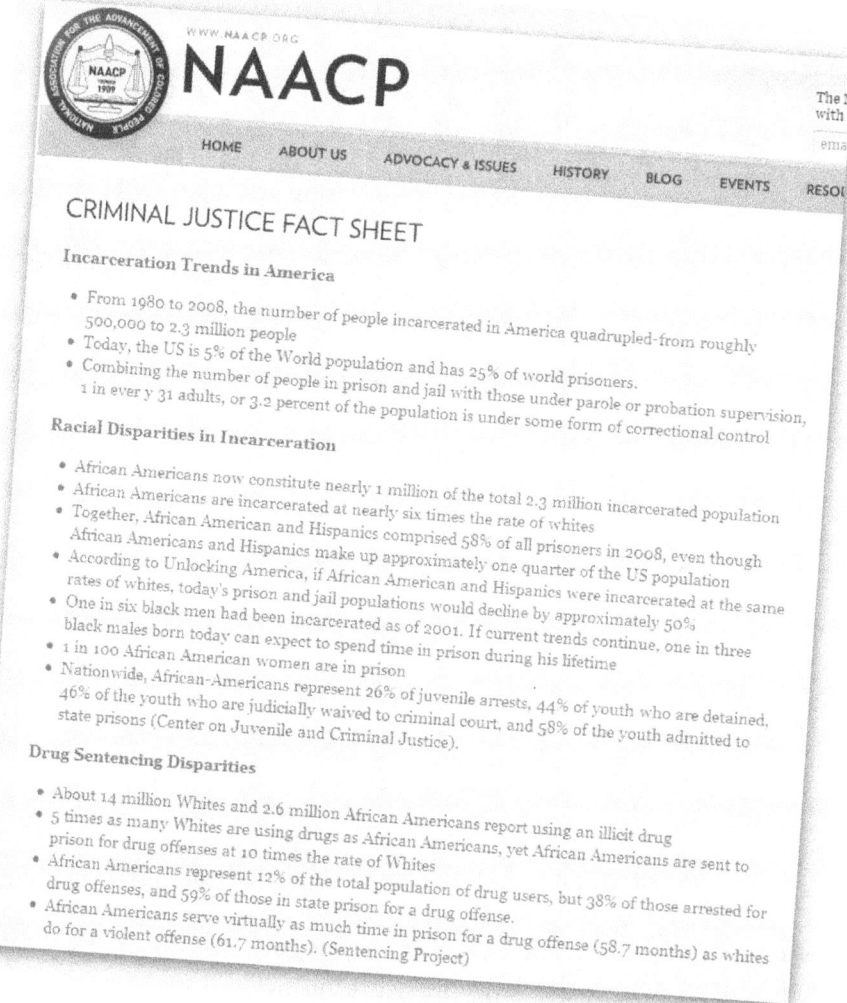

Criminal Fact Sheet[122]

---

[122] http://www.naacp.org/pages/criminal-justice-fact-sheet

Having this law, allowing slavery in the prison system, in the constitution, allowing the continuation of slavery in the penal system, as a legal basis, from here it would be easy to make laws that allow people to be incarcerated and thereby re-enslave them. After the civil war and after the 13th amendment, laws such as those against vagrancy, joblessness, etc. would allow the population in control (white people) to take non-whites at will and force them to work as prisoners for little or no wages, thus accomplishing the same goal of slavery but now in an unobtrusive manner that does not tarnish the veneer of civilized, free, open and upwardly mobile culture that the USA government representatives constantly try to present to the world.

It is this underbelly of unrighteous, unethical, immoral and greed-based policies, that are at the heart of the efforts to control nature, countries and crimes against humanity (in terms of wars and malfeasance)[123] that has caused untold misery around the world and stolen trillions of dollars of wealth from populations the world over. This practice continues today whereby corporations force inmates to work for slave wages. This practice of prison job sourcing, like job outsourcing to other countries such as Mexico, India or China, exacerbates the regular job market in such a way that all wages for all workers are depressed. Additionally, the masses of the population that make up 70% of economic spending that sustains the economy, are unnecessarily under pressure from out as well as in-sourcing low wage jobs by the corporatocracy (rule by power elite through corporations), that has only its own interests at heart and not that of the regular workers or the economy as a whole.

---

[123] See the book *Malfeasance and Immorality* -by Muata Ashby

1	United States of America	716
2	St. Kitts and Nevis	714
3	Seychelles	709
4	Virgin Islands (U.S.A.)	539
5	Barbados	521
6	Cuba	510
7	Rwanda	492
8	Anguilla (United Kingdom)	487
9	Belize	476
10	Russian Federation	475
11	Virgin Islands (United Kingdom)	460
12	Sint Maarten (Netherlands)	456
13	Bahamas	444
14	Guam (USA)	432
15	Grenada	424
16	El Salvador	422
17	Bermuda (United Kingdom)	417
18	Azerbaijan	413
19	Panama	411
20	Antigua and Barbuda	403
21	Thailand	398
22	Dominica	391

Entire world - Prison Population Rates per 100,000 of the national population

FINAL NOTE: Slavery should not be thought of as only an event that occurs when a person is incarcerated. There are open air prisons such as the neighborhoods established by the white population of South Africa to control the black population or the occupation and restriction of Gaza and the West Bank, by Israelis to control the Palestinians. These open air prisons restrict wages, food, medicines and all commodities, keeping people in abject poverty and impotent to change their situation. In the USA there is an illusion of freedom but in essence there is an open air prison whereby the majority of the population lives on slave wages[124] and or in fear of losing a job and being one paycheck

---

[124] Slave wages are wages that do not allow a person to have any economic life beyond subsistence level existence, meaning just enough to pay basic expenses of life or just under what is necessary to pay for the basic expenses of life such that a person even if they are working full time still has to seek public assistance from food stamps, welfare, charity, etc. Additionally, those on slave wages cannot afford to live in their own house, get a quality education or pursue the higher meaning of life or better their economic situation or their family. They are relegated to the position of dependent on the state or those who offer charity and thus they are also subject to the desires, opinions and dictates of those with means.

away from hunger, destitution and homelessness or where the next meal is coming from. In the USA, the UK and other places open air prisons are created by segregating people in accordance with their income. Neighborhoods with low income get food deserts, municipal dumps as well as toxic waste dumps, bad schools and minimal healthcare, if at all. Two shameful examples of the greed, cruelty and disregard by the power elite (owners of corporations and government leaders that allow their greed to express in grotesque and wanton ways) and the culture of capitalism and efforts to degrade laborers and break unions as well as indifference and contempt for human life occurred in the year 2013 when two of the world's largest corporations, that made vast profits, reduced their employees to such slave wages that the employees were going hungry.

You have to give it to them here. The balls. The balls are large. A Walmart in Canton, Ohio is holding a Thanksgiving food drive among its employees...*to benefit its employees*. Because some of them can't afford food for some mysterious reason. ..

Walmart makes billion-dollar profits off its employees' willingness/need to work whatever hours are available for whatever wage is available, and when that cycle of poverty causes problems (like, say, not being able to feed your children), Walmart foists the burden of finding a solution on to other employees. A literal wall would have more human empathy and shame.[125]

Cutting regular-size meals into many tiny bites, singing happy songs during trying times, and selling all your extra stuff on eBay and Craigslist are just some of the completely unhelpful tips McDonald's is actually, seriously suggesting to workers through its McResources employee portal. As advocacy group Low Pay Is Not OK's new video shows, the fast-food giant is also

---

[125] http://jezebel.com/wal-mart-asks-employees-to-donate-food-to-other-hungr-1466905123

admonishing employees to "quit complaining," you know, because that raises stress hormone levels.[126]

FINAL NOTE2: The USA is the country with most incarcerated persons per 100,000 residents.[127] It has 4.5% of the world population and 25% of the incarcerated persons in the entire world. The number of the incarcerated persons in the USA is 7% of the population. This means that USA residents have the highest chance (risk) of being incarcerated or falling under the control and or punishment (deserved or not) by some aspect of the prison industrial complex.

FINAL NOTE ADDITIONAL: Since African Americans and other persons of color make up the highest percentage of the incarcerated, considering that they make up a higher percentage of the prison population than their presence in the total population, this means that they have a higher chance of becoming incarcerated or being otherwise affected by the prison industrial complex than if they lived in other countries. In other words, the USA is an inherently more dangerous place to live from the standpoint of the risk of incarceration and falling under the control of the legal system, which has the additional effect of reducing a person's capacity to find jobs, career advancement, political participation, etc., all of which allows the police state to "legally" exercise additional control over those persons. These risks are highest for the poor of all ethnicities and more so for those people of color or other economically disempowered minorities.

---

[126] http://www.grubstreet.com/2013/11/mcdonalds-mcresources.html
[127] http://www.prisonstudies.org/info/worldbrief/wpb_stats.php?area=all&category=wb_poprate

THE HARD POLICE STATE AND THE CULTURE OF EXCEPTIONALISM

It is the contention of this study that the USA is currently experiencing what may be classified as a "*Soft* Police State" while the system imposed in East Germany may be classified as a "*Hard* Police State." Nevertheless, in the soft police state all the elements are in place to make the system "hard", that is to say, the infrastructure is there to apply physically repressive methods to physically menace the society, detain, jail or stifle dissent if necessary, that is, if the soft methods fail (welfare, food stamps, entertainments, drugs, and narcissistic propaganda such as repeating the scientifically debunked ideas such as the USA is the land of opportunity and upward mobility or the idea that the USA is an exceptional country and therefore able and justified in doing things that other countries cannot and should not be allowed to do such as attacking other countries.[128]

In a speech president Barak Obama repeated the idea of USA exceptionalism as part of an effort to excuse USA aggression towards the country Syria. The president of Russia, Vladimir Putin, responded to his speech and drew much negative attention from the USA political establishment instead of reflection on the deeper meaning of the critique on "American Exceptionalism" as a dangerous social pathology. One of the parts of Putin's Op Ed in the New York Times that drew the most ire was his challenge to the delusion perpetrated by the USA political establishment about USA exceptionalism in which he stated:

> If we can avoid force against Syria, this will improve the atmosphere in international affairs and strengthen mutual trust. It will be our shared success and open the door to cooperation on other critical issues.
>
> My working and personal relationship with President Obama is marked by growing trust. I appreciate this. I carefully studied his address to the nation on

---

[128] *Collapse of Civilization and the Death of American Empire* by Muata Ashby

Tuesday. And I would rather disagree with a case he made on American exceptionalism, stating that the United States' policy is "what makes America different. It's what makes us exceptional." It is extremely dangerous to encourage people to see themselves as exceptional, whatever the motivation. There are big countries and small countries, rich and poor, those with long democratic traditions and those still finding their way to democracy. Their policies differ, too. We are all different, but when we ask for the Lord's blessings, we must not forget that God created us equal.

-Vladimir V. Putin is the president of Russia.[129]

Even though the USA is not the only country that has freedom (in terms of capacity to vote), there are other countries where the population exercises the same political rights. What is the USA exceptional at? When compared to the other 191 sovereign nations of the world the USA is 7th in literacy, 27th in math, 22nd in science, 49th in life expectancy, 178th in infant mortality, 3rd in median household income. The USA leads the world countries in military spending, and most incarcerated people, also, it is possible that the USA is responsible for more coups, toppling of governments and destabilizations of economies, more people dead in wars and the spreading of more chemical and nuclear pollution than any other country in history. The USA engaged in wars of the late 2oth century that killed millions (millions dead in Korea, Viet Nam, Iraq, Afghanistan, Libya and Syria).

The superpower mindset was perhaps best demonstrated by Vice President George H. Bush in 1987. Before he became president, Iran was locked in war with Iraq. Iran started to gain the advantage over Iraq, so the US forces were sent to decisively support Iraq [Saddam Hussein] so that Iran would not win and gain control of Iraq. President Ronald Reagan and Vice President George H. Bush [of the republican party] sent a large US armada to the Persian Gulf to make sure that Iraq would receive weapons. A US gunship shot down an Iranian civilian airliner. They killed 290 passengers. In
response to that tragedy and loss of civilian lives Vice President Bush said:

"I will never apologize for America. I don't care what the facts are."

The statement above denotes hubris but also a complex of superiority that devalues life in the pursuit of the superpower's goals and objectives and allows the personality to act callously to protect the superpower economy and hegemony at the cost of the lives of soldiers or civilians. To the superpower president, the loss of human life is treated as a necessary part of maintaining the superpower supremacy.

---

[129] http://www.nytimes.com/2013/09/12/opinion/putin-plea-for-caution-from-russia-on-syria.html?pagewanted=all&_r=0#h[]

United Nations report: U.S. 17th happiest country in the world [130]
The role of demagogic religious, political and corporate leaders has been to fan the frenzy of patriotism and nationalism and mask the true detrimental and toxic expressions of USA politics that degrade the lives of people abroad as well as the domestic population despite their frantic flag waving at political and sports rallies, the indoctrination of the young with exceptionalistic ideas and outward displays of satisfaction. For these and other reasons Henry David Thoreau referred to the USA as a society in which:

---

[130] http://www.cbsnews.com/8301-204_162-57602077/

Maat Philosophy Versus Fascism and the Police State

"The mass of men lead lives of quiet desperation. What is called resignation is confirmed desperation."

Therefore there is no evidence that the USA is exceptional or the greatest country on earth. There is evidence however, that the unethical and immoral as well as amoral nature of USA politics and the delusion of exceptionalism have led to continual promotion of violence in the world in the 21st century[131] as it was in the 20th and 19th centuries. This reflection on history and current politics and economics prompted Martin Luther King Jr. to refer to the USA role in the world as:

"the greatest purveyor of violence in the world today [is] my own government"[132]

---

[131] http://www.huffingtonpost.com/michael-shank/march-on-washington-great_b_3797222.html
[132] http://www.hark.com/clips/zvpntckzzk-greatest-purveyor-of-violence

Maat Philosophy Versus Fascism and the Police State

Martin Luther King, Jr., speaking against the Vietnam War, St. Paul Campus, University of Minnesota on April 27, 1967

The idea of exceptionalism, which has been around USA politics since the 19th century, has underpinned justifications of USA wars and illegal actions to undermine the governments and economies of other countries such as the CIA instigated coups of Iran in 1953 and in Chile in 1973. The idea of USA exceptionalism also underpins the delusion of capitalism as the ideal economic system and thus justifying the use of USA military power to force compliance by other countries with the economic designs of the USA political establishment which serves to protect the exploits of the USA multinational corporations. Thus, the soft or hard police state is a tool of a capitalist minded government which serves the desires of the corporate state which requires a compliant, and consumer oriented population that will acquiesce to being subconsciously controlled to be consumers or soldiers to enforce the policies arrived at by those in government and those leaders of the multinational corporations and their related power elite which amounts to not democracy but fascism. Therefore, a police state is merely a tool for enforcement of fascism, and capitalism is a method of enforcing crony capitalism. Consequently, we are also forced to recognize that the USA is and has been for some time controlled by the power elite and the corporate class and is indeed a country controlled by a fascist government.

When we are discussing the topic of "police state" we can also not avoid the topic of a "prison industrial complex" for these are related. The police are used to repress the population and the prisons are not there primarily for the purpose of rehabilitation or to protect society from violent criminals but rather to provide an excuse to intimidate the population as a whole and substitute for the previous slavery system since the law allows for corporations to use an incarcerated person's labor for free or near free while the prison system, especially the private prison system, assuming the position of the old slave masters and plantation owners, benefits financially from the arrangement. The government and power elite benefit from the bribes (political contributions) and profits but the society also keeps indigent segments of the population from disrupting the wider society and this also allows them to point to someone other than themselves as the supposed "trouble makers" of society and thus deflect the spotlight away from their own corruption. Therefore, there is a strong incentive for corporate owned jails to incarcerate more people in order to make more money off the state, which pays per bed occupied in the jails. The benefit for the state is that there is more cheap labor, more persons locked out of the workforce and outside the political system and destitute, depending on the government and thus not in a position to offer independent political opposition. In recent years, private prison companies have lobbied congress to make laws in such a way that it is easier for the police to arrest people for lesser infractions while the sentences for all infractions are longer, thereby allowing the companies to have more prison populations for longer periods of time and thus insuring and raising profits.

So, the lawmakers, judges, medical establishment, corporations, banks and media, that they own, are all in collusion by being in favor of their own interests, regardless of the law and this is the mechanism by which the power elite profits on the backs of the general population and at the same time control society. In the neo-police state [soft police state] there is no necessity for a large and extensive police apparatus since the mass mainstream media, which is owned by bigger corporations and billionaires, constantly spews propaganda about how the USA is the best country that ever existed and it is the "land of opportunity" even for people starting with nothing, despite the evidence that shows otherwise and despite the violations of human rights and the depravity of its leaders who allow hunger, homelessness and lack of opportunity for the majority of its citizens in the supposedly "wealthiest country on earth" to exist. It has been now found that the USA is not a land of opportunity as other countries rank higher in social mobility. The USA is a land where cronyism and nepotism as well as racism, and sexism, all of which still define the social, economic and political order, are promoted and managed by the power elite (upper 1-2% of the population). The following studies provide insight into the delusion of the "American Dream" and similar delusions in other populations around the world, which are oppressed by class struggle against a capitalist/neo-liberal system. The delusions inspire people to hang on and continue striving for a life they can never have, even as their wealth and quality of life diminish year after year.

> The American Dream Report, a study of the Economic Mobility Project, found that Americans surveyed were more likely than citizens of other countries to agree with statements like

- "People get rewarded for intelligence and skill",
- "People get rewarded for their efforts";

and less likely to agree with statements like

- "Coming from a wealthy family is 'essential' or 'very important' to getting ahead,"
- "Income differences in my country are too large" or
- "It is the responsibility of government to reduce differences in income."[133]

In the US only 32% of respondents agreed with the statement that forces beyond their personal control determine their success. In Europe, in contrast, majorities of respondents agreed with this "fatalistic" view in every country but three (Britain, the Czech Republic and Slovakia).[134] The Brookings Institute found Americans surveyed had the highest belief in meritocracy — 69% agreed with the statement "people are rewarded for intelligence and skill" — among 27 nations surveyed.[135]

Another report found such beliefs to have gotten stronger over the last few decades.[136]

According to journalist Jason DeParle

At least five large studies in recent years have found the United States to be less mobile than comparable nations. A project led by Markus Jantti, an economist at a Swedish university, found that 42 percent of American men raised in the bottom fifth of incomes stay there as adults. That shows a level of persistent disadvantage much higher than in Denmark (25 percent) and Britain (30 percent) — a country famous for its class constraints.[137] Meanwhile, just 8 percent of American men at the bottom rose to the top fifth. That compares with 12 percent of the British and 14 percent of the Danes. Despite frequent references to the United States as a classless society, about 62 percent of Americans (male and female) raised in the top fifth of incomes stay in the top two-fifths, according to research by the Economic Mobility Project of the Pew Charitable Trusts. Similarly, 65 percent born in the bottom fifth stay in the bottom two-fifths.[138]

The Economist also stated that "evidence from social scientists suggests that American society is much 'stickier' than most Americans assume. ... would-be Horatio Algers are finding it no easier to climb from rags to riches, while the children of the privileged have a greater chance of staying at the top of the

---

[133] Economic Mobility Project
[134] Ever higher society, ever harder to ascend Whatever happened to the belief that any American could get to the top? economist.com 29 December 2004
[135] International Comparisons of Economic Mobility Julia Isaacs| brookings.edu, 2008
[136] CAP: *Understanding Mobility in America* - April 26, 2006
[137] American Exceptionalism in a New Light: A Comparison of Intergenerational Earnings Mobility in the Nordic Countries, the United Kingdom and the United States Markus Jäntti et al.| January 2006
[138] Harder for Americans to Rise From Lower Rungs | By JASON DeParle | January 4, 2012] Economic mobilities of Families Across Generations Brookings Institute

social heap. The United States risks calcifying into a European-style class-based society."[139]

So the police can be used to legitimately keep order and peace but in the police state it is also used in the fascist manner, to maintain the power of the power elite and to promote "law and order" based on the laws set by the power elite and the socio-political-economic order of power over the population. The other order protected by the police is the hierarchy of the power structure with the wealthy at the top, enforcing the rules, regulations and laws established by that power elite through politicians and the judges they sponsor.

---

[139] Ever higher society, ever harder to ascend Whatever happened to the belief that any American could get to the top? economist.com 29 December 2004
via Brendan Nyhan's Blog

Chapter 5: The Illusion of the American Dream and the Reality of a Corporate backed Police State

So the American Dream" is a sham, perpetrated to maintain an illusion and the duping of a perpetually buzzed population that has been convinced that there are actually two separate political parties instead of one party with two wings that are both controlled by and work for the benefit of the same power elite. Under these conditions, the classical "hard" police state is not necessary as long as people remain deluded, believing that the government and or economic system can somehow benefit them or not hurt them, even if it hurts others in the society (minorities, the poor or others whom the society deems as undesirables and or as undeserving. The heavy handedness of the classical police state, where police are always around asking for a person's ID or frequently doing warrantless searches and seizures is not necessary as long as people remain deluded and compliant, believing that, out of fear of being singled out for terrorist treatment (arrest and torture) and for the sake of perceived security from terrorist attacks that the police state projects, that someone else will be targeted and they should support the police state.[140] The classical police state is not necessary as long as people remain taken in by the ideology of capitalism and personal responsibility, where capitalism cannot be questioned and all bad outcomes are the fault of the individual and not institutions of government or corporations. The classical police state is not necessary as long as people continue believing that they cannot do anything about the state of political, economic and income disparities in society even if they know the system is corrupted and rigged against them. This corruption of society and the acquiescence/collusion of the masses (continued belief in the systems of government and corporate capitalism and the hope they too can somehow partake in the bounty of capitalism by getting rich or at least buying consumer goods at Wal-Mart) will continue as long as the masses get enough (at least sufficient to maintain a subsistence level deluded existence) drugs, entertainments, food to eat even if they have no opportunity for advancement.

---

[140] [people support government excessive police and military force and loss of civil liberties even though more people die from car accidents and household accidents every year than die from terrorist attacks.]

THE CORPORATE SOFT POLICE STATE AS A TOOL OF FASCIST GOVERNMENT AND ECONOMIC POLICY TO CONTROL THE COMPLIANT MASSES

What has been instituted in place of the previous system of government is now fascism and that fascism has expanded to include police state despotism in all the matters of social, political and economic life that are consequential and meaningful.[141] Other areas of life such as lifestyle, gay marriage, discrimination, etc. are not considered as consequential and therefore are left to state legislatures or local determination; these areas also serve as distractions and or false areas of conflict that people can occupy themselves with, thinking that they have a say in matters that affect their lives. All the while, decisions about matters that implicate all human life are removed from the purview of mass influence. The police state now insures that the state of affairs remains in place. Regular policing now includes arbitrary pat downs, searches and even body cavity searches without warning or probable cause. Protesters against corporate lawbreaking or destruction of the environment by corporations or protesters against animal cruelty and now whistleblowers are now treated as terrorists; all that so as to intimidate the population generally into accepting and submitting to police authorities, that may show up in full menacing military gear, regardless of if any law has been broken. In the event that the propaganda, drugs and entertainments are not enough to confine the masses to a perpetual state of subjection in the face of state/police power, an effort has been engaged to prepare for an eventuality that the population may not only show signs of discontent but begin acting out in the form of protests or civil disobedience that could become a consequential challenge to the existing political and economic order. Large capacity "Fema Camps" and the paramilitary police (otherwise known as SWAT) as well as the general militarization of regular police departments throughout the country, have been made ready to be deployed at the sign of any inkling of substantial (consequential) physical and now also even vocal protest. Any physical protest (includes marching in the streets or mass communication such as the internet) be it violent or peaceful can now be arbitrarily treated as "terrorism" and therefore, "lawfully" open to policing without warrants or probable cause (indication of malicious or criminal intent).

---

[141] (including the laws for the wealthy and corporations versus laws for the masses, the economic arrangement between the 1% and 99% of the population, what type of healthcare system will be used, what type of environmental protections will be used, what type of fuels will be used, what type of government will be used, etc.).

In the neo-police state, free speech is not specifically prevented, unlike in the classical police state, where it is specifically repressed along with suppression of freedom of assembly. In the neo-police state (soft police state) the claim to legitimacy and the illusion of the masses, of having freedom, is maintained by the delusion of being able to speak out against injustices, and the ability to protest as a real and effective political strategy, even though it is in reality inconsequential if it does not have freedom to assemble politically and act legislatively on the demands. Those who experience the crackdown, who feel the brunt of the hard police state tactics, act as a warning to the others, who remain afraid of losing what they have and falling under the scrutiny of the police. If the protest or protest movement were to become consequential then it would be treated harshly with hard police state tactics, such as infiltration, surveillance and ultimately confronted with paramilitary force and suppression as was done to the Occupy Wall Street Movement. Meanwhile, as people pat themselves on the back thinking "well we really told those politicians off" or "we really protested and put them in their place" or "they really got what was coming to them when we got in their face and disrupted their speech", etc. those politicians and corporate heads continue doing what they were doing, controlling the "commanding heights"[142] of the social, political and economic order. So business as usual and the free speech and protest had no effect but to palliate the protester and encourage and embolden the corrupt leaders. The palliative allows people to feel better that they expressed their anger or even outrage, not realizing that it was inconsequential and that their protests actually served the designs of the police state and was what the establishment wants. However, if the protest should become such that they were to attract a substantial gathering or affect materially (through the electoral process), the social, political or economic order, then the corporate controlled media turns from ignoring the protests to denigrating and ridiculing them so as to degrade their following. If that does not succeed then the brutal militarized police puts down the protests in a manner such as was done to the recent "Occupy Wall Street" movement.

The "Occupy Wall Street" movement gained notoriety through physical protests since they did not have well funded "think tanks" and media outlets to project their image and ideals, as do the power elite with the mainstream media they control ["mainstream media may be defined as media (print, television, cable, internet or other) outlets that serve a mass audience, promote a biased point of view or suppress dissenting or differing points of view and or which are controlled by corporations and or members of the 1% (wealthy) members of the society].

---

[142] control the levers of power in the central social, political and economic institutions that determine the course of society and the power structure in society.

WHO OWNS THE MEDIA?

> Back in 1983, approximately 50 corporations controlled the vast majority of all news media in the United States. Today, ownership of the news media has been concentrated in the hands of just six incredibly powerful media corporations.
>
> The six corporations that collectively control U.S. media today are Time Warner, Walt Disney, Viacom, Rupert Murdoch's News Corp., CBS Corporation and NBC Universal. Together, the "big six" absolutely dominate news and entertainment in the United States. But even those areas of the media that the "big six" do not completely control are becoming increasingly concentrated. For example, Clear Channel now owns over 1000 radio stations across the United States. Companies like Google, Yahoo and Microsoft are increasingly dominating the Internet.
>
> ***Who Owns The Media? The 6 Monolithic Corporations That Control Almost Everything We Watch, Hear And Read*** By Michael Snyder, on October 4th, 2010

So in the neo-police state, the media message is controlled in order to control what people think and the alternative media is kept out of the mainstream and marginalized. Therefore, in the neo-police state, the free speech is encouraged as long as it does not materially affect the interests of the media corporations and their owners and as long as it relates to things that are inconsequential to the fundamental interests of the power elite. So subjects such as gay-rights, gun control, school vouchers, abortion, etc. are allowed because these areas of social life are ancillary and inconsequential to the levers of social, political and economic power, but if it should deal with something more substantial such as anything relating to corporate profits, then it is ignored by the mainstream media, or met with media suppression, ridicule or outright attack. If that fails to squelch it, it is maligned and also extinguished through drying up its finances, media coverage and maintaining its individuals fearful of losing their jobs if they follow the alternative message. Therefore, a minimum threshold is to be maintained just above the level where people en mass would lose the fear of opposing the state (those in a position of power-the power elite and their servants -the politicians) en mass for having nothing to lose, due to having insufficient resources to sustain even a subsistence level existence with its requisite entertainments, drugs and other diversions.

Utah Data Center[143]

> According to another top official also involved with the program, the NSA made an enormous breakthrough several years ago in its ability to cryptanalyze, or break, unfathomably complex encryption systems employed by not only governments around the world but also many average computer users in the US. The upshot, according to this official: "Everybody's a target; everybody with communication is a target."[144]

Since the recent revelations, by Edward Snowden, a NSA whistleblower, have proven that the government surveillance agencies and their contractors are apparently tracking individuals through ALL their phone, internet and financial records. A move to digitize those records so that they can be controlled from a central location and or agency has been underway. In this environment what would be the need for prohibiting assembly of people in groups? Actually the meeting of groups would be encouraged so that the meetings can be easily spied upon. There would be no need for heavy hard police state tactics and overtly intrusive means of surveillance when the soft means (digital records of vital information and digital live records of current whereabouts, miniature drone surveillance) are available. Thereby a person who would get out of line (criticize or oppose the government) could have their police, medical or financial records altered, restricted or blocked so as to preclude them from certain jobs, government services, travel, social mobility and or advancement, suspend their bank account, drivers license, phone, medical records, passport, student loans, etc. which could be instantly cut off for non compliance. Electronic surveillance of groups can also be conducted electronically and then

---

[143] https://en.wikipedia.org/wiki/Utah_Data_Center
[144] THE NSA IS BUILDING THE COUNTRY'S BIGGEST SPY CENTER (WATCH WHAT YOU SAY) BY JAMES BAMFORD 03.15.12 HTTP://WWW.WIRED.COM/THREATLEVEL/2012/03/FF_NSADATACENTER/ALL/

also upgraded with infiltrators who monitor first hand and can, as has been done in the past, and recently, incite violence or commit violence to frame the group so that the authorities may use that as a pretext to shut down the group. This would be the full realization of what NSA whistleblower, Edward Snowden, called *Turnkey Tyranny.*"[145] Without investigating or waiting to discover evidences of Snowden's claims, critics of Snowden, politicians and supporters of the spy industrial complex, in the mainstream media, which is supposed to be a watchdog on government officials (was here assisting them to protect an illegal surveillance program), labeled him as 'a monster of self-importance who has failed to produce a single concrete example of abuse of a spy apparatus'. Of course, subsequent evidences of the violations of the constitution did come out that vindicated Mr. Snowden. This demonstrates a primary tactic of smearing and character assassination to squelch the whistleblower and thereby not have to be confronted about the revelations.

> There is no evidence to support Edward Snowden's fears of a surveillance state… Edward Snowden has become a monster of self-importance. Commentary by Peter Foster, US Editor.

---

[145] http://www.telegraph.co.uk/news/uknews/defence/10188209/Edward-Snowden-is-a-self-regarding-idealist-whose-warnings-of-tyranny-ring-hollow.html

[Glenn]
If your motive had been to harm the US and help its enemies, or if your motive had been personal material gain, were there things you could have done with these documents to advance those goals that you didn't end up doing?

[Edward]
Oh, absolutely. Anybody in the position of access with the technical capabilities that I had could, you know, suck out secrets, pass them on the open market to Russia-- they always have an open door, as we do. I had access to the whole roster of everyone at the NSA, the entire intelligence community, and undercover assets all around the world, the locations of every station that we have, what their missions are, and so forth. If I had just wanted to harm the US, you could shut down the surveillance system in an afternoon. And I think for

anyone making that argument, they need to think, if they were in my position--and you know, you live a privileged life, you're living in Hawaii, in paradise and making a ton of money--what would it take to make you leave everything behind? The greatest fear that I have regarding the outcome, for America, of these disclosures is that nothing will change. People will see in the media all of these disclosures, they'll see the lengths the government's going to to grant themselves powers unilaterally to create greater control over American society and global society, but they won't be willing to take the risks necessary to stand up and fight to change things, to force their representatives to actually take a stand in their interests. And the months ahead, the years ahead, it's only going to get worse until, eventually, there will be a time when policies will change, because the only thing that restricts the activities of the surveillance state is policy. Even our agreements with foreign governments, we consider that to be a stipulation of policy rather than a stipulation of law. And, because of that, a new leader will be elected, they'll flip the switch, say that because of the crisis, because of the dangers that we face in the world--some new and unpredicted threat-- we need more authority, we need more power. And there will be nothing the people can do at that point to oppose it and it will be turnkey tyranny[146][147].

The advent of facial recognition and computer behavioral algorithms now portend to allow police the supposed and unproven possibility of "preempting" crimes by "predicting" where crimes will be committed, and by whom, through analysis of movement patterns, body temperature analysis, and facial recognition, to determine mental disposition, feelings and emotions and ultimately thought waves. The implementation of such systems are already being tested and rolled out in some police jurisdictions. Currently possible is surveillance on what people are typing on their computer in real time so that the police or NSA can preemptively stop a person in the planning stages of any action. This capacity was demonstrated in an erroneous search that revealed the capacity and potential for harm of this new surveillance capability.[148]

---

[146] Here Snowden is adapting a metaphor from the tech industry, which was in turn adapted from the consumer goods, housing, and legal realms:
The term turnkey is also often used in the technology industry, most commonly to describe pre-built computer "packages" in which everything needed to perform a certain type of task (e.g. audio editing) is put together by the supplier and sold as a bundle. This often includes a computer with pre-installed software, various types of hardware, and accessories. Such packages are commonly called appliances. A website with a ready-made solutions and some configurations is called a turnkey website. Turnkey websites are becoming more popular as the internet grows.
In other words, the government in this scenario will have a tyranny conveniently bundled, set up, and ready to go.
[147] news.rapgenius.com/Edward-snowden-interview-on-nsa-whistleblowing-full-transcript-lyrics#note-1854674
[148] http://reason.com/blog/2013/08/01/innocent-couple-gets-visited-by-feds-aft
http://www.theatlanticwire.com/national/2013/08/government-knocking-doors-because-google-searches/67864/

Maat Philosophy Versus Fascism and the Police State

Innocent Couple Visited by Feds Cops After Google Searching for Backpacks and Pressure Cookers (Now With Updates!)[149]

---

[149] http://reason.com/blog/2013/08/01/innocent-couple-gets-visited-by-feds-aft

Update: Now We Know Why Googling 'Pressure Cookers' Gets a Visit from Cops[150]

This event of the police receiving information through an internet search for information and arriving at the home of innocent people in full military gear points to an issue of a choice made by authorities to use the pretexts of terrorism and law and order to escalate the military aspects of policing and "National Security" surveillance. It was revealed that a previous system of surveillance ("Thin Thread") did not violate privacy rights and was more effective at watching for true potential terrorism, Yet a system of surveillance that collects ALL information was chosen, which allows the state vast power over those who are surveilled, apparently in real time and in perpetuity.

The idea is also being advanced that a person's records can be contained in computer chips that would be implanted into each individual, thus rendering

---

[150] http://www.theatlanticwire.com/national/2013/08/government-knocking-doors-because-google-searches/67864/

them completely and utterly as subjects (without freedom or independence), nay, objects of the neo-police state (modern post digital age police state). These prospects are orders of magnitude in intensity and capacity for control of the masses much greater than older concepts of pre digital era empire, of pre digital era feudalism, of pre digital era capitalism, and even slavery since even in slavery there was active force needed to maintain the slave economy; in the neo-police state the individuals are controlled through media propaganda about an illusory "American Dream", drug dependency, entertainments, financial debts and the threat of being singled out or cut off from being allowed to participate in the society which at least appears to have some people who are "still doing well" and avoid the alternative of being cut off, incarcerated and tortured; here also there is a lure to the power elite through the illusion of the possibility of somehow being able to be one of them someday or at least partake in their "glory", which is constantly idolized in entertainments, the political and business arenas. So due to the mis-education of an educational system that has been co-opted by the wealthy, teaching less liberal arts and history (or rewriting history to deceive and or make the police state and fascism look appealing). The rewriting of history can be related to political matters or to social or religious matters so as to promote a particular economic system, religious tradition or political agenda.

Texas schools board rewrites US history with lessons promoting God and guns[151]

---

[151] http://www.theguardian.com/world/2010/may/16/texas-schools-rewrites-us-history

Maat Philosophy Versus Fascism and the Police State

Door to Door Search by the police leads the homeowner out at gunpoint and with raised hands

Rewriting history and constant propaganda in the media in support of the police state contributes to public acquiescence to illegal searches and seizures. The bombing of the Boston Marathon occurred on April 15. Then on Friday April 22, several days earlier, the police engaged in a door to door search of an entire town. The idea has been advanced (see article below: *Can the Police Search My Home for a Bomber?*)[152] that the police did not violate the law because of the *exigent circumstances* exception to the 4th amendment to the USA constitution that allows police to enter premises without a warrant if they are in pursuit of someone who might cause harm; however, what is the period of exigency? As applied in this situation can the police search anywhere, without a warrant, several days after a crime? Why not a month after or years after or whenever they deem exigency is in effect? The point is that there is no oversight or control by citizens over their policing and this inevitably leads to abuses and violations of legal and moral standards of human rights.

---

[152] http://www.slate.com/articles/news_and_politics/explainer/2013/04/boston_bomber_manhunt_is_the_watertown_door_to_door_search_by_police_for.html

Maat Philosophy Versus Fascism and the Police State

Can the Police Search My Home for a Bomber?[153]

---

[153] http://www.slate.com/articles/news_and_politics/explainer/2013/04/boston_bomber_manhunt_is_the_watertown_door_to_door_search_by_police_for.html

April 19, 2013: Police in tactical gear arrive on an armored police vehicle as they surround an apartment building while looking for a suspect in the Boston Marathon bombings in Watertown, Mass. Source: AP[154]

---

[154] http://www.foxnews.com/us/slideshow/2013/04/19/huge-police-presence-as-authorities-swarm-boston-suburb/#slide=1

Maat Philosophy Versus Fascism and the Police State

Another Major Police Lie About the Boston Bomber Search[155]

The reason for out the example of the police door to door searches of a town in Massachusetts is that it is emblematic of a systematic escalation of the use of police power in general and militarized police power in specific. In effect this escalation also serves the purpose of training or grooming the population into accepting further and further intrusions and physical inspection and submission to the police state officers and officials. Even those who think they will go into the woods and live off the land with their guns and off the grid are deluded since there is no place within the country that is beyond the reach of the police and or military and the weaponry of the police and military is not far beyond that of any individual gun owner or any survivalist group. The police state, owned by the wealthy, has the power to pay the police and they have carefully selected persons to be police officers who's IQ tests have revealed them to be most

---

[155] http://www.economicpolicyjournal.com/2013/04/another-major-police-lie-about-boston.html

capable of following orders, being willing to hurt others if necessary and not deeply thinking for themselves about the ethics of their actions even when hurting the population and this coupled with the fact that they (police officers) too do not want to get cut off. An example of direct financing of the police was a large "donation" to the police by wall street bankers just prior to the crackdown that broke up the occupy wall street protests. Even with the reporting of the "bribe" the crackdown proceeded and no court objected to the collusion between wall street and the police and the media never followed up on this issue.

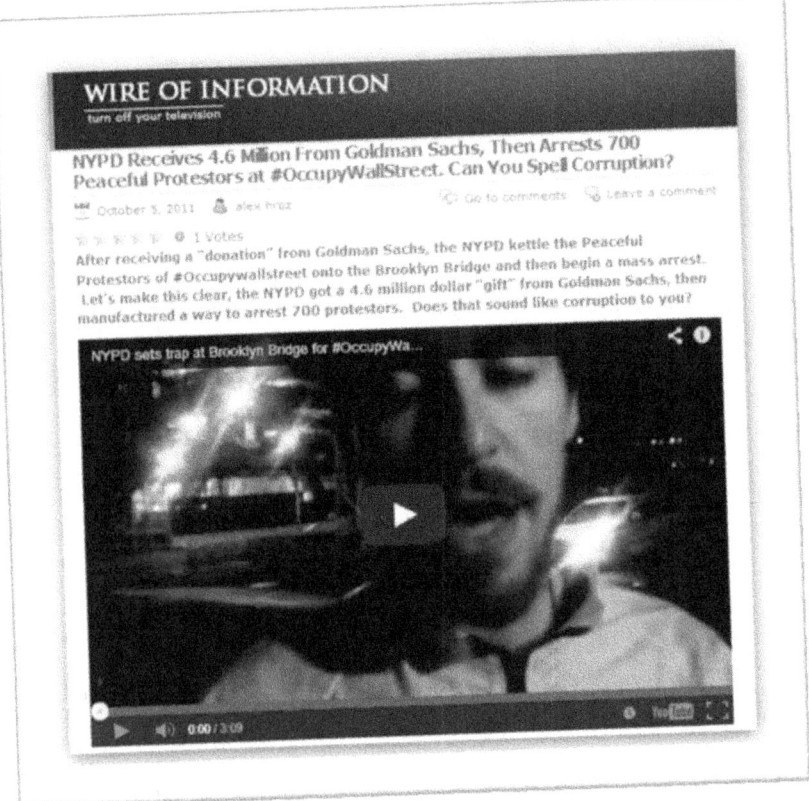

NYPD Receives 4.6 Million From Goldman Sachs, Then Arrests 700 Peaceful Protestors at #OccupyWallStreet. Can You Spell Corruption?[156]

---

[156] ttp://wireofinformation.wordpress.com/2011/10/05/nypd-receives-4-6-milllion-usd-from-goldman-sachs-then-arrests-700-peaceful-protestors-at-occupywallstreet/

Quelle Surprise! "J.P. Morgan Chase "donates" $4.6 Million to NYPD" #OccupyWallStreet[157]

Despite the well publicized donation from Wall Street banks to the New York Police department, and the subsequent crackdown on the OccupyWallStreet protests that were beginning to get worldwide attention, focusing the spotlight on immoral and criminal policies perpetrated by the Wall Street banks, the media did not question the ethics of the police, the collusion between the police and wall street and judicial system or present the injustices and double standards that portray the state, corporations or power elite as unjust or present the views of those who do question leaders and the injustices of society, but rather, the media presented such events as either the fault of the protesters and police brutality as anomalies or the perpetrating police officers or soldiers who commit abuses, atrocities or even extrajudicial killings as "rogue" or "isolated cases. The lack of questioning or seeking for the truth, by the mainstream media, goes on while never questioning the ethics of the leaders, the legitimacy of institutions of power (government and corporate, or the ethics of the society or culture as a whole) and policies that accepts imbalances between rich and poor that support

---

[157] http://stopforeclosurefraud.com/2011/10/01/quelle-surprise-j-p-morgan-chase-donates-4-6-million-to-nypd-occupywallstreet/

discrimination, racial fears and have been proven to lead to poverty and increased crime.[158]

LEADERSHIP FOR THE FASCIST GOVERNMENT

What follows is a stark example of how corporatist politicians and the judiciary of a government ignore decades of precedent law and redefine the meaning of the application of the law. In this case the president and his attorney general claim and indeed are unopposed by any congress person or judge in applying a legal standard that is unprecedented.

"Some have argued that the President is required to get permission from a federal court before taking action against a United States citizen who is a senior operational leader of al Qaeda or associated forces. This is simply not accurate. "Due process" and "judicial process" are not one and the same, particularly when it comes to national security. The Constitution guarantees due process, not judicial process."[159]

---

[158] http://www.poverties.org/poverty-and-crime.html
[159] http://www.theatlanticwire.com/national/2012/03/holder-due-process-doesnt-necessarily-mean-courtroom/49509/

But the crux of Holder's argument as set forth in yesterday's speech is this:

> Some have argued that the president is required to get permission from a federal court before taking action against a United States citizen who is a senior operational leader of Al Qaeda or associated forces. This is simply not accurate. **"Due process" and "judicial process" are not one and the same, particularly when it comes to national security.** The Constitution guarantees due process, not judicial process.[160]

Who decides when an American citizen has had enough due process and the Hellfire missile fairy pays them a visit? Presumably the group of top national security

---

[160] http://www.salon.com/2012/03/06/attorney_general_holder_defends_execution_without_charges/

officials—that, according to Defense Secretary Leon Panetta, decides who is targetable and forwards its findings to the president, who gives final approval.[161]

How does Att. Gen. Eric Holder define "due process":

He laid out three sufficient (but perhaps not necessary) conditions for the targeted killing of "a U.S. citizen who is a senior operational leader of al Qaeda or associated forces, and who is actively engaged in planning to kill Americans" (as Anwar al-Awlaki was alleged to be): First, the U.S. government has determined, after a thorough and careful review, that the individual poses an imminent threat of violent attack against the United States; second, capture is not feasible; and third, the operation would be conducted in a manner consistent with applicable law of war principles.[162]

The Orwellian[163] practice of turning known policies, terms and procedures towards an opposite or self-serving meaning and or application of a legal standard reversing or adjusting it to avoid legal review and impose a tyrannical application that serves the desires and policies of those in power and their executive (government officials) is a hallmark, not only of the sociopathic personality that has no compunction about lying to get his or her way but also of the fascists who use rhetorical double speak for explaining reinterpretations of previous norms and justifying previously unethical, unlawful and unreasonable actions as reasonable, justified and even desirable. So now, not only do no laws or basic human dignity need to be of concern for the president and his executive ministers but now also no laws need to be applied when dealing with USA citizens that the president and his executive employees, deem to be against the "interests" of the USA, meaning against the interests of the power elite and the corporations. This conception is now apparently named "Due process", meaning that a person has been duly considered by the president and his employees to be worthy of being killed and it is no longer necessary for that person to be captured and evidence presented in an open court against them so that they have a chance to defend themselves. This latter procedure would be the longstanding legal precedent of habeas corpus, taking the power away from the king of abducting a person and keeping them detained indefinitely without charge or

---

[161] http://www.motherjones.com/mojo/2012/03/eric-holder-targeted-killing
[162] http://reason.com/blog/2012/03/06/eric-holders-definition-of-due-process-a
[163] In Orwell's novel, all citizens of Oceania are monitored by cameras, are fed fabricated news stories by the government, are forced to worship a mythical government leader called Big Brother, are indoctrinated to believe nonsense statements (the mantra "WAR IS PEACE, SLAVERY IS FREEDOM, IGNORANCE IS STRENGTH"), and are subject to torture and execution if they question the order of things.[http://civilliberty.about.com/od/historyprofiles/g/orwellian.htm]
Orwellian" is an adjective describing the situation, idea, or societal condition that George Orwell identified as being destructive to the welfare of a free and open society. It connotes an attitude and a policy of control by propaganda, surveillance, misinformation, denial of truth, and manipulation of the past, including the "unperson" — a person whose past existence is expunged from the public record and memory, practiced by modern repressive governments. Often, this includes the circumstances depicted in his novels, particularly *Nineteen Eighty-Four*. [https://en.wikipedia.org/wiki/Orwellian]

outside communication, but to them it would also be an inconvenient and time consuming "judicial process". Now we are back to kidnapping and disappearing persons, what is now called by the Orwellian term, "rendering" and "enhanced interrogation", which is really torture by its correct name. Avoiding the judicial process allows the government and the executive in particular to accumulate vast concentrations of power that lead to despotism and tyranny on the masses in the long-term, but in the short term serve to expedite the efficiency of the hard police state applied to individuals and groups.

What does Ancient Egyptian Maat philosophy say about killing citizens?

> Beware of punishing unjustly,
> Do not kill anyone, it does not serve you or bring what you desire.
> Punish instead with beatings, and detention,
> By these actions the land will be well ordered;
> -Teachings to MeriKaRa

The obvious dangers of any government leader assuming the power to personally decide who should be killed, and then order those killings, as presidents, including Barak Obama, have done should be apparent. As the point that was made in the movie, *The Godfather Part 2* suggests, the difference between a gangster who orders a killing as opposed to a government leader, a senator or a president, who orders a killing is that the government leader is in business and has he veneer of legitimacy as well as the power of media propaganda to convince the masses that the killings are to protect the society whereas the gangster openly does it for profit, without the pretences used by the politician. When those policies become normalized and accepted by the population other harsher measures usually follow, tightening the grip of power and the loss of civil liberties for all. The killings can be for political reasons, and or of foreigners, then domestic citizens or anyone who opposes the power that be, seemingly the killings and police brutality appears random and then becomes systemic until the population is intimidated and under constant threat of harassment not directly but through the media or knowing someone personally who was harassed or killed by the state in an extrajudicial manner. What difference is there between a president with that power to kill anyone and an absolute monarch that can order the execution of any subject without any legal review or justification? In this sense the president of any country with such power, should be more accurately considered as a temporary monarch (this system may be termed *Temporary Monarchy,* or *Revolving Monarchy*) instead of a hereditary monarch for life; and regardless of if the country calls itself democratic or otherwise, is indeed operating in a autocratic manner which is the most efficient manner of executive power for a fascist system of government. In this case there is no democracy but rather a façade of democracy, a mask that presents the illusion of democracy over the autocracy of the plutocrats, the modern day expression of aristocratic rule which would have been referred to as monarchy or feudalism in years past. We may refer to this form or feature of "head of state" in the illusory democracy, in other words "faux democracy", as "revolving monarchy".

The reason why a legal system needs review and why there should be more than one person making judgments is that individuals, especially those who have not been ethically trained, can make mistakes or be biased due to egoism and other imperfections or corruptions. They may operate not out of ethical conscience but egoistic desire or delusions related to their position, their friends or ideologies that have not been vetted with reasoned argument and reflection on how they impact the society as a whole but rather, some persons might be swept up in a frenzy of emotion or taken over by hubris and or delusions of grandeur. The fascist leaders (government leaders, leaders of corporations, owners of corporations and or vast wealth) want to nullify, if not eradicate the review or corrupt it so as it will not be able to thwart the fascism because to have a leader whose decisions are reviewed by judges or ratified by legislators in congress would hamper the ability to take fascistic actions (implement government policies and laws that benefit corporations and the wealthy) as the reviews might reveal the sinister machinations of the deeper strategies at work and might also disturb the social order of the masses. Another benefit of having a revolving monarchy is that a temporary monarch gives the political operatives a periodic chance to fool the populace into believing they have a choice of government systems and leaders. It also allows for regular relief of political tensions by allowing the masses to expend energy and effort, like hamsters running on a wheel but going nowhere, in pointless political debates and campaigns. In so doing people are duped into thinking they are "changing the system" by getting their "good" candidate into office or thinking they are "throwing the bums out of office", those whom they thought were bad leaders, not realizing they are going to get the same leadership under a new name and or political party brand. Furthermore, since the system itself is based on a corrupt "ideology" it would not matter if the elected person were trying to be ethical or not as the system as a whole and the majority of people in it, operating from sociopathic or egoistic, greedy or unethical standpoints, will force the system to operate in corrupt ways until it collapses under its own weight of malfeasance and criminal destruction of the environment, all for the benefit of corporations, the power of the power elite and for the personal pursuit of happiness and disregard for the common needs of all humanity. This expertly manufactured system of electoral prestidigitation has been a key component of the creation of a society with permanent upper and under classes with an electorate that is completely deluded about the nature of their power to change the system of government and the power structure headed by the aristocracy/plutocracy/power elite. Under such conditions the only hope for change would be economic and social collapse due to malfeasance and fascistic overreach or outright revolution by the over-drugged, overworked and "dumbed down"[164] population. If such an unlikely eventuality as the revolution by the over-drugged, overworked and "dumbed down population were to occur, the likely outcome would be the result of over-drugged, overworked and "dumbed down reasoning which could lead to disastrous results, no better than the present and possibly worse.

---

[164] see the book *Collapse of Civilization* by Muata Ashby

THE PRESIDENT MONARCH, INDEFINITE DETENTION, KILL LISTS AND INTIMIDATION OF CITIZENS AND NON-CITIZENS WORLDWIDE WITH THE THREAT OF REPRISALS

On Dec. 31st 2012 president Obama signed into law a new power, the ability to detain anyone, including USA citizens, indefinitely and without trial. This direct violation of the USA constitution was allowed to pass into law by the present president, congress and the judiciary.

The NDAA's historic assault on American liberty[165]

President Barak Obama and the leaders in congress and the military, continued and expanded a program of extrajudicial killing (murder) of those arbitrarily considered as enemies of the USA without legal proof of their guilt and even if it meant killing innocent women and children. Obama began a practice of

---

[165] http://www.theguardian.com/commentisfree/cifamerica/2012/jan/02/ndaa-historic-assault-american-liberty

secretly and personally reviewing a list regularly and deciding which people on the list should be killed. This review is without judicial process but is rather an expedient and executive decision. Reputed to be occurring on Tuesdays, the reviews have been dubbed "Terror Tuesdays."

Secret 'Kill List' Proves a Test of Obama's Principles and Will.[166]

Under the guise of national security, Obama has further justified, beyond the use by his predecessor, the use of drone attacks and killings of thousands of innocent women and children which amounts to war crimes and crimes against humanity.

---

[166] http://www.nytimes.com/2012/05/29/world/obamas-leadership-in-war-on-al-qaeda.html

Kill List Exposed: Leaked Obama Memo Shows Assassination of U.S. Citizens "Has No Geographic Limit"[167]

> "If you look at the memo ... there's no geographic line," says Jaffer. "The Obama administration is making, in some ways, a greater claim of authority [than President Bush]. They're arguing that the authority to kill American citizens has no geographic limit."

The kill list includes USA citizens deemed in violation of the USA constitution but president Obama and his attorney general are stating that they are following the constitution by giving due process (not judicial process). The due process is the due consideration when the president decides who to kill. As long as those who have the power to stop this policy do not do so they are in collusion with it and all citizens or non citizens are in danger from an unchecked presidency.

---

[167] http://www.democracynow.org/2013/2/5/kill_list_exposed_leaked_obama_memo

Who can't be on Obama's "kill list"?[168]

That's the most accurate label to describe the machinery of the government's ever-expanding drone war. As the white paper asserts, that war — which is likely creating more terrorists than it is neutralizing — cannot be curtailed by laws or the Constitution. Therefore, the argument goes, the president no longer merely claims the power to detain and torture people without due process, nor does he merely claim the power to execute American citizens without indictment or trial. Those extra-constitutional powers, which only a few years ago were seen as utterly illegal, are quaint compared to the new assertion that the president can now do all of this **without any concrete intelligence suggesting a citizen is linked to terrorist activity**.

Not only does the Obama administration claim to have the right to kill anyone they deem worthy of killing, without judicial review, but they also claim to have

---

[168] http://www.salon.com/2013/02/05/who_cant_be_on_obamas_kill_list/

the right to kill anyone related to them or around them at the time of the killings. They blame the person they targeted without presenting evidence in court as the responsible party for their own death and the death of the family member that was around in the area when they were killed, usually by drone (bomb) attack, and this applies to USA citizens or non-USA citizens. Another policy to facilitate extrajudicial killings is to assert that any male that may be killed who is over 15 is an "enemy combatant" and thus not an unlawful killing.

How Team Obama Justifies the Killing of a 16-Year-Old American[169]

The answer Robert Gibbs gave is chilling:
ADAMSON: ...It's an American citizen that is being targeted without due process, without trial. And, he's underage. He's a minor.

GIBBS: I would suggest that you should have a far more responsible father if they are truly concerned about the well being of their children. I don't think becoming an al Qaeda jihadist terrorist is the best way to go about doing your business.

From an ethical perspective, to justify the killing of an innocent person, let alone a child, for the unproven crimes of a parent or other relative, is on its face, illegal, unethical, patently negligent and a self-serving statement displaying reckless disregard for human life. From a moral standpoint, for a country and president that are supposed to be following Christian values which include forgiveness and not killing, this policy of killing people around the world, who either actively are or may possibly be working or even speaking against the USA government, including citizens of their own country (USA), and those policies of other presidents which have included assassinations and wars, should be considered as war crimes or crimes against humanity or at least antithetical to

---

[169] http://www.theatlantic.com/politics/archive/2012/10/how-team-obama-justifies-the-killing-of-a-16-year-old-american/264028/

Maat Philosophy Versus Fascism and the Police State

Christianity, in other words, anathema. In other words, these policies and statements should stir up the moral angst of the populace or at least the religious, ethics and moral leaders who should take action and publicly oppose such statements and policies and advocate for redress in the form of impeachment and prosecution for war crimes.

To the extent that the judiciary and the congress have not even criticized and at least tried to stop him speaks to the complicity in the attempt to institute not only worldwide empire through military bases that can attack countries if they stray from the USA corporatists policies but now, in addition, an attempt to implement a worldwide police state through intimidation and fear of death through the technology (drone attacks) that is cheaper and can be hidden from the view the public since it does not require large numbers of dead soldiers. The question is what is the difference between such a president and a mob enforcer, who goes around a neighborhood and beats up people who do not pay for protection from the mob enforcer? What is the difference between such a president and a mob boss who orders the hit man to kill those who oppose the mob boss and or his policy of rackets, controlling the neighborhood and or the city and its businesses all who must pay the mob boss; furthermore, what is the ethical difference between that and a country that enforces that control on another country or even on countries worldwide? In this sense the American empire[170] is a mob and the president is a mob boss but on an exponentially larger scale. A population that allows such assumption of absolute power and essentially the creation of an absolute[171], rotating monarchic presidency is also partly complicit with the unethical and or criminal acts of the leaders and will suffer the consequences of that acquiescence with such a leadership in the form of more ruinous economic policies, more wars, tyranny and enslavement to corporate designs and products that are harmful to health and the environment, etc. as outlined in this volume. Another conclusion that can be derived from the aforesaid is that that same domestic population is now mistrusted and targeted by the state as enemies of the state. In other words, the foreign peoples as well as the domestic population of the USA are now considered as and being treated as enemies to be spied on, intimidated to prevent challenges or rebelliousness against the power of the rulers. Those same techniques, war crimes, surveillance and non-judicial dispensations of the executive action are being applied to citizens as well as non-citizens.

---

[170] See the book *Collapse of Civilization and the Death of American Empire* by Muata Ashby
[171] From its inception, the US Constitution created a monarchic presidency with the power of kings, including the power of eminent domain, but only on a temporary basis and with some review by congress. Absolute monarchic presidency is here defines as a presidency that takes on itself the right to kill citizens, use their property, etc. without congressional or judicial review.

FBI director says surveillance drones used in US[172]

Why are increasing surveillance, violence and suppression of dissent being used in western countries and especially the USA? One answer is because eventually the financial malfeasance and indeed the fraud that is the electoral and legislative processes, the fraud of the banking system, income taxes, the impoverishing of the masses through inflation and the fraud of corporate subsidies, corporate looting of government funds through legalized bribery (campaign donations) and laws like the Affordable Care Act, bailouts and capture of state government will eventually lead to a situation in which masses of dispossessed people will become vocally and physically disgruntled. The Occupy Wall Street (OWS) movement was a peaceful call to the establishment that was brutally put down by the establishment. However, the real protest

---

[172] http://www.telegraph.co.uk/news/worldnews/northamerica/usa/10131364/FBI-director-says-surveillance-drones-used-in-US.html

movement and social disruption that is expected will be much more serious, widespread and threatening to the establishment than what was presented by the OWS and will elicit more harsh measures. The creation of more jails and detention centers, the escalation of drones flying domestic skies, the increased police brutality and mass incarcerations, etc. may be considered as a grooming process,[173] to prepare the population for those harsher measures that have been prepared.

Where does the callous disregard for human life come from that justifies killing women and children in supposedly accurate drone attacks (that are not actually accurate and kill indiscriminately) targeting supposed terrorists? Where does the callous disregard for the well-being of other human beings come from that justifies businesses seeking profits regardless of the cost to human life or the environment? These are sociopathic behaviors, based on sociopathic ideologies engaged in by sociopathic individuals who have convinced others, who are not necessarily sociopathic themselves, not only to follow such ideas but to allow them to assume positions of leadership in corporations and the government including presidents. Sociopathic individuals who advocated such ideas include Ann Rand (writer), Milton Friedman (economist), and Paul Ryan (congressman). Milton Friedman openly advocated such ideas as that business should have no concern for the community or the society and only be concerned about profits.[174]

So there is a type of personality that does not have compunctions about initiating sociopathic behaviors; these may be referred to as dull/gross minded. There are others who are borderline sociopathic and others who under some pressure will follow the sociopaths out of ignorance, greed, overwhelming desires, or other psychological issues. This latter group is referred to as agitated mind, containing a mixture of positive and negative mental impressions (of vice and virtue). Maat Philosophy can help to rectify the ethical conscience of those who are not psychologically impaired, like sociopaths, the clinically insane, etc. The practice of Maat Philosophy leads to a Lucid Mind, which includes an advanced level of ethical conscience and wisdom to lead society.

There is a particular feature in the human mind whereby ordinary people can fall into a kind of group or mob mentality, where they do things they would not

---

[173] [process of gradually preparing the population through increasing displays of violence, surveillance and intimidation as well as suppression of dissent in the media through corporate media ownership and control of reporting and editorials] The grooming process can include false flag terrorist attacks to instill fear and as an excuse to display police power, increased deployment of police donning paramilitary equipment, constant advocacy by subsidized experts to advocate war, fear of terrorism, and the beneficence of corporatism.

[174] America's Sociopathic Leadership: Reversing The Downward Spiral by Jerome G. Manis

normally do because others are doing it. They may start looting when others are looting but would never have initiated that action on their own. Also, there are some personalities who will follow orders to hurt other people by deferring to authority, thinking that the person in authority has the right to give such orders. They do not question the authority and are even comfortable following the authority and desire to be followers, like a child who clings to the parent to feel safe. Such degraded personalities are weak and even if they have some moral sense their fears and intellectual weakness precludes their capacity to think and then act for themselves, in a way that is reasoned, ethical and moral. This kind of personality is what the resolutions that were arrived at after World War II (Nuremberg trials) were trying to discourage, the notion that a soldier could use the defense of "I was just following orders" was rejected. One cannot suspend moral judgment even in war. Yet, this is what the current fascist police state regime is encouraging and doing. That kind of personality is what the fascist wants to cultivate, through propaganda in the mainstream media, rewriting history, cancelling liberal arts classes and humanities in schools and universities, making sure that people have to work two and three jobs to survive, etc. and thus not allow people the time, resources and education to be able to think critically, ethically and freely about the nature of their lives, the ethics of the established leaders, and to have imagination and a sense of history about how things were and how they can become better. Hence, in the state of intellectual, emotional and financial destitution, the present leaders with their certainty and apparent authority become the only trusted and supported entities.

Sociopathic ideas and policies are considered, from the perspective of Ancient Egyptian Maat philosophy as not only immoral, callous and cruel but criminal. The following examples of sociopathic statements and policies are presented below so that the reader may be able to clearly discern what is sociopathic versus what is in agreement with Maatian values (ethical, caring for individuals and community for the benefit of society as a whole and not for the benefit of an elite or the benefit of one country over another):

Madeline Albright, the 64th U.S. Secretary of State

On May 12, 1996, Albright defended UN sanctions against Iraq on a *60 Minutes* segment in which Lesley Stahl asked her "We have heard that half a million children have died. I mean, that's more children than died in Hiroshima. And, you know, is the price worth it?" and Albright replied "we think the price is worth it."[175]

Ayn Rand, American novelist, philosopher, playwright, and screenwriter

Rand's political philosophy emphasized individual rights (including property rights),[176] and she considered *laissez-faire* capitalism the only moral social system because in her view it was the only system based on the protection of those rights.[177] As a follower of *objectivism,* Rand had the main character in her book *Atlas Shrugged,* John Galt say the following words which summarize the objectivist ethics philosophy:

> "I swear—by my life and my love of it—that I will never live for the sake of another man, nor ask another man to live for mine."

Persons in congress such as congressional representative Paul Ryan, who believe in and follow the philosophy of people like Rand and try to implement those policies so that society is more guided by individual values, and less caring for the community, more corporate freedom and less regulation are agreeing with and implementing sociopathic ideals and agendas which are favorable for capitalist enterprises and criminals who can then say that it is not their fault that others were hurt but rather that others should have been looking out for their own best interest. This is of course the same idea behind the concept of caveat emptor or *buyer beware,* which is in complete contradiction

---

[175] *The mighty and the Almighty ... – Google Books*. Books.google.com. Retrieved 2010-09-09.
[176] Peikoff, Leonard (1991). *Objectivism: The Philosophy of Ayn Rand*. New York: E. P. Dutton. ISBN 0-452-01101-9. OCLC 28423965.
[177] Gotthelf, Allan (2000). *On Ayn Rand*. Wadsworth Philosophers Series. Belmont, California: Wadsworth Publishing. ISBN 0-534-57625-7. OCLC 43668181.

with the idea that "I am my brother's keeper". It is an ideology that absolves the immoral, unethical or criminal activity by placing the onus on the victim. So if the criminal succeeds it is good on him or her but if the victim succeeds in thwarting the plans of the criminal then it was good on them. So with this conception, if the criminal gets away with the crime they did well and there is no moral or unethical question they need to be concerned with. If the victim got victimized it was their own fault because they should have taken better care to protect themselves. This is the philosophy used by criminals in jail, Wall Street and by presidents. This may be referred to as "Sociopathic Ethics", but many people who are not sociopathic, also follow this ideal because it is self-serving. Even though they know it is wrong, they have so much negative psychological impressions in the mind that they overwhelm or even atrophy their moral and or ethical sense. Some people, knowing the acts are wrong and even feeling guilt, still willingly pursue the unethical path and thus degrade their mental capacity to discern truth from untruth as they more and more convince themselves they are in the right. This feature can be observed in many politicians and those who work closely in politics, including the lobbyists, rationalizing that if they can get it passed into law it is good and acceptable, even if it is immoral or unethical; they end up convincing themselves of the morality of their position, being blinded by their greed, lust for pleasure, fame or fear of poverty or retribution by the powers they serve.

> "I grew up reading Ayn Rand, and it taught me quite a bit about who I am and what my value systems are and what my beliefs are. It's inspired me so much that it's required reading in my office for all my interns and my staff."
>
> -- U.S. Representative Paul Ryan, Republican vice presidential candidate, in a 2005 speech[178]

According to the objectivist philosophy, all human beings are left to their own capacities to survive and be preyed upon by those who are stronger or more clever. So people should just care about themselves and not about other people. These ideals are in complete contravention with Maatian ethics.

---

[178] http://www.atlassociety.org/ele/blog/2012/04/30/paul-ryan-and-ayn-rands-ideas-hot-seat-again
http://www.atlassociety.org/ele/blog/2012/04/30/paul-ryan-and-ayn-rands-ideas-hot-seat-again

Maat Philosophy Versus Fascism and the Police State

Milton Friedman

> No modern leader has provided a more effective justification for actions that have harmed so many Americans than has Milton Friedman. As a Nobel award-winning economist, his views have been widely disseminated and adopted—especially by economists. Not aimed at well-being or justice, they have clearly led to much and extremely antisocial actions supposedly guided by an "invisible hand of the marketplace."
>
> His version of the "free trade," which guides the marketplace, is expressed most specifically in a 1970 article in the *New York Times*. Its title makes clear his views: "The Social Responsibility of Business is to Increase its Profits." Throughout the article, he made clear that "only people can have responsibilities" while business can have no other purpose than to "increase its profits."
>
> As "only people can responsibilities," expecting business to have responsibilities is not desirable. Friedman does not mention that many businesses are owner operated. As businesses, their sole purpose is making profits and without any social responsibility.
>
> In the same report, he wrote, "What does it mean to say that a corporate executive has a 'social responsibility?' If this statement is not pure rhetoric, it must mean that he is to act in some way that is not in the interest of his employers."
>
> To Friedman, the executive who spends corporation money for social benefits is wasting its money. In his view, the notion of responsibility involves "the socialist view that political mechanisms, not market mechanisms" are proper for business owners. To him, social responsibility is a political, not an ethical matter.

Sociopathy is a mental abnormality. Webster's Dictionary traces "sociopathic" usage to 1944, defining it as "characterized by asocial or antisocial behavior, or a psychopathic nature." "Sociopathy" is used in the Diagnostic and Statistical Manual of Mental Disorders, Fourth Edition (DSM). Especially notable and influential has been Adam Smith. Sociopaths are not the same as unethical persons who know right from wrong but acquiesce to the sociopathic policies out of fear of losing their possessions or their life or those who choose to go along with the sociopathic ideas even though they know it is wrong but their desires compel them to go along for personal gain or fear of loss. Sociopaths are a small segment of the population (2-4%) but Western culture in particular, and its forms of social order and government allow sociopaths easy access to leadership positions. Under the guise of democracy, free speech and the pursuit of personal happiness, those sociopaths have been able to spread those ideas which almost exclusively serve the designs of the sociopathic leadership.

ABSENCE OF RELIGIOUS CRITICISM IN THE FACE OF FASCISTIC POLITICS AND ECONOMICS

Where have the church leaders been on the issues of killing citizens and non citizens policies as contradictory to supposedly Christian values of the Ten Commandments and the Beatitudes of Jesus which speak against killing and for forgiving enemies, for taking care of the poor and not supporting moneychangers? Up to now and throughout the history of the country we can scarcely find any pointed, sustained criticism, calling out any president on those issues. This means that the Christian leaders, including those of the mega-churches, such as Rick Warren, Joel Ostein and T.D. Jakes, are acquiescent and thus complicit in the hypocrisy and corruption of politics and economics. Such religious leadership gives religious cover to the supposedly law abiding leaders.

Casting out the money changers by Giotto, 14th century.

The very idea of fascism/corporatism/crony capitalism, etc. which amounts to collusion of government and corporations is also intersected with religious fascism, the mutual support between corporations and churches. The indiscriminate killing of women and children in countries where terrorists supposedly live, through drone attacks, committed by presidents Bush and Obama, the collusion between Washington and Wall Street to make laws and take financial risks that damage the national economy and many other serious and wide-ranging crimes, would seem to be at least immoral if not unethical and illegal and thus antithetical to the very principles of the church doctrine as embodied in the Christian gospels by Jesus' exhortation to take care of the poor and the lesson of casting moneychangers out of the temple. Yet, the silence in criticism of the lack of ethics and open lawbreaking with impunity in government and by corporations belies collusion between religious leaders and the corporate state.

179

Despite being the figurehead of a organization, the Vatican and the Catholic Pope, that has committed crimes by harboring pedophiles, and also committed financial crimes through the Vatican bank, including money laundering and collusion with corrupt politicians and organized crime leaders, a notable mention, but virtually a lone voice, among the influential religious leaders in Christianity, is the new pope, who spoke out even more forcefully than his predecessor, Pope Benedict, who did speak out on the issue of "Ethical Financial Regulation". Pope Francis spoke forcefully and unambiguously and critically about the practices of capitalism and its supposedly beneficial "free markets" which are in reality not free and fair but free of regulation and free for criminal behavior, defrauding retail investors and are rigged for the benefit of big banks and wealthy investors. Not surprisingly, other major Christian leaders, especially those in the West, in the countries from where capitalism is headquartered, have not followed the Pope's lead and the mainstream media has not followed up on the Pope's words. We may also understand this dynamic in the context of the fact that Western religion in the form of Protestantism and its offshoots, which make up the bulk of Western religious followings, was created, among other reasons, to allow the European royalty in varied countries, to be able to have a separate power center of religious authority in order to be able to ignore the dictates of the Vatican and thus be able to chart a different path by controlling the religious authority to support their divergent policies. This is how versions, sects of Christianity, came into being. In modern western society, the church does not serve as an agent of change or of moral force to keep corporate and government leaders honest. Rather, it serves as a place where people can go to

---

[179] http://www.huffingtonpost.com/2013/01/01/pope-slams-capitalism-ine_n_2392653.html

shout "halleluiah" and relieve their stresses of life; since they feel powerless and have been inculcated, from the time of their youth, with the idea they must have faith in God to solve their problems and on the other hand, that wealth is not a sin, their understanding of their plight as being caused by an unjust system of politics and economics and their capacity to do anything about it is futile, that it is in God's hands to save them. Thus, life goes on and their god given intellectual and ethical capacity to right the wrongs of society are impaired with the facilitation of codependent and illusory religiousity.

A blunt Pope Francis targets free market economics[180]

No major political or corporate leaders had any comment on the statements. It may not be surprising that this Pope would be the person to make such statements since he has personally followed a path of real service to the poor and not just lip service. It is, however, notable that other Christian leaders, who supposedly agree with the same values, regardless of denomination, have not commented or added their voice to confront what is obvious to the Pope, a utter distortion of human and social balance in favor of the wealthy and detrimental

---

[180] http://www.cnbc.com/id/100931792

consequences for everyone else. In this sense the western countries, which created capitalism and have instituted their imposition of it throughout the world, have developed their own form of Christianity that supports the values of corporatism as much as they might like to increase their own religious influence and power and even impose their religious vision through the theocratic control of government. Therefore, the main western forms of Christianity may be considered as not just in collusion with the fascism but they have an important role in facilitating it by firstly not calling out immoral, unethical or even criminal leaders, providing charity where the government falls short of its responsibilities to take care of the populace, whipping up support for political leaders that support the Churches and their exemptions and subsidies. Added to this is the issue of corporate leaders who support churches with donations. Thus, the western churches would seem to be replete with moneychangers and permeated by corporate leaders and their supporters, who would not support them if they do not support the government leaders. In other words, they are in the pockets of the corporations as much as the media and other institutions of society that are supposed to be looking out for the welfare of the population as a whole but are in reality captured and corrupted by the same moneyed interests, the power elite.

CHAPTER 6: CORPORATE MEDIA, AND CRIMINALITY AT THE TOP, NEGLECT AND ABUSE OF THE POOR, AND THE ATTACK ON TRUTH-TELLERS AND WHISTLEBLOWERS

In the following article by dissident Chris Hedges, he points out the degradation of USA government as manifest in the support of the corporate agenda by the government and in particular the presidency. He also highlights Dr. Cornel West's examination of the deterioration of the "Black Prophetic Tradition's role in speaking truth to power and being a moral conscience for those in power. Nevertheless there is acknowledgement of the setting up of the police state in the USA and the abject acceptance of criminality not limited to but especially "on top", i.e., the political and corporate leaders. It is this deficiency that acts to eat away at the social infrastructure as a cancer whose metastasized creation is the birth of fascism and its accompanying hard police state. {underlined sections are by Ashby}

Cornel West and the Fight to Save the Black Prophetic Tradition[181]

Posted on Sep 9, 2013

---
[181]
http://www.truthdig.com/report/item/cornel_west_and_the_fight_to_save_the_black_prophetic_tradition_20130909/

Maat Philosophy Versus Fascism and the Police State

The wide swath of destruction Obama has overseen on behalf of the corporate state includes the eradication of most of our civil liberties and our privacy, the expansion of imperial war, the use of kill lists, abject subservience to Wall Street's criminal class and the military-industrial complex, the relentless persecution of whistle-blowers, mass incarceration of poor people of color and the failure to ameliorate the increasing distress of the poor and the working class. His message to the black underclass in the midst of the corporate rape of the nation is drawn verbatim from the Booker T. Washington playbook. He tells them to work harder -- as if anyone works harder than the working poor in this country -- and obey the law.

West said... "We are talking about crimes against humanity—Wall Street crimes, war crimes, the crimes of the criminal justice system in the form of Jim Crow, the crimes against our working poor that have their backs pushed against the wall because of stagnant wages and corporate profits going up," West said. "Abraham Heschel said that the distinctive feature of any empire in decline is its indifference to criminality. That is a fundamental feature of our time, an indifference to criminality, especially on top, wickedness in high places."

West said. "With corporate media and the narrowing of the imagination of all Americans, including black people, there is an erasure of memory. This is the near death of the black prophetic tradition. It is a grave issue. It is a matter of life and death. It means that the major roadblock to American fascism, which has been the black prophetic tradition, is gone. To imagine America without the black prophetic tradition, from Frederick Douglass to Fannie Lou Hamer, means an American authoritarian regime, American fascism. We already have the infrastructure in place for the police state."

What occurred to the economy in 2008 (economic crash) and since may be characterized as a crash and depression, which occurs periodically in a capitalist system of economy, especially when there are imbalances of wealth and income amongst the population, but it would have been a collapse were it not for the bailouts by the Federal Reserve bank and the US Government. The bailouts to save the domestic and international banks and the wealthy, have been using public moneys (funds belonging to the masses and not the power elite). This temporarily held back a collapse but made the initial situation worse and the eventual inevitable collapse much harder than it would otherwise have been. So the usual destruction of wealth, caused by the Federal Reserve and the debt based monetary system, through inflation and fractional banking system has been compounded by massive transference of wealth through the bailouts. Now, additionally, the events of 9-11-2001 have allowed the ushering in of what can be termed "soft police state" including unlawful mass surveillance, widespread suppression of political and economic dissent, massive corporate frauds and a two tiered justice system (one for the wealthy and one for the rest of the population) and widespread surveillance, suspension of the rule of law for the super rich and politicians, and the national security agencies and now restriction of financial freedom and later to come, restrictions in freedom of movement. A complete collapse of the economic system would likely lead to economic, social and political chaos and inevitably harden the current soft police state we have at this moment. A hard police state would mean restrictions in travel and movement, restrictions of financial freedom, devaluation of currency, widespread violent crime and extrajudicial or more corrupt judicial dispensations of the law, possibly leading to martial law and not just selectively ignoring the constitution, which is what we have now, but complete abrogation of it and full corporate rule. Incidentally, if the new Trans Pacific Partnership Treaty is approved it will constitute that abrogation of the constitution in favor of international corporate commercial law which will place corporations above consumers and consumer rights.

> Teachings to MeriKaRa:
> (23) When free men are given land,
> They work for you like a single team;
> No rebel will arise among them,
> -Ancient Egyptian Wisdom Texts
>
> Teachings of Ptahotep:
> Inspire not men with fear, else Ptah (God) will fight against you in the same manner. If anyone asserts that he lives by such means, Ptah will take away the bread from his mouth; if any one asserts that he enriches himself thereby, Ptah says: I may take those riches to myself. If anyone asserts that he beats others, Ptah will end by reducing him to impotence. Let no one inspire men with fear; this is the will of Ptah. Let one provide sustenance for them in the lap of peace; it will then be that they will freely give what has been torn from them by terror.
> -Ancient Egyptian Wisdom Texts

The societal philosophy of western countries, the guiding idea underlying social, political and economic activity, as instituted by the leaders of those countries, is that human beings should be motivated by fear. This includes fear of poverty, fear of authority, fear of insecurity about losing a job, about being a victim of crime, etc. The state reserves the right to administer its laws while people are more or less kept in a state of perpetual stress and ultimately living under a police state, dictatorship or outright military rule. According to Ancient Egyptian wisdom the aforesaid is not the way for a society to survive, mature and prosper over millennia. People need a more noble form of motivation which will allow them to achieve their goals and realize the potential opportunities a rich society can offer; then people will be naturally industrious, without coercion or the external imposition of stress or fear. In this context a rich society is one in which its members come together to cooperate and allow the fruits of all labor to benefit the society as a whole instead of just an elite minority. Then all members of society benefit and the society will be well ordered. Therefore, the police state exists, among other reasons, to force the population to accept the hierarchy of society but also the format of the labor structure, how commerce is conducted and what wages are paid. In essence, the police serve as enforcers for the power elite, not unlike the service of enforcers for organized crime syndicates. These two competing ideologies are in constant struggle in quasi-democratic forms of government but the fear and violence based ideology invariably wins out because the leaders who decide on such matters, acting out of egoistic conscience instead of "Maat Ethical Conscience," end up moving towards protection of their own elite positions at the expense of the rest of the population. Sage Ptahotep wrote about the personality that comes into power, is lauded, and develops arrogance and conceit to such a degree as to become dependent upon and corrupted by the adulation and position they hold. Then when it comes time to do service for the society their preference becomes that which will allow pursuit of their desires and passions instead of the good for the society. This is what the power elite has become, vainglorious self indulging egos with self-serving ideologies that enrich them at the expense of the environment and the impoverishment of others, all that so as to satisfy their exalted (exceptional) idea about themselves and to retain their "privileged"[182] positions.

> Teachings of Ptahotep:
>
> If you are with people who display for you an extreme affection, saying: "Aspiration of my heart, aspiration of my heart, where there is no remedy! That which is said in your heart, let it be realized by springing up spontaneously. Sovereign master, I give myself to your opinion. Your name is approved without speaking. Your body is full of vigor, your face is above your neighbors." If then you are accustomed to this excess of flattery, and there be an obstacle to you in your desires, then your impulse is to obey your passion. But he who . . . according to his caprice, his soul is . . ., his body is . . . While the man who is master of his soul is superior to those whom Ptah has loaded with his gifts; the man who obeys his passion is under the power of his wife.
>
> -Ancient Egyptian Wisdom Texts

Over-concern with personal desires, vanity, narcissism, etc. leads to being susceptible to flattery and emotional appeals. That tilt towards emotions and lack of balance with intellect allows a person's actions to be swayed by the dictates or desires of others, which inevitably leads to a person's incapacity to think, feel and act in accordance with their own conscience, let alone, Maatian Ethical Conscience. Therefore, a person should shy away from self-importance, unearned praises and emotional appeals that are not supported by intellectual correctness. Then the ethical conscience will have the capacity to be expressed for the benefit of the individual, family, community and society.

---

[182] positions gained by rigging the economy and job market in their and their children's favor

WEALTH AND INCOME IMBALANCE AND POVERTY AS A SOURCE OF CRIME

> Poverty is the mother of crime.
> -Marcus Aurelius[183]

One of the arguments for the necessity of the neo or soft police state is because of increased terrorism but that issue is debunked by the fact that there is more chance of dying in a car accident than being hurt in a terrorist plot. Another reason for the establishment of a police state is to combat ever increasing crime. However, studies show that crime is increasing because poverty is increasing and poverty is increasing because of the greed and malfeasance of the power elite, perhaps as many as 2000 people who are the wealthiest in the country of 310 million, who control corporations and the government. So the reason for the police state is not to confront terrorism but to, among other things, feed the insatiable greed for corporate wealth created by arms dealing, which has now expanded to local municipalities and which supports local SWAT police teams with military gear, the new customers of the military industrial complex, and to protect the wealth and income imbalance in favor of the power elite from being interfered with by anyone including the domestic dissenters.

> Place where he lives is God plenty of names
> Slums, ghetto and black belt, they are one and the same
> And I call it Soulsville"
>
> Any kind of job is hard to find
> That means an increase in the welfare line
> Crime rate is rising too
> If you are hungry, what would you do?
>
> Rent is two months past due and the building that's falling apart
> Little boy needs a pair of shoes and this is only a part of Soulsville
>
> - Isaac Hayes - Soulsville Lyrics | MetroLyrics (1971)

---

[183] http://www.brainyquote.com/quotes/keywords/poverty.html#eWKYGCKwd20ayaas.99

Maat Philosophy Versus Fascism and the Police State

Poverty and Crime: Breaking the Vicious Cycle[184]

The unmistakable connection

Poverty and crime have a very "intimate" relationship that has been described by experts from all fields, from sociologists to economists. The UN and the World Bank both rank crime high on the list of obstacles to a country's development.

Unemployment, poverty and crime
Starting from the 1970s, studies in the US pointed more and more at the link between unemployment, poverty and crime. After that other connections with income level, time spent at school, quality of neighborhood and education were revealed as well. Fresh research from the UK even indicates that economic cycles may affect variations in property and violent crimes.

But most importantly, what reveals the unmistakable connection between poverty and crime is that they're both geographically concentrated - in a strikingly consistent way. In other words, where you find poverty is also where you find crime. Of course this doesn't include "softer" crimes such as corruption which causes massive damage to people's lives but in a more indirect type of violence.

Poverty causes crime
In the countries where the social discrimination factor isn't very strong, results have shown that less education meant more criminal offenses ranging from property crime to "casual" theft and drug-related offenses (again, mostly theft). But not violence. It appears that in fact, poverty itself is more tied with violence, criminal damage and also drug use - as a catalyst for violence.

The effect of inequalities & mixed populations
Another study across 20 cities in the US analyses how local inequalities and

---

[184] http://www.poverties.org/poverty-and-crime.html

heterogeneous populations can influence crime rates.

As ever more countries face problems related to immigration, policymakers should be aware that inequality, even within one ethnic group, is a major cause of crime.

The key? Re-building the social fabric
Income inequalities generate pockets of poverty and crime concentrated in the same ghettos, not only between but also within ethnic groups.

Unemployment means more property crimes
In the end, it's no big surprise that unemployment is also connected with crime as it's an important factor of inequalities. It's only recently that studies have revealed that unemployment causes not only higher property crimes but violent ones too.

Besides, joblessness has a deeper impact on the community because it destroys entire communities and whatever social cohesion that kept people living together in peace. This is a process that is all the more difficult to reverse. Eventually, it leaves a community completely helpless towards the growing cycle of poverty and crime.

Instead of focusing on fundamental imbalances and injustices in government, the courts and the economy, that lead to poverty, suffering and crime, the authorities focus on white and blue collar crimes or crimes of the poorer segments of the population while ignoring the injustices, perpetrated by corporations or the state and federal government that promote crime while glorifying police raids, chases, crackdowns, warrantless "stop and frisk", etc. as virtuous actions to keep the public safe and events of police brutality or killings as unfortunate solitary events. Often what happens in such cases is police departments may pay a fine and the officers involved may be reprimanded but the policies do not change.

If the intimidation fails there are being prepared FEMA Camps and other facilities are being prepared to detain large numbers of persons who may be deemed disruptive or terrorist[185] elements. However, just as every other government and empire from the Persian empire, the Greek empire, Genghis Khan, Attila the Hun, Napoleon, the British empire, the Ottoman empire, the Soviet Union, etc. has discovered is that when sufficient people are unsatisfied there is no government or police state that can cope with them. However, the digital age offers the police state more flexibility and capacity to exercise preemptive power, yet the sheer numbers of persons, when acting in concert, would still pose an overwhelming force to contend with. Of course that would be a situation of extreme social, political and economic unrest and possibly even revolution, which is another fear most people, the power elite as well as the

---

[185] The new laws now being enacted allow protesters who interfere with the activities of corporations to be considered and treated as "terrorists"

general population, are avoiding, for obvious reasons. Even though revolution could possibly be the only solution, since the power elite have shown no intention of changing the social hierarchy with themselves at the top or changing the nature of the economy, the possible negative outcome such as is being currently experienced in revolutions such as that of Egypt (Arab Spring that began in 2011) and other places may give people pause; though when the current system may become unbearable, then the masses will be forced into revolutionary actions.

> Do not waste your time on Social Questions. What is the matter with the poor is Poverty; what is the matter with the rich is Uselessness.
> -George Bernard Shaw[186]

> Poverty is the worst form of violence.
> -Mahatma Gandhi[187]

Finally, it is important to understand that poverty in a society, that has means, is a choice. Therefore, countries that have wealth such as the USA and other countries that allow wealth and income imbalances are doing so by choice. Furthermore, in such cases poverty is not just a cause of crime and social degradation, but the perpetrators, the government, corporate and church leaders of society that allow the poverty to exist are perpetrators of violence and suffering against those who are caused to be in the state of poverty by the economic system that is allowed to operate and impoverish people for the benefit of a minority.

> In a country well governed, poverty is something to be ashamed of. In a country badly governed, wealth is something to be ashamed of.
> -Confucius[188]

> Where justice is denied, where poverty is enforced, where ignorance prevails, and where any one class is made to feel that society is an organized conspiracy to oppress, rob and degrade them, neither persons nor property will be safe.
> -Frederick Douglass[189]

---

[186] http://www.brainyquote.com/quotes/keywords/poverty.html#eWKYGCKwd20ayaas.99
[187] ibid
[188] ibid
[189] ibid

POVERTY AS A CHOICE BY SOCIETY AS A GROUP

The following quotations are provided so that the reader may see that the current system of economics that promotes and allows the existence of poverty is neither natural to human political and economic organizations and has been recognized as a flaw by careful researchers and scholars of economics over the last few centuries. This means that poverty does not have to exist but is allowed to exist for the purpose of also allowing some members of the society to become fabulously rich and also maintain power over those who are poor or indigent.

To understand what the state of society ought to be, it is necessary to have some idea of the natural state of mankind, such as it is at this day among the Indians of North America. There is not, among the Indians[190], any of those spectacles of human misery which poverty and want present to our eyes in all the towns and streets in Europe. Poverty, therefore, is a thing created by that which is called civilized life. It exists not in the natural state.

—Thomas Payne (1752–1831) (from the book Agrarian Justice 1795):

---

[190] Native Americans

Maat Philosophy Versus Fascism and the Police State

Overcoming Poverty is not an act of charity, it is an act of justice. Like slavery and apartheid, poverty is not natural, it is manmade and can be overcome and eradicated by the actions of human beings. When poverty persists, there is no true freedom. (speaking in the 1990s)

—Nelson Mandela (1918-2013):

Thus, poverty is not a feature of society that existed among the Native Americans and it did not exist among the Ancient Egyptians. It is a byproduct of what European society called "civilized life". Another way of putting it is, poverty is an acknowledged and accepted consequence of having the type of economic system that produces wealth and income imbalances between members of a society. It is not a normal or inevitable condition of human society but rather, it is a choice to have things that way. Therefore, a choice can be made to not have things setup that way. What is necessary to make that choice to eradicate poverty is ethical conscience, and maturity as a human being to feel empathy and understanding for others beyond one's immediate family or social group and especially in the leadership of society. Additionally, that ethical conscience needs to actively prevent the ascension, by those members of the society who are unscrupulous, greedy or sociopathic, to positions of power in the leadership positions of government and or the commanding heights of the economy. Both conservatives (republican party) and democrats (democratic party), have supported the policies of capitalism and neo-liberalism. However, the republicans have historically been most extreme in the direction of hoarding wealth, producing wealth and income imbalances in society, favoring corporations over the general public, etc. In the following quote by John Kenneth Galbraith, we can see that this pursuit was true over 80 years ago as it is today.

Maat Philosophy Versus Fascism and the Police State

T he modern conservative is engaged in one of man's oldest exercises in moral philosophy; that is, the search for a superior moral justification for selfishness.

— John Kenneth Galbraith (1908-2006)

CONCLUSIONS

In closing, I suggest you read the follow-up ebook *MALFEASANCE & IMMORALITY: An Analysis of the World Economic Crash of 2008, the Corrupt Political and Financial Institutions that Caused it and Strategies to Survive the Future Collapse of the Economy,* which details more issues based on the themes discussed in the earlier books *Collapse of Civilization and the Death of American Empire* and *Dollar Crisis.* These texts contain further recommendations of how to protect yourself and what actions can be taken to promote Maat (truth, justice, righteousness) in society. Though the police state is bound to become more oppressive and controlling as the economic situation, the healthcare situation, the environmental situation and overall social, political and religious (spiritual) confidence worsen, it is probable that the society will fall into disarray or even chaos and despair or that in order to distract the population and promote patriotism and allegiance to the state, more wars may ensue until there is collapse of the economy and social order. Perhaps after such a collapse there may be a possibility to rectify the iniquities of the current system but due to the lack of integrity and education of the populace it is more likely that there will be polarization, infighting, intensification of class divisions and a neo-feudal order if not even a breakup of the USA as an integrated country, which would eventually, if the cultures were to remain with their current ideological points of view (ideology is a way of thinking regardless of facts and or taking into account the legitimate needs of others) could also lead to interstate wars.

It is important to understand that poverty and the relentless pressure of the capitalist society, of rising inflation and charges for all aspects of society have another important and insidious quality, its capacity to keep people in their state of poverty. Poverty and the lack of services and resources for the poor has the capacity to cause malnutrition which leads to lowered capacity to think effectively, learn in school and thus discover a skill or acquire a trade as well as act politically in a responsible way. Aside from the malnutrition issues, the rat race for survival itself has the effect of preventing thoughts other than about the poverty; thoughts like why is this happening to me, how did this happen, is society rigged against me and for the rich, and have the injustices of society played a part in causing my deplorable condition? Thus, poverty also acts as a mechanism to prevent protest and or revolt against the unjust conditions. In the book *Riches for the Poor: The Clemente Course in Humanities,* Earl Shorris [(C)2000] summarizes this condition in the following way:

> There is a point at which the forces that surround the poor become insurmountable, when there is no time or energy left to be anything else but poor.[191]

The pressure that comes from being manipulated into a position of poverty, by the capitalist society that accepts the existence of poor and indigent populations within the society, coupled with the innate human struggle for human development, that is, finding one's way in the world and discovering meaning in life, creates an incapacity to search for and discover the higher purpose of human existence. The overwhelming pressure from the practical life struggle causes a person to be incapable of engaging in a search for the meaning of life and the psycho-spiritual aspect of their personality becomes dull and untapped; This facilitates and promotes the development of harder, cold and bitter sentiments that operate out of base emotions instead of maturing into thoughtful well adjusted adulthood.

Poor and forsaken, the poverty-stricken also feel the effects of alienation and that alienation drives them to actions that are aberrant and self-destructive. At the same time, they are blamed for their actions and labeled with the stigma of being referred to as a form of undeserving, lazy, responsible for their own condition because of individual responsibility, "low life" or of being "uncivilized", etc. Detroit Michigan and Camden, New Jersey are examples of cities that benefitted from capitalism in the beginning, then thrived when workers were able to get decent wages and then collapsed and went bankrupt when the capitalist corporations moved away in search of low wage workers. This self-serving labeling of the poor by the rich and or the "privileged", and those who agree with them justifies their separation from and mistreatment of them. This self-serving idea ignores the adage: *"when a person has nothing to lose they lose it!"* Therefore, if there is suffering or destitution in a segment of the population it may be considered morally wrong, and rightly so. However, it is also the fault of society that it has failed to look after all its members.

---

[191] pp131

Maat Philosophy Versus Fascism and the Police State

Camden, New Jersey is the poorest city in the United States. Camden suffers from unemployment, urban decay, blighted neighborhoods, poverty, inability to pay for basic services like police and many other social issues. Much of the city of Camden, New Jersey suffers from urban decay.

When the residents of Watts or Detroit riot in their own neighborhoods, it is because they are not citizens of Watts or Detroit or the United States of America. There is no polis they can call their own; they have been excluded and dishonored, condemned to privacy. In the private panic of the surround, people become enemies of each other, even of themselves.[192]

---

[192] ibid pp73

Maat Philosophy Versus Fascism and the Police State

Burning buildings during the riots. Whole city blocks were gutted by arson and mob set fires that the fire department was powerless to control due to sniper attacks.

So society suffers by not taking care of all members of the society. Therefore, it is bad public policy and social management, for that suffering will eventually become a scourge on the social fabric leading to a morally bankrupt, corrupt and crime ridden society, which is of course what we see in all levels of society from the poor to the middle class, the political class, the corporate class and the ruling class of the modern fascist and capitalist society. Prime examples of this deteriorating form of society are the United States of America, England (and Europe in general), and Japan.

"The test of our progress is not whether we add more to the abundance of those who have much; it is whether we provide enough for those who have too little."
— Franklin D. Roosevelt

USA: RICH IN NAME ONLY

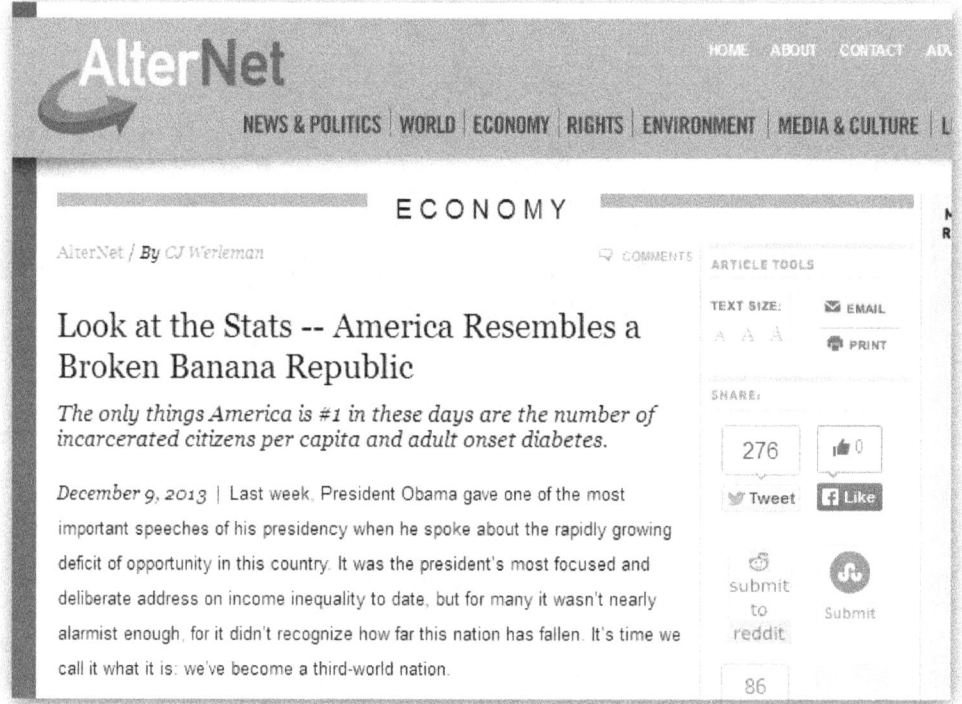

Look at the Stats -- America Resembles a Broken Banana Republic... America has become a RINO: rich in name only. [193]

It is ironic but not unexpected or surprising that the impoverishment of the USA population has led to a situation where higher economies can now see and treat the USA population as a low wage population. Due to the "race to the bottom" in terms of wages, where US corporations in collusion with the Federal Reserve and government officials have, for the last three decades striven to suppress wages and benefits, suppress or prevent unions from forming and open the US labor market to competition with lower wage countries, now the wages are so low in the USA that countries in economies with higher labor costs such as in Europe or Japan, where the minimum wage is over $14 can now open businesses in the USA where labor costs are lower. So, this means that Europe is to the USA what the USA is/was to Mexico, India and China. So to countries with higher wage labor costs, the USA is the low economy they can go to in order to exploit the downtrodden labor market where people are so grateful to get a job that they will accept anything that would pay a little more than the minimum wage. This is, of course, a humiliation, from the standpoint that the USA was in

---

[193] http://www.alternet.org/economy/america-rich-name-only-look-stats-we-resemble-broken-banana-state

the past a leader in the minimum wage and wealth distribution, that is after the Great Depression. Before the Great Depression, the USA was as it is now, a land where the rich took so much wealth out of the economy that it almost collapsed, and would have, were it not for the changes that were made in the "New Deal" whereby wealth and income were redistributed, rebalanced between the rich and everyone else in a more equitable fashion. The fact that the USA is back to where it was, at the brink of economic and political collapse, points to the fact that a capitalist system of economics and government inevitably leads to wealth and income imbalance, to boom and busts and ultimate collapse.

THE TRIUMPH OF CAPITALISM FOR THE WEALTHY AND THE FAILURE OF CAPITALISM FOR EVERYONE ELSE – BY DESIGN

Roman Empire → Feudalism/monarchy → Slavery → Capitalism → Neo-Feudalism

Capitalism is an evolution of the old feudal system of government and economy where the wealthy lord owned the land and people on it and allowed the people to farm the land for subsistence, while taking the surplus and increasing their own wealth. The workers, or serfs, were no better than slaves. In Capitalism the capitalist aggregates [hoards] wealth and power to him/her self while blocking the rights and wealth of the masses. Capitalism is an undemocratic system of economy, unlike the coop system,[194] in which workers decide what is to be produced, where the production and consumption of goods will take place, what materials will be used, how income will be distributed among them and what to do with excess profits, etc.

> "The wealth of those societies in which the capitalist mode of production prevails, presents itself as 'an immense accumulation of commodities,' its unit being a single commodity." (First sentence of Capital, Volume I.)
>
> - Karl Marx

In Capitalism the capitalist owns not simply the land but the capital that sustains it, industries, politics and the media while allowing the masses to believe they are not serfs and that they have freedom to control their lives. All the while the capitalist is the one who owns the mortgages and municipal government politicians who control all lands and industries so that wherever a worker might go, in the capitalist domain, they are confronted with the same conditions. Meanwhile, the capitalist class increases its wealth while the masses struggle to compete for meager wages against others willing to work for less; so laborers are kept in a condition of begging for work in order to survive and in competition with others who are struggling to survive. If the labor market were to get smaller, that is, less workers available, then the value of labor and wages would go up. Taxes and immigration are used as tools to keep the population from becoming wealthy through unfair taxation and in large numbers to reduce competition and allow capitalist corporations to have the pick of laborers and the capacity to dictate the terms of compensation. Laborers do not control immigration but when there is a flare-up of tension due to low wages, the politicians may blame the economy, another country, or single out some ethnic

---

[194] http://rdwolff.com/
http://www.democracyatwork.info/

group or minority as the guilty party that is "stealing" jobs away from the larger group of laborers; but never blame their immigration policies or the policies of businesses and corporations, that work in concert to constantly undermine laborers. Yet, the political and corporate leaders are orchestrating higher taxes for laborers, low tariffs that allow goods made with cheap labor to be imported, and a surplus of laborers domestically to keep labor costs to corporations down by using the excuse that immigration is needed to sustain the economy, though not in the numbers they allow to immigrate. This condition of labor, being subservient to capitalists is an integral aspect of capitalism, and constitutes an evolution of slavery whereby people are enslaved to debt and low wages and the slave master does not need to worry about controlling the slaves as in the chattel slavery system or the old feudalism system. Thus, it is imperative to prevent the formation of or the effectiveness of labor unions. This condition may be referred to as "Neo-feudalism".

> Neofeudalism entails an order defined by commercial interests and administered in large areas, according to Bruce Baker, who argues that this does not fully describe the extent of cooperation between state and non-state policing.[195] The significance of the comparison to feudalism, for Randy Lippert and Daniel O'Connor, is that corporations have power similar to states' governance powers.[196]
>
> The widening of the wealth gap, as poor and marginalized people are excluded from the state's provision of security, can result in neofeudalism, argues Marina Caparini, who says this has already happened in South Africa.[197] Neofeudalism is made possible by the commodification of policing, and signifies the end of shared citizenship, says Ian Loader.[198] A primary characteristic of neofeudalism is that individuals' public lives are increasingly governed by business corporations, as Martha K. Huggins finds.[199]

The lesson is clear that in order to avoid the problem of serious levels of crime it is important to prevent poverty. Capitalism is an economic system that by its very nature produces disparity in income distribution and therefore inevitably leads a society to have a segment of the population that will be "privileged" and another that will be "dispossessed". Therefore, Capitalism does not work to produce a well ordered and balanced society, but rather, the opposite. It works to

---

[195] Baker, Bruce (2004). "Protection from crime: what is on offer for Africans?". *Journal of Contemporary African Studies* **22** (2): 165–188. doi:10.1080/cjca0258900042000230005.
[196] Lippert, Randy; O'Connor, Daniel (2006). "Security Intelligence Networks and the Transformation of Contract Private Security". *Policing & Society* **16** (1): 50–66. doi:10.1080/10439460500399445.
[197] Caparini, Marina (2006). "Applying a Security Governance Perspective to the Privatisation of Security". In Bryden, Alan; Caparini, Marina. *Private Actors and Security Governance*. LIT Verlag. pp. 263–282. ISBN 3-8258-9840-7.
[198] Loader, Ian (1999). "Consumer Culture and the Commodification of Policing and Security". *Sociology* **33** (2): 373–392. doi:10.1177/S003803859900022X.
[199] Huggins, Martha K. (2000). "Urban Violence and Police Privatization in Brazil: Blended Invisibility". *Social Justice* **27** (2). ISSN 1043-1578.

benefit a minority. This is why capitalist systems cannot be allowed to operate freely and most governments who allow capitalism also eventually see they are forced to institute elements of socialist government like government run healthcare, social security, as well as other common aspects of society that capitalists do not care about but yet all use, such as roads, legal systems, and other social services that serve all of the population including police departments and the military; otherwise, capitalism would lead to such a concentration of power and wealth that it would strangle the life of the greater society in short order. Since Capitalism cannot work any other way, the socialist elements work only to alleviate, and not resolve or fix, the force of capitalist greed which eventually does mature into full ownership and control of mass wealth through apparently logical ideologies such as "Privatization" and "what is good for business is good for all", etc., the capitalist class and media convinces the masses that society would work better if everything were privatized, meaning owned by individuals and or corporations, as opposed to the government which in theory is owned by all. However, the only class that has sufficient wealth to own and operate the privatized elements of society is the wealthy class. With their ownership and greedy nature, their intent is to hoard and protect the wealth they have hoarded through changing laws to their favor and privatizing more resources. This process has the effect of crowding out the general society and precipitating social, political and economic imbalances that can lead to revolution or even an end to that society.

However, today capitalists are leaving the developed world ("First World") where they first applied capitalism and are moving to countries where they can get cheaper labor like originally Mexico, then it was China, later Viet Nam and now Bangladesh. In leaving cities in the "First World" for lower paying countries the capitalists left a vacuum wherein regional economies collapsed. Examples of this are Detroit, Michigan and Camden, New Jersey.

Lately, the workers of those cheaper labor countries have been fighting back against the slave-like conditions and eventually all labor will reach parity but not before capitalists and the resource depleting corporations do serious damage to the environment and wreck havoc with the countries they are enslaving and the devastation they are leaving behind as the cities they leave fall into economic depression. The next step would be for the capitalists to return to those devastated cities and try again to enslave the first world population as they did at the beginning of capitalism more than 200 years ago and through the middle of the 20th century now that the populations of those areas have been impoverished and are desperate for any meager wages. Those who are interested in the topic of how the capitalist class exploited and devastated the poor of society in the 19th and 20th century's and the disastrous conditions that were experienced by the poor and the middle class should read the works of John Steinbeck and Charles Dickens.

CONCLUSION

> Teachings to MeriKaRa:
> (23) When free men are given land,
> They work for you like a single team;
> No rebel will arise among them,
> -Ancient Egyptian Wisdom Texts

The teaching to Meri Ka Ra explains simply and succinctly that if people are well taken care of and treated fairly, compensated for their service as equals with the managers and owners of enterprises, then they reciprocate and work for the benefit of the organization, city or country devotedly and willingly. In the neo-feudal culture, capitalists and fascists do not have that ideal in mind. The ideal in capitalism/neo-feudalism is to hoard wealth and squeeze laborers in an adversarial relationship where laborers and business owners are not partners but rather combatants to see who will get the most wealth at the expense of the other. But since capitalists have most of the wealth they have most of the power to set the agenda in the media, the laws and government policies. This coupled with arrogance, hubris, greed, amorality and corruption leads to the current condition of society that we have today where the greed is so acute and blind that it does not see or care about the deterioration of society and the economy which may be likened to a bone whose marrow and calcium has been sucked dry and it is so weak and brittle that it can collapse and break catastrophically at any time. Since the marrow and calcium (wealth) has been sucked out of the society, it is feeding on itself in the form of infighting between groups for the scraps that are left, high unemployment, people working two and three slave wage jobs (just to pay for basic bills), young people can't move out of their parent's homes because they cannot afford to, and there is increased crime, stress, drug use, disease and desire for mindless entertainments.

Maat Philosophy Versus Fascism and the Police State

WHAT DOES ANCIENT EGYPTIAN MAAT PHILOSOPHY SAY ABOUT THE ISSUE OF HOARDING WEALTH?

> "Knowledge without action is like hoarding precious metals, a vain and foolish thing. Knowledge is like wealth, intended for use; Those who violate the universal law of USE conflict with natural forces."
> -Ancient Egyptian Proverb

Wealth is intended for use. This means that it is intended to be used and circulated for the benefit of humanity as a whole and not just for the benefit of a minority, while the rest of the population languishes for want and need of basic sustenance.

> "An immoderate desire of riches is a poison lodged in the mind. It contaminates and destroys everything that was good in it. It is no sooner rooted there, than all virtue, all honesty, all natural affection, fly before the face of it."
> -Ancient Egyptian Proverb

Immoderate desire means "GREED". Greed is a scourge of human life and the bane of human society. It corrupts the mind allowing a person to commit heinous acts of cruelty while justifying those as "just business", or the "it's the market" and not personal. Greed is a kind of cancer that consumes the ethical capacity of the mind, rendering it callous, shallow and weak in the face of personal safety, pleasure and prosperity even at the expense or pain and suffering of others. No ethical, caring society or individual person, banker or police officer, would ever dispossess another human being from their home and then say "it's just business, not personal" or it's the market that has done this to you and it's not my fault, it's not my fault you are being thrown on the street. I'm just doing my job."

> "Any riches you have are useless without the many."
> -Ancient Egyptian Proverb

Without the masses to do the work of production of goods, farming and other services of life, where would the wealthy be? They would have to do the work themselves. Therefore, their status as wealthy depends on the status of the masses and the willingness of the masses to remain in their place even as the wealthy rig politics, taxation schemes, wages and banking systems in their favor, to systematically increase their wealth while systematically impoverishing the masses.

Maat Philosophy Versus Fascism and the Police State

"Know your friends and then you prosper. Don't be mean to your friends. They are like a watered field and greater than any material riches that you may have, for what belongs to one belongs to another. The character of one who is well born should be a profit to him. Good nature is a memorial."

-Ancient Egyptian Proverb

Maatian wisdom unequivocally demonstrates that balance in the distribution of "riches' of a society is desirable because all human beings are part of a self-same nature manifesting in a variety of personalities but which is nevertheless one single family of humanity. Therefore, as such, all are deserving of a sufficient portion of riches. Further, when this fair sharing is accomplished, another kind of riches is revealed, the richness of good nature that allows a person to experience a kind of satisfaction and contentment that hoarding riches cannot bring forth. This higher nature of the human heart, is the source of what is beneficial in one's own life as well as the environment we all live in. Maat philosophy is also practical and always striving for balance in all things. From a practical perspective it is better to have a society with balance in wealth because then all will prosper and the wealthier segments of the population will still become wealthier; they will just not be able to hoard all the wealth and direct society in accordance with their ideological designs or egoistic desires or megalomaniacal tendencies. Therefore, this is the foundation of Maatian order that is the ideal for all followers of maat philosophy to develop, model and implement in government, economics and spiritual life.

FAILURE BY DESIGN: THE ILLUSION OF THE "BROKEN" SYSTEM

Many people are fond of saying that the USA government and or the USA economic system and or the USA medical industry, or the energy industry, or consumer economic system, etc. etc., etc., are "broken," that they don't work anymore. These statements are based on the idea that the underlying concept of the USA social, political and economic systems are legitimate and workable, as if there is proof somewhere in history or another country, that these systems can and have worked in the past, as if they ever worked for the benefit of all members of society. The fact of the matter is that they are evolutions of monarchy, feudalism and empire systems of the past. Thus, capitalism, consumerism, dictatorship, oligopoly, oligarchy, plutocracy, etc., are just as prone to direct wealth and power to the few as the modern form of representative democracy and crony capitalism (fascism) that he USA is experiencing now. Therefore, the USA systems of government, politics and economics are not broken and are working just as designed, to direct power and wealth to a minority, a power elite. The only difference is that we do not call the system monarchy, aristocracy, etc., and we do not have a king to blame for the problems. By creating a system of legalized debt and by controlling the legal system, the power elite does not have to hold title to land or property or physically appear as a leader; rather, the debt itself constitutes a shackle to control the society. So the system is not broken. It is actually working so well that the power elite may cause a collapse of the economy due to extracting so much wealth that the poverty levels rise so much that the poor and middle class cannot support the economy and thus it collapses under the weight of incapacity to sustain debt and incapacity to sustain demand in the economy. In such a scenario, social, political and economic collapse would be likely and additionally, an opportunity for revolution or at least to reform the system would be possible. However, as stated elsewhere, the system is corrupt, in and of itself, so no reform would work in the long run. What is needed is a change to a system based on righteousness, ethics, peace, environmental balance and concern for all humanity. This would necessitate a revolution and an institution of a system with human and environmental values as opposed to a system based on a societal philosophy of greed, profit and indifference to human suffering and environmental destruction.

Why is it that when government agencies fail to protect the environment, fail to protect civil rights, property rights, or the environment, the masses lose but there is always some corporation or wealthy land owner or government official benefitting? Why is it that when government agencies fail to serve the needs of people and yet the bureaucrats and agency heads are rewarded with higher pay, higher honor and positions? Why is it that corporate executives (board members and CEOs especially) lead their companies into bankruptcy, need for bailouts or criminality and yet they get higher compensation, bonuses, move on to better positions, etc.? It is by design. An Institute for Policy Studies report[200] found that 40% of corporate leaders led their companies into failure, need for bailout or paying fines due to malfeasance or criminality while the executives were still compensated handsomely, despite the supposed failure.

---

[200] http://www.ips-dc.org/reports/executive-excess-2013

Maat Philosophy Versus Fascism and the Police State

In the political field, the Bush, Obama and Reagan administrations violated the constitution and did not suffer any consequences. Another example is Henry Kissinger,[201] a secretary of state in the Nixon Administration, he oversaw the toppling of South American and South East Asian governments and the killing of leaders as well as citizens of those countries so as to maintain USA control over those countries and stopping those countries from electing governments that would oppose USA political and corporate policies. Kissinger should have been tried for crimes and is wanted for arrest by some countries and would be arrested if he were to travel to some countries around the world.[202] Yet, he is accorded respect and still acts as an advisor to government leaders. He was also awarded a peace prize even though he admitted to breaking the law purposefully, which tells us something about the organization that made the award.

---

[201] a German-born American statesman and political scientist. A recipient of the Nobel Peace Prize, he served as National Security Advisor and later concurrently as Secretary of State in the administrations of Presidents Richard Nixon and Gerald Ford. After his term, his opinion was still sought by some subsequent US presidents and other world leaders. https://en.wikipedia.org/wiki/Henry_kissinger

[202] http://www.thirdworldtraveler.com/Kissinger/CaseAgainst1_Hitchens.html

Kissinger: "The illegal we do immediately; the unconstitutional takes a little longer."[203]

> A just-released transcript of a meeting between Henry Kissinger and a Turkish Foreign Minister 35 years ago provides a bombshell quote that will go a long way toward solidifying the former Secretary of State's reputation as one of the most Machiavellian insiders of American politics and diplomacy in the 20th century.
>
> During a secret meeting on March 10, 1975 in the Turkish Capital of Ankara with Mehli Esenbel, Turkey's Foreign Minister, Kissinger, then Secretary of State and Assistant to the President for National Security Affairs, told Esenbel:
>
> Before the Freedom of Information Act, I used to say at meetings, "The illegal we do immediately; the unconstitutional takes a little longer." [laughter] But since the Freedom of Information Act, I'm afraid to say things like that.
>
> Ironically, it was a Freedom of Information Act (FOIA) request that finally pried loose the transcripts of the meeting, albeit three and a half decades later. The transcripts were posted November 5 on the website of the National Security Archive, a research institute and library located at the George Washington University.

THE ILLUSION OF CONSTITUTIONAL GOVERNMENT AND THE REALITY OF CORPORATE GOVERNMENT

The USA government is also run like a corporation. The legislature, together with the Supreme Court and the Federal Reserve members may be considered as the board members and the president is the CEO. Just as corporations are run as dictatorships and the employees have no say in the company policies, so too the corporation USA government leaders are dictators who are not concerned with the needs or higher aspirations of the population at large; rather, they are more concerned with the dictates of the corporate power elite. Therefore, the policies of the power elite routinely get enacted while only basic the needs of the masses are provided.
Increasingly, from the 1980s onwards more intensively, beginning with specific policies instituted by Ronald Reagan, and subsequent presidents, began to be implemented including underfunding government agencies so they do not have leadership and/or financial resources to do the job they were intended for and placing someone at the head of the agency who either is a fool, incompetent, or who does not have expertise in the given area (example Michael D. Brown as

---

[203] http://www.thenewamerican.com/usnews/politics/item/3492-kissinger-the-illegal-we-do-immediately-the-unconstitutional-takes-a-little-longer

head of FEMA during the Katrina Hurricane disaster)[204]. The other tactic is to place someone in the position who is a crony, someone who was previously working in the industry that the agency regulates and who will do no regulation in accordance with their real bosses who will hire them back after their time heading the agency. This is the proverbial "revolving door" between government service and industry. This is someone who knows what they are doing and will intentionally lead the agency to failure, which also happens to benefit corporations and the power elite. If a government agency fails, then the argument is made that government can't work so there is supposed "need" for a "private" company to take over and scale back government. Of course the private company is controlled and or operated for profit and the benefit of its owners and not for the public good but since the corporate failures cannot be questioned due to the corporate ethos of being the best system to give opportunity for wealth, then the wider population degrades in a morass of propaganda and intentional failure that is instituted by the power elite and believed in as well as followed by the masses. The stooge who is placed at the head of the government agency also serves as a convenient fall person whenever there is failure or complaint about the services provided but never is the issue of cronyism and the tactic of intentionally sandbagging and or sabotaging the government agencies discussed.

The better the corporate executives and government bureaucrats serve the needs and dictates of the power elite, the more they are rewarded and compensated. An example of the "failure" executive head of government agencies is Timothy Geithner, the head of the New York Federal Reserve who supposedly completely missed the impending crash of 2008. He was rewarded with a higher position, that of head of the USA Treasury. Another example is Alan Greenspan, who was the head of the USA Federal Reserve, and oversaw the period of the crash and admitted the fault in the concept of unregulated capitalism and yet has not lost credibility, or favor in the halls of government or Wall Street. Even when the failures are evident and even admitted, the government officials, including the president, and media praise them as knowledgeable, or as the best and brightest who are doing the best that anyone could do and if there is failure it was not their fault, it was just a difficult or unprecedented situation or it was someone else's fault who did not follow their instructions properly, etc.. This is also known as "failing upwards". So the greater the "failure" the greater the reward and the higher the position, exactly the opposite of what would occur in an ethical system. Rather, if there is any failure it was due to individual inadequacies of the members of the organization and never should the mission and structure of the organization be questioned. This is the argument of

---

[204] Before joining the DHS/FEMA, Brown was the Judges and Stewards Commissioner for the International Arabian Horse Association, (IAHA), from 1989-2001.
[https://en.wikipedia.org/wiki/Michael_D._Brown]

"individual responsibility" whereby failure or success is the fault of the individual not trying hard enough, regardless of the system they are operating in. Under this argument, Africans were enslaved by their own fault and the oppression they suffered was in no way the fault of the slavery system they were surrounded by. Never are those who warned of the failed policies or the impending failure acknowledged, mentioned or consulted. This is because the failure is desired, as the policy is designed to lead to "failure" since it is a concerted effort to carry out a policy that fails for the majority and succeeds for the power elite. If any criminality should be discovered, it can be redressed by retroactively making a law that legalizes that. An example of this tactic was what was done with warrantless wiretapping during the administration of president George W. Bush, an impeachable offence. After saying that he would not support retroactively legalizing the lawbreaking by the Bush administration, Barak Obama, as a senator before becoming president, did vote to retroactively pass a law that let president Bush and his operatives get a free pass on violating the constitution. However, since the law passed by congress was not a constitutional amendment, the law was and is invalid and the criminality still exists but now with new accomplices, those who voted for that law, trying to legalize what was previously and is still illegal. The power elite make sure the bureaucrats who run government and industries are protected from criminal prosecution while making sure they are well compensated for their services to the power elite and not to the general public.

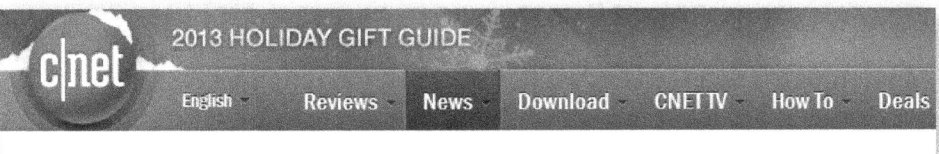

Senate endorses retroactive FISA immunity for warrantless wiretapping

Bush wins hard-fought battle after Senate immunizes telecom companies that illegally opened their networks to the Feds. There's a chance a suit against AT&T could continue.

by Declan McCullagh | July 9, 2008 1:29 PM PDT
Follow @declanm

The Democratic-controlled Senate handed President Bush a major political victory on Wednesday by voting to derail lawsuits against telecommunications companies that unlawfully opened their networks to the National Security Agency.

Senators voted 69 to 28 for the bill, which would rewrite federal wiretap laws by granting retroactive immunity to telecommunications companies as long as the government claims the request was "lawful" and authorized by the president.

> Wednesday's vote followed a last-minute effort by liberal and libertarian activists to convince enough Democrats to kill or modify the bill. DailyKos called the bill "a pardon to Bush"; some activists created a Wiki to hone their message; a *Salon* columnist dubbed the bill a "coverup of surveillance crimes."
>
> Many of those efforts were aimed at Sen. Barack Obama, the Democratic presidential candidate, who told us half a year ago that he would definitely not support retroactive immunity. That was then. Now he does--and he voted for the final bill on Wednesday.[205]

---

[205] http://news.cnet.com/8301-13578_3-9986716-38.html

Chapter 7: Maat Philosophy as a Foundation for Good Government and a Well Ordered Society That Does Not Need a Police State

> (15) "I have not laid waste the ploughed lands."
> (36) "I have never befouled the water." <u>Variant: held back the water from flowing in its season.</u>
>
> -Ancient Egyptian Precepts of Maat on protecting the environment and natural world

A Society based on Maat Philosophy, as was the Ancient Egyptian culture, would conduct society on a foundation of righteousness and truth based on a premise of universal interrelationships whereby human beings, nature and indeed the universe, are inexorably linked and interdependent. Indeed, there were police in ancient Egypt and the courts were run by judges who were also priests and priestesses who based their judgments on the philosophy of Maat. In Ancient Egypt, t o be seen as biased against the poor or for the rich would have been anathema and cause for removal, punishment and incarceration of any court official. In contrast today we see rampant corruption in politics and business where government officials from the president to the congress violate laws and do not enforce laws on corporate and political leaders but enforce laws on the general public in collusion with the courts which do not prosecute corporations, the rich or government officials. The equal dispensation of the law is the foundation for a well ordered society that administers a proper balance between the needs of all citizens and the care of the environment. So the wanton misuse of resources and destruction of the environment for profit would be a direct violation of Maatian law. Therefore, such a society that ruthlessly and profoundly violates natural laws and the laws which express human and natural balance (Maat) is in complete contradiction with itself and the very order and balance of nature as well as the balance of human society; therefore, eventually there has to be a movement in nature and in society to return to the balance and when humans do not heed the natural laws of nature and the needs of humanity, then the rebalancing, the swing of the Maatian scales are inevitable and can be violent and also ruthless; this reordering of nature and society is what we are facing as a humanity as a result of the massive unrighteousness that has been expressed on society, economics, in the environment and in the psychic space.

Maat Philosophy Versus Fascism and the Police State

In Chapter 125 of the *Prt M Hru* Text (Ancient Egyptian Book of the Dead), in affirmation of having practiced and fulfilled the precepts of Maat the person uttering the declarations states:

> "I have done God's will. I have given bread to the hungry, water to the thirsty, clothes to the clotheless and a boat to those who were shipwrecked. I made the prescribed offerings to the gods and goddesses and I also made offerings in the Temple to the glorious spirits. Therefore, protect me when I go to face The God." (For the full text see the *Book of the Dead* -translated by Sebai Muata Ashby)

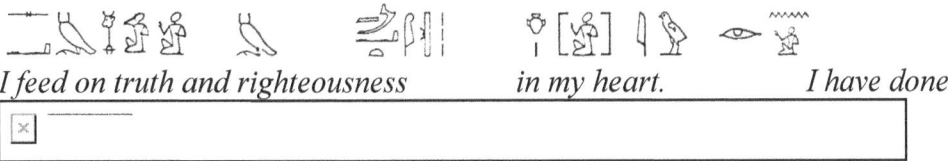

I feed on truth and righteousness   in my heart.   I have done the commanded things to men and women that satisfy the gods and goddesses. Thus I have brought peace to the Divinity.

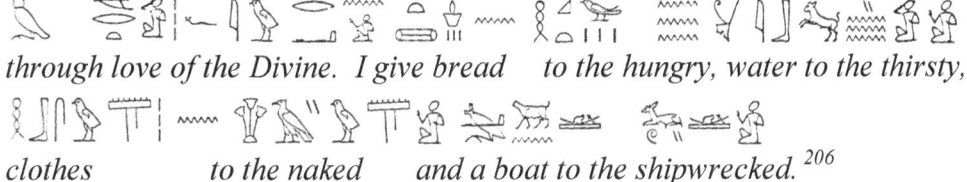

through love of the Divine. I give bread   to the hungry, water to the thirsty, clothes   to the naked   and a boat to the shipwrecked. [206]

In terms of social responsibility and charitable caring for all members of society, these declarations mean that one who practices Maat Philosophy ("God's will") expresses that wisdom by not just professing faith but rather by acting in accordance with those precepts in the following ways:

- Feeding the hungry
- Giving drink to the thirsty
- Giving clothes to the clotheless
- Giving Shelter to the homeless
- Giving a boat, i.e., ability to move, to work, to travel, in short, opportunity to those who do not have opportunity to better themselves, to start over if they have fallen on hard times, to find their life's purpose, to not be tied to a dead end job, to be destitute without income and capacity to invest in themselves and their family so as to grow and prosper, etc. Ultimately, this means the capacity to achieve the goals of life that all human beings aspire to.

---

[206] *Pert M Heru*, Ancient Egyptian Book of Enlightenment (Book of the Dead). Translation by Muata Ashby

Maat Philosophy Versus Fascism and the Police State

The teachings of Maat constitute a foundation of ethical conscience for a well ordered, fruitful and just society. The Ancient Egyptian system of government sets the personality at the top, the Pharaoh, which could be a male or a female, as the *Shepherd* (Heka) parent of the society and as a figurehead that person is also regarded as a representative, if not manifestation of the Creator, the Divine Spirit that created and sustains all life. As such, that person is responsible, as an executive position, to execute the laws that protect and provide for the well-being of all members of society. A parent in a family does not allow the children and family members to fend for themselves or favor some over others. That would be unethical, uncaring and cruel. In the same way, the Pharaoh, under the guidance of the council of priests and priestesses was charged with seeing to it that all members of society have a basic safety net and that if some fall on hard times that the society as a whole steps in to assist them to get back on their feet.

The Ancient Egyptian God Asar (Osiris) The "Good Shepherd"

This social responsibility and caring between citizens for other citizens and indeed other human beings is a viable societal responsibility based on the balances observed in nature and not to be seen as charity or welfare and it is not the purview of the rich or of donors. Again, it is a common responsibility of all citizens to help other citizens and thereby the health of the society as a whole. In this way, everyone's capacity to find fulfillment in life and reach their potential, is enhanced and society overall achieves a higher standard in terms of physical and mental health, security from crime, etc. In such an ethically conscious society, as the Ancient Egyptian, the members of society agree and understand that food, shelter, opportunity, healthcare, etc, are rights all members of the human family are deserving of and not just for the minority of rich and powerful. In such an ethically conscious society as the Ancient Egyptian, the rich and powerful are not to be allowed to exploit the weak or less fortunate or even other wealthy persons. In such an ethically conscious society as the Ancient Egyptian, excessive imbalance in income and wealth would not be allowed. In such an ethically conscious society as the Ancient Egyptian it would not be allowed for some to have healthcare and others not, etc.

It is important to understand that the above wisdom does not apply to isolated charity but it is to be applied by individuals and by the state. Of course this conception would be most similar to the modern concept of socialism as is practiced in present day Denmark, Norway, Sweden, Finland, and Germany, which have the lowest poverty rates among nations of the world. Comparing those countries to the USA, the USA has among the worst poverty rates among all nations [207] of the world and especially when compared to other developed nations. This Kemetic style of socialism is managed by the council of priests and priestesses of the entire country who insure that no one, especially children and the elderly, would go hungry, homeless or without opportunity. This means that everyone's basic human needs were provided for by all members of the society contributing to a system that was similar to but more comprehensive than the present day Social Security of the USA and would be more like the Social

---

[207] http://www.epi.org/publication/ib339-us-poverty-higher-safety-net-weaker/

Security system of modern Northern European nations. This practice would preclude social unrest as everyone would have the capacity to be free from basic wants and then they would be able to pursue the higher goals of life, be they professional and secular or non-secular. Of course this means that there could not exist a large disparity in wealth and income distribution and a economic power elite that would impose heavy taxes, own most of the capital and hoard most of the income of the society as is done in the empire, feudal, capitalist, etc. systems. In the environment where Maatian wisdom is upheld and applied to all members of the society, there would be a sufficient level of balance and order in the society such that members of the society would be disposed to support and uphold their communities and local economies, thereby promoting prosperity for all. Another point is that when the injunction talks about Feeding, Giving, etc. it is not to be understood as giving something to the undeserving. All members of a society are deserving if we consider that all members are actually related by culture and ethnicity but also by human genetics. Additionally, in giving of ourselves we also receive for ourselves in our own time of need. This is what it means to be a true family and community and Maat Philosophy is an ultimate expression of how the family of humanity can coexist and prosper by following divine regulations that are actually derived from the logic drawn from thousands of years of observations of nature, which always seeks balance, removal of pain, caring for its parts and evolving the higher consciousness that it in its sentient inhabitants. Secondly, Maatian wisdom recognizes that cooperation allows the sum of human efforts to become more than their constituent parts and this is how a great civilization can be built but also sustained. Furthermore, it is important to understand that the bounty of nature is to be shared because it is given by nature, that is to say, God; therefore, no human being, or living being, has the right to hoard it or withhold it from others and indeed no one "owns" it and all have a "right" to it. Conversely, no one has a right to steal in such a society that upholds this balanced order for there should be no need and thus no legitimate purpose for stealing. Above and beyond the sharing, when all basic needs are met, then industrious individuals may accumulate more surplus depending on their efforts and thereby create an even higher standard of living but if a situation arises are where the basic needs (food, water, shelter, opportunity) of the many are not met then the wealth of the wealthy is to be applied towards those needs. This idea was similar to the concept of the "Estate Tax" of the USA in which upon death, the wealth of a person's estate was taxed and used for the benefit of the whole society. This also served the purpose of preventing large family wealth accumulation in such a way that would allow certain families and groups to develop generational wealth and thereby develop into an oligarchy. In recent years, the political class, which does the bidding of the power elite and neglects the needs of the masses, and groups financed by the power elite like members of the republican party, libertarian party and the "tea party", has taken to calling the Estate tax a "death tax" so as to denigrate, reduce and eventually do away with it and in so doing allowing even further massive wealth inequalities to ensue and the vision of balance and social responsibility in the society to erode regardless of the factor that the continuation of this policy will eventually lead to a social breakdown.

Therefore, it behooves all who would seek to follow a Maatian path, to promote Maat in their personal lives and in their physical, social, political and economic spaces. In other words, to face the coming disruptions, what is the best way to promote Maat in relationships? What is the best way to promote Maat in your community? What is the best way to promote Maat in your local and national politics? What is the best way to promote Maat in your finances? and if it is found that the environments are too toxic to be reformed to make use of your efforts what can you do where you are and with others of like mind? or where can you go where you r efforts can have the best chance to protect you from these issues and allow you to protect your family, finances and allow you to continue a viable spiritual practice? How would it help your spiritual practice and capacity to uphold Maat if you are made destitute or rendered powerless in your society? You may need to consider communicating with and allying with others of like mind, forming cooperatives and legal advisories, protecting your finances, changing banks, moving to a different dwelling, or a different state, or a different country. Consider the question of what were people thinking just before the social disruptions that led to the genocides by the German Nazis? or the genocides of Rwanda, the depression of the 1930s or the civil war? If the populations of those countries had realized where the country was headed what would they have done differently? Surely some people who did not leave Germany were thinking that it was too hard to move to a different country and start over economically, or too difficult to learn a new language or too unbearable to leave family members behind, etc. etc. Surely some were hoping that things would not get too bad or that things would somehow change for the better or that everyplace is the same so why bother going through the trouble? Another rationalization is why worry about the future when those future dire scenarios may not occur at all? If they had the wherewithal to take different actions to protect themselves would they have done so or were they thinking that things would never get too bad - until it was too late to take any action. Certainly it is possible that the dire predictions may never come to pass, that somehow there may be a more positive outcome to these issues; is that realistic? Is it probable? Is it worth not being concerned about the possible outcomes that may occur and possible consequences and not at least be prepared to take some action to protect oneself? Is it better to face truth and take action the ego is against and or rationalize what is in favor of the ego's desires, that the likelihood of such dire predictions is low and that those who are in power are trustworthy people looking out for your best interests and there is no need to worry?

Maat Philosophy Versus Fascism and the Police State

"Truth and knowledge produce courage."

"Are not the enemies made by truth, better than the friends obtained by flattery?"

-Ancient Egyptian Proverbs

Under a government which imprisons any unjustly, the true place for a just man is also a prison.
-Henry David Thoreau -**Civil Disobedience**

These are questions for reflection and the above publications have more ideas on these issues. The time is now to consider these issues and to take the actions that will allow the best chance of success in upholding Maat in your life and thereby you will have the best chance of helping your family, community, society and the world. Since people who do not belong to the power elite do not control their fate as they are living in a police state controlled by the power elite, then it follows that the laws of the power elite that contravene the ethical culture of Maat or other similar ethical philosophies, are invalid. Since the police state itself is an illegitimate system of government and social organization, then it follows that its subjects are not legally or morally bound to uphold its tenets, policies or designs including subjugation of segments of the population or the subjugation, wars or damages to other countries. It is the right of every individual to follow the dictates of their conscience and to follow truth to the best of their understanding in so far as that effort does not violate the rights of other individuals or the community; however, since the police state is invalid and illegitimate, neither the individual nor the community or the masses are bound to protect or uphold the usurped rights of the police state. What we are witnessing is how a society drowns in its own orgy of selfish and unhindered pursuit of profit, power and pleasure seeking. As the society breaks down, the seeker of righteousness must stand for truth and also make a decision about whether or not their efforts are best served by allowing him/herself to be hurt or imprisoned by the police state or to leave the police state until it more fully implodes and there is sufficient awakening in the masses that would allow a significant revolution an rebuilding of the state along more ethical lines.

The fundamental difference between a fascist police state and a just system of government is the existence or nonexistence of a rule of law. In the soft or hard fascist police state the rule of law is subverted and those at the top, the ruling class (capitalists and the politicians they control) are protected from the legal system or rather, excluded from it, exempt from penalties or criminal consequences beyond fines. In the Maatian system of government, maat, or ethical conscience and caring for the wellbeing of all citizens and indeed all human beings and the natural world, are primary. Therefore, a system of government and social order that has, as its foundation, the welfare of living beings at heart as opposed to the wellbeing of corporations and the protection of people's right to pursue happiness even at the expense of others or at the expense of the environment, such a system will be a purveyor of life and health instead of violence and death in the form of wars and polluted environments.

A police state is necessary when the leaders presume that the population needs to be controlled as by not doing so could lead to a revolution and their ouster, and rightly so, for if the media were to fully and relentlessly point out the shortcomings of the fascist style of government then driving the message home through repetition as they do with endless mindless advertisements and reality shows, the population would come to understand how they are being hurt and would overturn the leadership. In the fascist police state the media is compliant with the fascist leaders and do not highlight or follow up on the damage done to the economy, the environment or the erosion of civil rights or the rule of law. Thus a slow boiling frog situation ensues in which the population remains oblivious to the ever increasingly deteriorated condition they are in and gradually lose power and wealth so as to end up in the status of serfs in a neo-feudal condition, poor and at the mercy of the fascist leaders, the neo-feudal lords.

ANCIENT EGYPTIAN POLICE

The chief of police Shemai
Aswan, 12th dynasty[208]

---

[208] Manuelian 1996, Vol.1, p.94

Maat Philosophy Versus Fascism and the Police State

Ancient Egypt did have police officers and in the pre-Persian conquest period, their duties were related to guarding facilities, border patrols, protecting persons and property and apprehending violators of the law, Maat. They were not used to repress the population or go after political enemies but to ensure public order in accordance with the precepts of Maat, which are a body of regulations composed of 42 special declarations of ethical conscience, the upholding of the three values of social justice: society's capacity and duty to provide food, shelter and opportunity for all citizens, and confessions of Maatian personal purity.

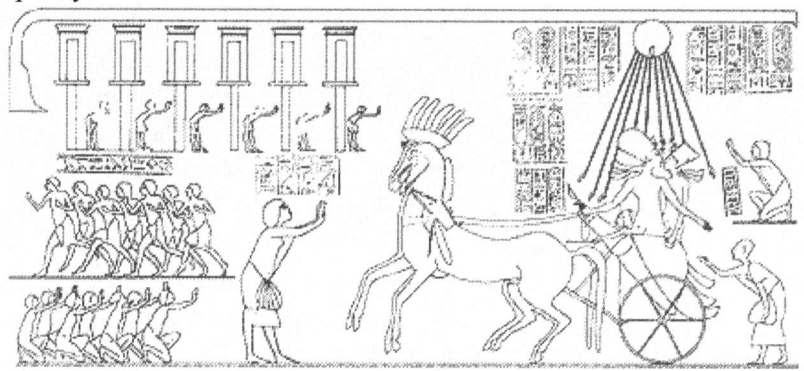

The chief of police Mahu and his men greeting the royal cavalcade
Tomb of Mahu, Akhetaten

Mahu was chief of police at Akhetaten under the Pharaoh Akhenaten. He decorated his tomb with scenes from his working life such as escorting robbers to court and looking for fugitives.[209] Just as there are today many persons who are sociopathic, prone to violence or even sadism or are otherwise corrupt, who join the police forces, so in ancient times there is a record of the same types of personalities serving in the ranks of the police. However, unlike the present, citizens were able to report them and their actions would not have been dealt with by imposing simple fines or dismissal but would have been more harsh. In the Ancient Egyptian story of the *The Eloquent Peasant, the peasant* was not afraid to call for justice in a case of police corruption:

> *Behold, you are a policeman* (SnT) *who steals...*
>
> -*The Eloquent Peasant*

There is also a record of the breakdown in the legal and ethical conduct of the police especially when there was a breakdown of the central command of the society which was headed by a council of priests and priestesses and the Pharaoh and his vizier. The major difference between the ancient Egyptian policing and the policing of the present would be that the police could not break the law with impunity and the standard of law would not be allowed to deteriorate in a way that there ensues a gradual degradation of legal dispensation

---

[209] Rice 2001, p.104

in which corruption and maltreatment by the police is tolerated, accepted and even expected, especially to the extent that ordinary or noble cause police corruption[210], including brutality and extrajudicial killings or planting of evidence, etc. are commonplace followed by police being exonerated of any wrongdoing and incidents are often characterized as isolated incidents or perpetrated by "bad apples", ignoring the corruption of the policing as a whole, which includes a code of silence and the ignoring of the gangs, the graft of politicians and corporations that donate to police organizations and make laws protecting them from prosecution and ignoring the distributors and importers of drugs into the country.

MAAT PHILOSOPHY AND ANCIENT EGYPTIAN LAW

There is no record of a period of normalization where police corruption was tolerated and allowed to become an endemic aspect of society in Ancient Egypt. This is because the practice of Maat philosophy is not just an intellectual exercise but an expression of a living aspiration to be in balance with nature and with spirit in such a way that allows a human being to discover transcendental consciousness and this was the highest goal not only of the priesthood but of the society as a whole, unlike modern culture, whose goal is pleasure seeking and political power for worldwide domination. This is the force that maintained an impetus in Ancient Egyptian society for a movement towards ethical conscience and a rejection of immorality and corruption.

> *Forget not to judge justice. It is an abomination of the god to show partiality. This is the teaching. Therefore, do you accordingly. Look upon him who is known to you like him who is unknown to you; and him who is near the king like him who is far from his house. Behold, a prince who does this, he shall endure here in this place.*
>
> The Instructions of Rekhmire
> From "The Wisdom of Ancient Egypt" by Joseph Kaster.

What may be considered the central difference underlying the dispensation of justice between the Ancient Egyptian system and the modern western system? The answer is *bias*. In the modern fascist system of government and economics there is bias in favor of the wealthy and this bias eventually leads to greater and greater disparities in which a two tiered justice system emerges, one for the wealthy and the other for the masses that is especially harsh on the poor of all ethnicities and also especially harsh on poor ethnic minorities. The bias leads to an ossified elite that cares not for anyone but themselves so they set out to hoard all wealth even to the detriment of the entire society including themselves and

---

[210] According to the field of Police Ethics, noble cause corruption is police misconduct "committed in the name of good ends."

their children. Bias is antithetical to the very nature of Maatian law and could never be allowed in the Ancient Egyptian legal system.

Maat
Tomb of Nefertari
Picture source: Jon Bodsworth

Thou art Re, thy body is his body. There has been no ruler like thee, (for) thou art unique, like the son of Osiris, thou hast achieved the like of his designs Isis [hath not loved] a king since Re, except thee and her [son]; greater is that which thou hast done than that which he did when he ruled after Osiris. The laws of the land proceed according to his position.....

From an eulogy to Ramses II
James Henry Breasted *Ancient Records of Egypt* Part Three, § 270

Maat means law, order, balance, union and truth. The concept of balance is presided over by a goddess of the same name, who is the daughter of Ra, the Creator. Thus Ra created creation and set Maat in it so that there would be order. Maat is therefore the order of the physical universe and that which transcends it, the realm of Ra, God. Thus, Maatian law is derived from the balance and order of the universe as determined by the principles of balance and order as displayed by nature including physical nature, as reflected in the sciences of physics, chemistry, etc. and the spiritual nature that is discovered by those who practice Maat philosophy and the meditative lifestyle of Maat wisdom that leads to a harmonizing of individual consciousness with the spirit, i.e. Ra by harmonizing their ethical conscience with the practice of Maat in day to day life. This is called being *Maa kheru* or "true of speech", in other words, a person who has discovered higher consciousness and who therefore speaks truth of existence. A person who speaks without benefit of discovering higher consciousness can only speak from a standpoint of their own egoistic limited understanding even though that limitation can be improved by the study and practice of maat. Nevertheless, only one who has experienced the ultimate order and balance of life known as *Hetep* (balance between the opposites of Creation), by dissolving the opposites of creation, the dissolution of the opposites of nature, can speak from a standpoint of ultimate balance and order and thus freedom from bias. Judges were recognized as priests of Maat. When a society follows a path based on maat philosophy that society does not produce extremes such as the imbalances between rich and poor, men and women, etc. that are being observed in the present day. Thus, such a society would not have to fear its own citizens since a well ordered society based on maat would look after the basic needs of the masses and thus there would not be a situation of massive crime or anarchism due to hatred against the state or between ethnic groups or between workers and corporate leaders, etc. There would be no need to fear the masses because the state itself would not be pursuing immoral or illegal policies.

A MAATIAN PARADIGM OF LEADERSHIP

From the Ancient Egyptian Wisdom we learn how a poor person should act and who they should follow in order to promote balance, order and truth in society, which ultimately is following a path that leads to social justice and balance.

> "If you are poor, serve a good person so that your conduct will be well with God. Do not mention the fact that they were once poor or feel arrogant or resentful about it. Respect them for their position of authority, since fortune has its own laws; it is God's gift. God protects them or may turn away from them."
> -Ancient Egyptian Proverb

From the above we learn that fortunes can change through life and a rich person can end up poor just as a poor person can end up rich but either way there should not be arrogance or hubris but rather, peace and effort to improve one's situation. In the following teaching we learn about the type of person a poor person should follow.

> "If you are mighty and powerful, then gain respect through knowledge and through your gentleness of speech. Don't order things except as it is fitting. The one who provokes others gets into trouble. Don't be haughty lest you be humbled. But also, don't be mute lest you be chided."

> "If you are in authority, then you should do perfect things, those which will be remembered by posterity. Never listen to the words of flatterers or words that fill you with pride and vanity."

> "Do not conspire against others. GOD will punish accordingly. Schemes do not prevail; only the laws of GOD do. Live in peace, since what GOD gives comes by itself."

"Help your friends with the things that you have, for you have these things by the grace of God. If you fail to help your friends, one will say "you have a selfish KA". One plans for tomorrow, but you do not know what tomorrow will bring. The right Soul is the Soul by which one is sustained. If you do praiseworthy deeds your friends will say "welcome" in your time of need."

"Do not plunder your neighbor's house or steal the goods of one that is near you, lest they denounce you before you are even heard."

-Ancient Egyptian Proverbs

Those persons who are in leadership positions through subterfuge, deceit, schemes, greed or who are selfish, arrogant, vane, egoistic, one who plunders his/her neighbor's property, unethical or corrupt are persons that should not be followed. Maat philosophy exalts virtue in leadership. They who seek order and truth also seek balance and true happiness which comes from contentment, that is to say, the gratification that comes from discovering an end to personal conflict and the scourge of constant dissatisfaction and unrest in life. The order of society comes through the proper distribution of wealth ("division of things") and the moderation in the pursuit of material wealth.

"Do not be greedy in the division of things. Do not covet more than your share. Don't be greedy toward your relatives. A mild person has a greater claim than a harsh one. Poor is the person who forgets their relatives; they are deprived of their company. Even a little bit of what is wanted will turn a quarreler into a friendly person."

-Ancient Egyptian Proverb

The Ancient Egyptian sagely teachings to MeriKaRa, the king, inform us that wealth is found in having noble acquaintances. The same sentiment is echoed in the following Ancient Egyptian proverb extolling caring for others who will also care for one in one's time of need.

"Wealthy is he who is rich in his nobles acquaintances."

- Teachings to MeriKaRa

"Help your friends with the things that you have, for you have these things by the grace of God. If you fail to help your friends, one will say "you have a selfish KA". One plans for tomorrow, but you do not know what tomorrow will bring. The right Soul is the Soul by which one is sustained. If you do praiseworthy deeds your friends will say "welcome" in your time of need."

-Ancient Egyptian Proverb

Maat Philosophy Versus Fascism and the Police State

Clearly, the idea in Maat philosophy is not just the detriment of hoarding but the need to proactively share. Those who are in a state of want ("One whose belly is empty...") are prone to mental agitation, stress, disease and animosity which destabilize society and ends up costing more in terms of conflict, disease, stress and sometimes even violence and war. This Ancient Egyptian statement is echoed by Albert Einstein: "An empty stomach is not a good political adviser." Consequently, the person who is in a state of want will likely not be in mental balance and will not be capable of being a righteous or rational citizen. Therefore, those who are in a state of material deficit may suffer from partiality. However, those who have been materially poor in the past can suffer from fear and anxiety over falling once again into poverty and that pressure may cause them to act in corrupt ways so as to maintain their positions.

"Be generous as long as you live. What leaves the storehouse does not return. It is the food in the storehouse that one must share, that is coveted. One whose belly is empty becomes an opponent. Therefore, do not have an accuser or an opponent as a neighbor. Your kindness to your neighbors will be a memorial to you for years."

-Ancient Egyptian Proverb

"...one who is rich in his house will not be one-sided, for he who does not lack is an owner of property; a poor man does not speak truly, and one who says, "Would that I had,' is not straightforward; he is one-sided toward the possessor of rewards...

-Teachings to MeriKaRa

Finally, perhaps the most important teaching given in the Teachings to Merikara, for the proper balance of society is an injunction on equal treatment and rejection of classism, caste systems or rule by a privileged class.

Do not prefer the well born to the commoner, Choose a man on account of his skills, Then all crafts are done — ...

-Teachings to MeriKaRa

The far reaching implications of this injunction for the proper and orderly conduct of social balance are staggering. This injunction partially explains how the Ancient Egyptians were able to foster a society that was able to thrive for thousands of years without internal social conflict or neglect of segments of the population that would lead to internal strife or degradation of the society. Classism, racism, nepotism, and other forms of social stratification for the purpose of segregating people and pitting one group against others is an effect of unrighteous leadership and lack of wisdom. Unrighteous leadership and lack of wisdom are features of spiritual ignorance and egoistic feeling that promote partiality, injustice and corrupt, criminal politics. Such a society with this type of leadership cannot exist in balance or peace and cannot thrive for extended periods of time and thus will lead to eventual degradation and collapse.

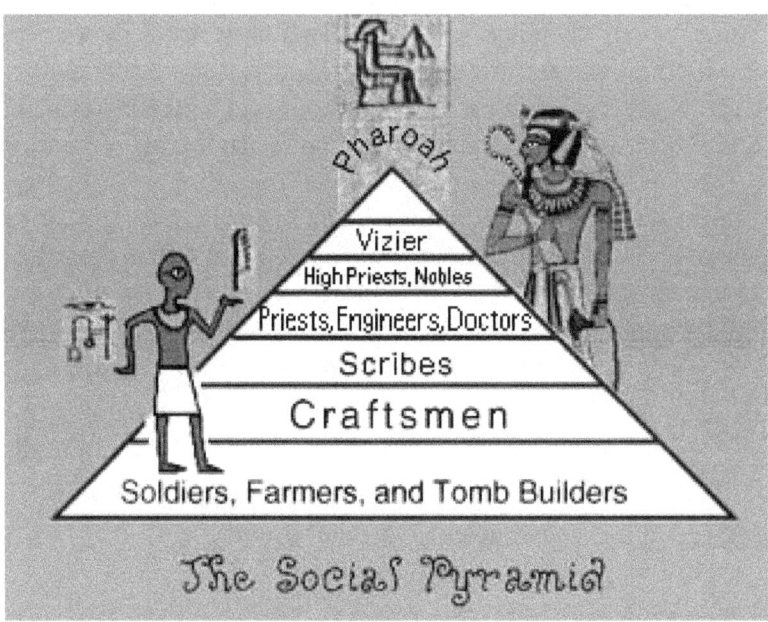

In Ancient Egypt the ideal was to judge all equally on the basis of their ethical conscience and their actions as opposed to ideologically pegging people in a prejudicial manner, based on ethnicity or family heritage or economic standing. Therefore, any person could rise to higher social standing but regardless of their position on the Ancient Egyptian social ladder, the social security system protected all from destitution by guaranteeing food, clothing, shelter and opportunity.

"It's becoming conventional wisdom that the U.S. does not have as much mobility as most other advanced countries," said Isabel V. Sawhill, an economist at the Brookings Institution. "I don't think you'll find too many people who will argue with that."[211]

Maatian Law also prohibits social, legal, political or economic disparities between genders. The income and wealth imbalances that are allowed to exist between men and women in western cultures would not be allowed to exist in Ancient Egyptian culture.

---

[211] http://www.nytimes.com/2012/01/05/us/harder-for-americans-to-rise-from-lower-rungs.html?pagewanted=all&_r=0

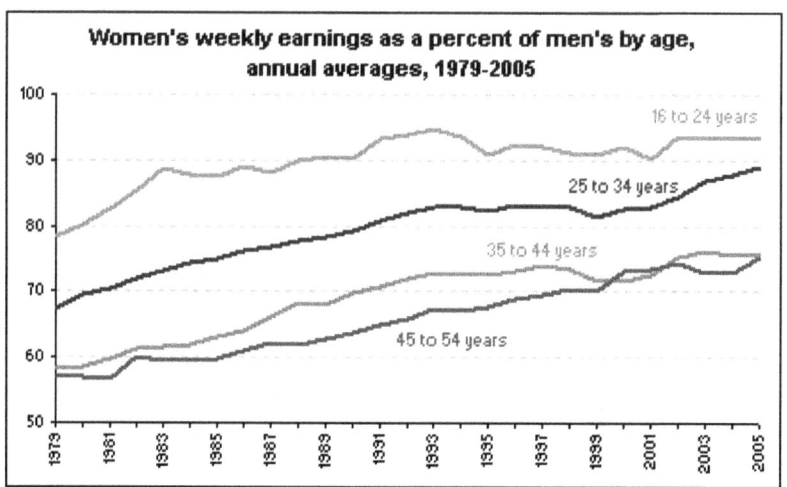

United States Congress Joint Economic Committee. *Graph: Federal Workforce – Gender Pay Gap Unchanged.*[212]

Looking at the gender pay gap over time, the United States Congress Joint Economic Committee showed that as explained inequities decrease, the unexplained pay gap remains unchanged.[213]

---

[212] http://www.bls.gov/opub/ted/2006/oct/wk1/art02.htm   U.S. Bureau of Labor Statistics, Division of Information and Marketing Services
[213] United States Congress Joint Economic Committee. *Graph: Federal Workforce – Gender Pay Gap Unchanged.* Retrieved on March 31, 2011.

THE MAATIAN IDEAL OF JUST GOVERNMENT AND LEADERSHIP FOR THE BALANCED ETHICAL HUMAN PERSONALITY AND THE WORLDLY PERSONALITY TYPES THAT COMPOSE PRESENT DAY NON-MAATIAN SOCIETIES

> "There are two roads travelled by humankind, those who seek to live MAAT and those who seek to satisfy their animal passions."[214]

Proviso: The following essay on the Ancient Egyptian Maatian Philosophy concept of *aryu*, the wisdom about the personality, and the other teachings presented elsewhere in this volume, from the perspective of Maatian Philosophy, should be understood as a exploration of the underlying process that undergird the tensions, prejudices, faults as well as complexes of the human mind that operate outwardly as the world of human experiences including the exalted achievements as well as the depths of human degradations. Yet, for all the achievements of humanity, human beings remain affected by the inner workings of their unconscious minds, which are scarcely understood by them and which often compel them to commit regrettable acts. For this reason, the wisdom of Maat should be studied, understood and practiced so as to cleanse the mind and thus be capable of creating a well ordered and sane society that lives by a societal philosophy of life and the pursuit of the meaning of life, spiritual enlightenment, what the Ancient Egyptians called *Nehast*, instead of mindless pleasure-seeking, greed, the lust for power and the myriad of human desires that lead human beings to conflict and unhappiness.

According two Maat Philosophy there are to paths that human beings naturally fall into in accordance with their propensities. Those propensities are referred to as *aryu*. The term "Aryu" means the residues or remnants of actions and feelings that remain from past deeds. Those past deeds create mental impressions that persist and color present and future thoughts and feelings about one's experiences. The Aryu, mental impressions, can impel and if strong enough, also compel the personality to act, think, and feel in certain ways about varied things as they move through life. Human beings develop through social interaction, genetic tendencies and innate psycho-

---

[214] see the book *Egyptian Proverbs* by Muata Ashby

spiritual tendencies developed based on lifetimes of experiences that have left residues of feelings from the past experiences, embedded in the unconscious level of mind. The acquired impressions from past experiences, including the conditioning effect of socialization (upbringing by parents and experiences with others during formative years of life) from the present life as well as from past lives, coupled with genetic predispositions from the physiological makeup of the body, all of this goes to compose the personality of a person and it is what is called *aryu*. Maat Philosophy demonstrates how that *aryu* leads a person's soul to their place of birth (incarnation) and to the family they will be born into. That aryu directs a person's thoughts and actions and can be so strong as to impel the person towards certain tendencies or compel them to act on desires even if the rational mind tells them they are doing something harmful or negative. Such is the power of mind and its positive or negative development. As such there are a myriad of variations but two major movements in human psycho-spiritual evolution, the movement towards Maat, the ethical, the orderly, peaceful, truthful and good or the movement towards an-maat or that which is opposite to what is ethical, the orderly, peaceful, truthful and good, i.e. what is based on delusion, ego, selfishness, haphazard, greedy, lustful, self-serving, etc. It is also important to understand that the sum total of the past experiences is a strong impelling and compelling force in a person's life but the present actions, feelings and reasoning's that a person can engage in at present, have the potential to change the destiny by changing the contents of the unconscious impressions as well as physically change the brain itself to accommodate the different conscience perspectives (outlook) a person may have about life. The brain is not the source of the soul but is an instrument that the soul uses to perceive the relative reality that is human life on earth. Just as electricity flows through a refrigerator, so too the soul or spirit of a person flows through the nervous system and body. If the nervous system and body are sound and healthy or damaged and diseased, those states of being produce a predilection towards certain psychological tendencies. Therefore, the soul (consciousness) will experience life through those filters of the personality (mind and body) to the extent that the body and mind are seen as the reality, the only and abiding truth of their experience. It is to be understood that the mind sees the world through the senses and those sense impressions are projected unto the nervous system, which receives the impressions from the senses; but the soul also feels about the world based on its acquired storehouse of impressions from past thoughts and feelings about and from past experiences. If the person believes entirely in the reality brought in by that mind and senses, that person is said to be deluded because the mind and senses are limited to perceptions and realities based on time and space which is only one form of reality and therefore by definition illusory. A life lived in accordance with Maat allows a person do discover a higher reality of order and truth that exists beyond the world of human interactions, the world of opposites, good and bad and that can be righteous or corrupt. Maat transcends the world of opposites when a person discovers how to balance the scales of Maat in the heart.[215] Maat Philosophy substitutes the illusory philosophy of life for an ethical and veracious vision of life. This higher vision, born of thousands of years of observation and experience, led to the creation of a way of life and values that recognize the balance in nature and the connection between objects in nature as well as the cosmic order that can be perceived by individuals and a society when a certain level of peace, order and balance is achieved and maintained. The Maat societal philosophy allows a human being to rise above the "animal passions" and thereby partake in higher consciousness and immortality.

Unconscious Reactions Separate Liberals and Conservatives[216]

How does this wisdom manifest in ordinary modern society which has developed based on a societal philosophy of egoism and ignorance about the deeper order of nature? In terms of a Societal Philosophy, the guiding belief

---

[215] Balancing the scales means ones aryu or unconscious mind has been cleansed sufficiently to be in harmony with life, nature, humanity and spirit. See the book Introduction to Maat Philosophy by Muata Ashby
[216] http://www.scientificamerican.com/article.cfm?id=calling-truce-political-wars

system of a culture, the ideal of capitalism, empire, elitism, aristocracy, plutocracy, etc. as viable and beneficial frameworks for government institutions, financial institutions, legal institutions and healthcare institutions has throughout history demonstrated its insufficiency. Societies based on these kinds of societal philosophical premises tend to self-destruct because those ideals tend towards what is selfish, egoistic and even criminal and thus society is moved towards imbalance, ill health and conflict. The Ancient Egyptian proverb recognizes two aspects of human personality though we may include a third and that is the mixed, containing both elements of Maat and an-Maat features. In countries such as the USA those groups are referred to as conservatives (republicans) and liberals (democrats) and independents. Each group has extremists, however, the extremist right wing conservatives tend towards what is closed, exclusiveness, exceptionalism, xenophobia, kainotophobia (fear of change), and dogmatism while the Liberals tend towards exploration, what is open, inclusive and understanding. Conservatives listen to and obey authority and patriarchy more, which makes them more susceptible to political and religious fundamentalism, demagoguery and dictatorship. The conservative mind also tends towards intransigence, absolutism, intolerance and dictatorial behavior. Liberals tend to question authority more and to include more views in decision-making and toleration of others opinions and ethnicities. Conservatives, neo-conservatives and neo-liberals are more open to terrorphobia, the irrational fear of terrorism, even as their own exclusive behavior, selfishness, fear of change and hoarding of wealth and resources in order to protect (conserve) their way of life, that causes criminal behavior and the mistreatment of other human beings is a primary source of the hatred they receive from others in the form of crime and retaliation [which they out of fear or self-serving designs (as an excuse to strengthen the police state), refer to as terrorism]. These groups are in turn reinforced by the crime and retaliations, which were reactions to the conservative, neo-conservative and neo-liberal policies, to believe that their fears are rational which causes them to increasingly act with more extreme, unethical and negative conservative values and ideals thereby increasing animosity towards them etc. This pattern leads to isolation even as the negatively complexed conservative mind tries to control the world around them even by illegal manipulation of markets or criminal behaviors. Liberals can also be corrupted but their corruption and criminality will tend to be less cruel and callous. The differences between the brains and behavioral tendencies of conservatives versus liberals has been documented in several peer reviewed scientific journals:

- **Conservatives spend more time looking at unpleasant images, and liberals spend more time looking at pleasant images.**[217]

---

[217] Michael D. Dodd, PhD, Amanda Balzer, PhD, Carly Jacobs, MA, Michael Gruszczynski, MA, Kevin B. Smith, PhD, and John R. Hibbing, PhD. "The Left Rolls with the Good; The Right Confronts the Bad.

Maat Philosophy Versus Fascism and the Police State

- Reliance on quick, efficient, and "low effort" thought processes yields conservative ideologies, while effortful and deliberate reasoning yields liberal ideologies.[218]
- Liberals have more tolerance to uncertainty (bigger anterior cingulate cortex), and conservatives have more sensitivity to fear (bigger right amygdala).[219]
- Conservatives have stronger motivations than liberals to preserve purity and cleanliness.[220]
- Republicans are more likely than Democrats to interpret faces as threatening and expressing dominant emotions, while Democrats show greater emotional distress and lower life satisfaction.[221]
- Conservatives and liberals react similarly to positive incentives, but conservatives have greater sensitivity to negative stimuli.[222]
- Conservatism is focused on preventing negative outcomes, while liberalism is focused on advancing positive outcomes.[223]
- Compared to liberals, conservatives are less open to new experiences and learn better from negative stimuli than positive stimuli.[224]
- Conservatives tend to have a stronger reaction to threatening noises and images than liberals.[225]
- Liberals are more open-minded and creative whereas conservatives are more orderly and better organized.[226]

Yet both conservative and liberal mindsets, if operating without the benefit of Maatian psychology insight into the nature of mind, are operating in a self-made world of personal ideals and delusions created over many lifetimes. They are

---

Physiology and Cognition in Politics." *Philosophical Transactions of the Royal Society B: Biological Sciences*. Mar. 5, 2012

[218] Scott Eidelman, PhD, Christian S. Crandall, PhD, Jeffrey A. Goodman, PhD, and John C. Blanchar. "Low-Effort Thought Promotes Political Conservatism," *Society for Personality and Social Psychology*. 2012

[219] Ryota Kanai, PhD, Tom Feilden, Colin Firth, and Geraint Rees, PhD. "Political Orientations Are Correlated with Brain Structure in Young Adults," *Current Biology*. Apr. 7, 2011

[220] Erik G. Helzer and David A. Pizarro, PhD. "Dirty Liberals! Reminders of Physical Cleanliness Influence Moral and Political Attitudes," *Psychological Science*. Mar. 18, 2011

[221] Jacob M. Vigil, PhD. "Political Leanings Vary with Facial Expression Processing and Psychosocial Functioning," *Group Processes & Intergroup Relations*. 2010

[222] Mindi S. Rock, PhD, and Ronnie Janoff-Bulman, PhD. "Where Do We Draw Our Lines? Politics, Rigidity, and the Role of Self-Regulation," *Social Psychological and Personality Science*. Jan. 2010

[223] Ronnie Janoff-Bulman, PhD. "To Provide or Protect: Motivational Bases of Political Liberalism and Conservatism," *Psychological Inquiry: An International Journal for the Advancement of Psychological Theory*. Aug. 2009

[224] Natalie J. Shook, PhD, and Russell H. Fazio, PhD. "Political Ideology, Exploration of Novel Stimuli, and Attitude Formation," *Experimental Social Psychology*. Apr. 3, 2009

[225] Douglas R. Oxley, PhD, Kevin B. Smith, PhD, John R. Alford, PhD, Matthew V. Hibbing, PhD, Jennifer L. Miller, Mario Scalora, PhD, Peter K. Hatemi, PhD, and John R. Hibbing, PhD. "Political Attitudes Vary with Physiological Traits," *Science*. Sep. 19, 2008

[226] Dana R. Carney, PhD, John T. Jost, PhD, Samuel D. Gosling, PhD, and Jeff Potter. "The Secret Lives of Liberals and Conservatives: Personality Profiles, Interaction Styles, and the Things They Leave Behind," *International Society of Political Psychology*. Oct. 23, 2008

egoistic from the standpoint of Maat Philosophy though the Liberals are closer to what is truly ethical and have the capacity to lead themselves towards an even higher perspective of Liberal culture or progressive culture and that is the mystic aspect of Maat Philosophy. It is important to understand that, barring physiological or genetic abnormalities or abnormalities brought on by physical or emotional injuries, especially in the formative years of youth, those tendencies do not define the innate person but control their outlook and actions and therefore make them a slave to their tendencies. If the wisdom of Maat or any similar teaching that reveals the higher aspects of human existence, beginning with ethical conscience and ending in spiritual realization of the higher self were applied by those personalities, to transform themselves, they could expand their horizons to move towards a higher truth. The higher truth from a perspective of worldly human interactions is that some conservative ideas are correct and some liberal ideas are correct and a middle ground, a Maatian balance based on truth, and not just compromise, is to be struck which would produce a viable, balanced and well-adjusted society; this is a necessary step in the creation of a balanced and long-lived, self-sustaining society but even this is not the ultimate goal of Maat Philosophy. That Maatian balance is the necessary fertile ground for human beings to be able to discover the higher aspects of their own humanity and then their universal spirit being. This was the goal of Ancient Egyptian society as a whole and was the source from which a viable society was created that lasted for thousands of years. So, the Maatian balance could allow a greater spiritual realization to occur and this is the goal of Maat Philosophy as well as the very source of power and goodwill which manifests in those human beings who have evolved to become compassionate, understanding, charitable and caring human beings. This is the group from which Maatian leaders are selected to be part of the council that directs the course of the society; these are the wise leaders of an Ethiocratic government. Maat Philosophy has two aspects, the secular and the non-secular. So the practice of secular Maat Philosophy is enjoined for the purpose of creating a just, balanced and harmonious society so that the individuals of the society may have the foundation and thus the capacity to explore higher and more abiding aspects of human existence beyond the rat race of life based on the artificial and unnecessary struggle for survival created by capitalist, objectivist, imperial and neo-liberal forms of economics, and the egoistic fear over losing possessions and the ultimate fear of death.

Maat Philosophy Versus Fascism and the Police State

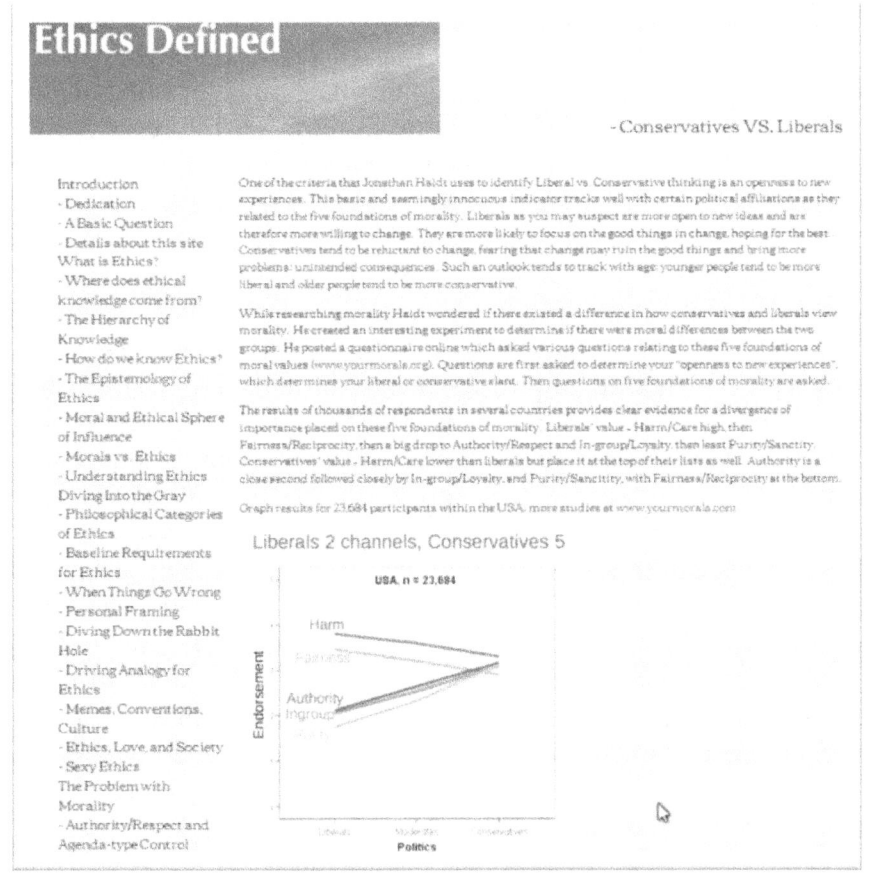

Conservatives VS. Liberals[227]

Following this theme of the liberal mind and conservative mind in politics or in terms of Maat philosophy the ego driven mind and the altruistic mind, studies demonstrate that the conservative personality views the world in terms of Authority, In-group and Purity while the liberal personality views three worlds through a prism of "Harm" and "Fairness." This means that for the conservative, Authority, In-group and Purity are more important than Harm and Fairness. Therefore, the liberal personality will tend to be more open and ethical as defined by Maat philosophy (concerned with the wellbeing of all members of society) while the conservative mind will tend to be more selfish, more concerned about the wellbeing of his or her group. Thus, the conservative mind displays a condition that is more closed off, more narrow, more constricted as opposed to the liberal mind. Consequently, racists, male chauvinists, con-artists, charlatans, demagogues, dictators and authoritarians will tend to be drawn to and found more among the ranks of conservative groups.

---

[227] http://www.ethicsdefined.org/the-problem-with-morality/conservatives-vs-liberals/

As such, the conservative personality, since it places less value on fairness and ethics and more emphasis on control, and personal and family wellbeing instead of group wellbeing, tends to more easily facilitate rationalizing being unfair and exclusive, protecting, providing for its own group. Therefore, philosophies like objectivism and libertarianism will be more appealing to the conservative mind than liberalism or progressiveness. Additionally, the conservative personality will more easily tend to rationalize unethical behavior and deception or even criminality in the pursuit of what they view as a higher moral cause, the purity of their vision of authority, family and community, regardless of whether or not it causes harm to others outside of their "in-group" since they have the delusion that they have a higher moral position due to the supposed virtue of their vision and intensions. The delusion of having a higher moral standing gives license to the pursuit of their desires and relieves any guilt from hurting others or the environment as they pursue their goals. Their rationalizations excuse any brutality, and trespass of the law and any unethical act in pursuit of the purity of that ideology as manifested in the in-group; for them the ends justify the means. An example of the rationalization is the history of stealing land and killing Native Americans by rationalizing that they were heathens going to hell anyway so it was ok to kill, maim, rape them, etc. Another example was the imposition of slavery on peoples of African descent using the same kinds of rationalizations and even promulgating the idea that slavery was good for blacks because it civilized them, etc. Therefore, for this personality type, whose fears, rationalizations and delusions have wittingly or unwittingly warped their sense of morality and ethics, "the ends justify the means" since "every man is for himself" and after all "it's a dog eat dog world" and people should look out for their own best interest and if they get taken in by con artists that is their problem for not being smart and instead being stupid and easily deceived, etc., etc. Said another way, the conservative personality tends towards the rationalization that "everyone else is doing it and I'd better do it to them first before someone else does it to me" and "hey, if they didn't want to risk getting hurt they should have known better before playing with the big boys, so it's their fault I was able to defraud them, not mine." In the conservative mindset everyone, in the out-group, is not part of the human community and therefore, worth less as a living being. They are adversaries and legitimate targets, fair game for conquest, and exploitation since the in-group members are worth more because the in-group is more moral and worthy of survival and this ideal provides the moral justification for acts against those in the out-group. The out-group may be based on culture, gender, race, nationality, etc. In essence, the delusion of being more moral based on the distorted, egoistic vision of self-worth derived from the delusion of certainty about one's authority and the purity of one's ideas (ideology), leads that personality to be the opposite of moral. Such personalities are a danger to ethical government and a well-ordered, healthy society with sane, reasonable politics. In the extreme, the conservative (including neo-conservative, libertarian and neo-liberals) personality type becomes absolute and uncompromising, the more they are challenged, leading to incapacity of the in-group, no matter how empirical the evidences may be and even to their own detriment. One example of that is the denial of climate change in which all human beings (conservatives and liberals) are suffering the consequences, and despite the fact that there is a consensus in the scientific community that there is unnatural global climate change and that it is caused by human activity, especially industrial activity, yet, they continue denying because that information does not agree with their world view (ideology) which says it is acceptable to destroy the environment for one's own gains and can be seen in the following typical conservative argument: "after all what do scientists know anyway, I know the truth because I am more moral and faithful to my ideology while others are following less pure ideas so they are wrong and I am right; whatever is happening is due to regular world cycles so don't ask me to pay more taxes for your liberal causes that will cost me my business and lifestyle (which is more correct than yours)." Another example of denial is the scientific fact of the common origins and kinship of the human race. The conservative mind denies this scientific fact since it would blow up the ideology of exceptionalism and exclusivity, that a certain ethnic group, the in-group, is not the only ethnic group worthy of being considered as part of the human race and deserving of partaking of the bounty of human and natural resources of the world. Another example is the argument that slavery and exploitation of other people is acceptable because those people are not really people since the in-group has real worthy people while others are worthless and sub-human due to their ignorance for following other ideologies (other religions, other political systems, speak other languages, have different skin color, etc.). A similar argument is made to support the exploitation of the poor by the rich; that the poor should have gone to school, get a job, had a better inheritance, pull themselves up buy their bootstraps, etc. and bettered themselves instead of asking for "handouts". Never does the conservative, neo-conservative or neo-liberal personality want to discuss the institutionalized, racism, gender bias, and injustices of the system that systematically promote poverty and prevent upward social mobility since these discussions would blow up the ideology that the system is fair and anyone, the ethnic minorities, women and the poor who "just work hard" can better themselves even as things are currently, an unjust society.

EXAMPLES OF UNREPENTANT DECEPTION AND DISREGARD FOR FELLOW HUMAN BEINGS

A stark example of the unethical conservative personality can be found in the person of Senator Rand Paul, who thinks it was perfectly acceptable and desirable to deceive his fellow medical students so that they would fail a test and he would pass with better grades. So there was no regard for the welfare of his fellow students or the fate of their patients if they were to graduate from medical school; there was only one concern, what's good for Rand Paul and to hell with everyone else, neither they or the community are his concern.

Maat Philosophy Versus Fascism and the Police State

Lessons from Rand Paul: 'Misinformation can be very important'[228]

The example above shows that the unethical mind finds no contradiction in applying deception, obfuscation or outright lies in the pursuit of their goals. This is one of the personality types that are undesirable as government leaders, as they will have no compunction about lying to constituents about their real motives and for achieving whatever they think their goal is since to them "the ends justify the means." In terms of a Societal Philosophy, the Maatian Philosophy dictates an ideal of communal support and caring in business, government and healthcare. Societal philosophy should not be dictated by the worldly, the ignorant, the liberal or the conservative since their values are not necessarily correct all the time and each has the potential for extremes. For this reason, Ancient Egyptian government was not managed by business people or the ignorant masses or megalomaniacal empire builders. It was managed by a council of priests and priestesses, trained in Maat Philosophy, with a Pharaoh as a figurehead who could not have independent actions like a European King who could unilaterally and capriciously order the death of a subject. This means that the Ancient Egyptians recognized that empires, democracies, capitalism, etc, cannot work for the benefit of all people. Thus a system of government was instituted based on the wisdom of Maat Philosophy and its experts, the priests and priestesses of Maat. Therefore, Ancient Egyptian government was not a theocracy for that would mean government based on religious principles or theories. Wisdom by the wise based on Maat Philosophy would be similar to rule based on Confucianism or Buddhist Dharma. So we may term the Ancient Egyptian government as Wisdocracy, government by the wise, or "Ethiocracy," or government and social institutions based on Ethical philosophy or wisdom, in this case based on the wisdom of Maat Philosophy, which protects the interests and welfare of all members of society and not just the few wealthy or privileged minorities at the expense of the society as a whole. Thus, the conservative mindset, the mindset that is callous, cruel and inconsiderate, tends towards mental agitation, egoism, closed mindedness and self-importance (narcissism), which are all features of the egoistic personality that when coupled with Sociopathy, the remorseless disregard for the feelings and well being of others, is especially suited for positions in politics and as corporate leaders, since cruelty, callousness and cutthroat behavior as well as the capacity to deceive, with minimal remorse, are regarded as valuable personality traits due to the way in which society has been setup to favor such personalities in such positions. It favors those who can coldheartedly and relentlessly pursue profits above all other concerns, no matter who (including their own family and progeny) gets hurt in the process.

---

[228] http://www.dailykos.com/story/2013/10/18/1248682/-Lessons-from-Rand-Paul-Misinformation-can-be-very-important

AN EXAMPLE OF DUPLICITY TO UNDERMINE CONFIDENCE IN GOVERNMENT AND GIVE THE IMPRESSION THAT PEOPLE SUFFERING FROM THE WEALTH AND INCOME IMBALANCES ARE UNJUSTIFIED.

Fox News used a dishonest graphic that inflated a comparison between the number of people receiving federal benefits to those working full-time by 500 percent to misleadingly imply more people receive government benefits than work.

The October 28 edition of *Fox & Friends* aired a graphic which purported to compare the number of people who received means-tested federal benefits to the number of people with full-time jobs in 2011. However, the chart used a truncated y-axis, and showed the number of people on welfare -- 108.6 million -- as approximately five times greater than 101.7 million, the number of people with full-time employment. [229]

---

[229] http://mediamatters.org/blog/2013/10/28/dishonest-fox-chart-overstates-comparison-of-we/196618

One of many possible examples, the above report shows how a right-winged (Republican party/conservative) corporation uses subtle deception to shape public opinion with either overt (outright lies and mendacity) or covertly (subtle distortions as above) against government and against true democratic, liberal or progressive values. The idea is to purposely mislead or at least confuse the populace so that they will be unsure about those who are not in power and believe, with force of emotions of hatred and fear of other members of society, in the authority of the Republican Party in general and the rich segment of the population in particular. The following report shows that those who watch Fox News and similar corporate media outlets, are the most misinformed segment of the population.

People who watch MSNBC and CNN exclusively can answer more questions about domestic events than people who watch no news at all. People who only watch Fox did much worse. NPR listeners answered more questions correctly than people in any other category.

The survey of 1185 random people conducted by landline and cell phone in early February follows a similar poll FDU conducted last November, which surveyed only New Jersey residents and returned similar results.

Notice that considering the report on a scale of informed versus uninformed, in terms of this comparison between corporate mainstream news media versus the corporate influenced non-profit news outlet (NPR)[230] scored highest in informing its viewers while the corporate right wing outlet was worse, but the supposedly left or democratic mainstream outlets such as MSNBC which is considered by some to be supportive of the democratic party, still scored worse than the non-profit NPR, though not as bad as Fox News. The point is that left and right corporations have a vested interest in misinforming, confusing or misdirecting the populace for if they were to report and advocate the truth, their viewers might

---

[230] Alternative news outlets such as Democracy Now or Free Speech TV, Aljazeera, or RT.com are not included here.

develop ideas about politics that would lead to corporate dethroning from the commanding heights of government and economic institutions or perhaps worse, would leave the station in favor of another one that reflects their preconceived notions and prejudices.

BEST INFORMED Non-Profit	➡	NPR
--	--	--
LESS INFORMED Corporate Left wing/Democratic party leaning	➡	MSNBC and CNN
WORST INFORMED Corporate Right wing/Republican party leaning	➡	Fox News

The corporate mainstream news media (corporate republicans [Fox News] and corporate democrats [MSNBC]) outlets have a vested interest in promoting lies and deceptions but the right wing media is most extreme in this regard. The left wing media may not lie as much but they are perhaps more prone to hide or present less favorable news about their party and also they, are less prone to criticize members of the democratic party though and maybe considered, as the right wing media, apologists who explain away unpopular, unethical or criminal policies, errors and scandals of the administration they are supporting. However, the corporate democrat news outlets practice more fact-based reporting than the right wing media which is not as concerned with facts when reporting the news, but only in promoting their agenda by any means necessary including lies, deceptions, omissions or outright bold-faced lying. Why can we say that misinformation is not the only purpose of outlets such as Fox News and that the purpose if also to actively deceive? Another study showed that Fox News viewers were more misinformed than those people who do not watch the news at all. This means that Fox News viewers are being purposely given information that is wrong or deceptive.

Those who claim non-partisanship of the poll might be interested to learn that there was no difference in terms of Republicans who watched Fox, and Democrats who watched Fox. Both groups of people were, surprisingly, equally as misinformed.[231]

AN EXAMPLE OF DUPLICITY AND DISREGARD FOR THE SPIRIT OF THE LAW

Another example of the duplicity, showing disregard for the spirit of the law and displaying unethical conscience and disregard for the humanity of others is the willingness and sometimes even eagerness to circumvent the law using technicalities or outright lies, fictions, etc., to accomplish the desired illegal goal. In this case, the revelations of whistleblower Edward Snowden demonstrated how the spying agencies circumvented the law setup by congress, preventing them from spying on USA Citizens, by having other countries spy on them and then give the NSA that information; the idea is that the NSA could circumvent the intent of the law. This way they could say they themselves did not do the spying. This would be like a mob boss saying that he is innocent since he did not steal something but only told someone else to steal it

---

[231] http://www.examiner.com/article/study-finds-fox-news-viewers-more-misinformed-than-non-news-watchers

and then he exchanged it with that person in exchange for something that other mob boss wanted that he could not get directly. The embrace of technicality and ignoring of the spirit and goal of a law is a manifestation of the same immoral and or sociopathic behavior that the egoistic mind develops. That egoistic (conservative, dull, atrophied/stunted intellect and cold heart) mind justifies and excuses its immorality and is even surprised when called on its duplicity, and corruption since it does not recognize itself as such and any technicality is acceptable in furthering its goals to serve its own needs and or that of its recognized in-group. Therefore, this personality type will strain to experience remorse especially in a permissive environment where most politicians and corporations are corrupt as well. The personality being described is a person whose ethical conscience has been suppressed by so many desires and rationalizations of their wrongdoing that they deep down know is wrong. A further worst situation is the personality that has developed the negative qualities who is not only immoral, but is amoral, that is, has no scruples and no notion of ethical caring for others and no capacity to feel remorse or empathy for anyone and only are concerned for their own welfare and accomplishing their own goals, such as the sociopath. When sociopaths get into positions of leadership their actions can have severe repercussions for the entire society. Of course, the immoral person as well as the sociopath can be narcissists, which complicate and exacerbate the immoral or amoral acts of those personalities.

TWO EXAMPLES OF PROTECTING CRIMINALS, AND BECOMING AN ACCOMPLICE WITH THEIR CRIMES BY NOT ACTING WITHIN ONE'S POWER TO UPHOLD JUSTICE AND DISREGARD FOR THE LETTER AND SPIRIT OF THE LAW

Obama's justice department grants final immunity to Bush's CIA torturers[232]

Upon taking office and throughout his administration, president Obama made the decision to not prosecute president Bush, vice president Cheney and their associates for torture and warrantless wiretapping (spying on citizens) and are failing to prosecute bankers for drug money laundering and for malfeasance that led to the 2008 market crash and its aftermath. Obama has famously said he prefers to "look forward and not backward". These are direct and naked violations of ethics and the law and in collusion with the criminals. Good governance requires upholding ethical laws so that society should maintain proper functioning order and the confidence of its citizens. The failure to "look backward" and uphold this duty creates a precedent of corruption and criminality that will continue and expand, degrading society. How might an ethical, moral person view the behavior of president Bush, who broke laws or gave orders allowing them to be broken? As an accomplice? Also, how might president Obama be viewed for not prosecuting Bush and also the unethical and criminal violations of the Obama administration? If we consider that Mr. Obama

---

[232] http://www.theguardian.com/commentisfree/2012/aug/31/obama-justice-department-immunity-bush-cia-torturer

knows the law, having worked as a constitutional lawyer, then the incapacity to uphold ethical conscience may be considered as weak will or if there is agreement with such criminality then it may denote corruption and immorality. If he personally supports those acts, and agrees with the perpetrators and sees nothing wrong in what they have done, then it may indicate Sociopathy.

THE DELUSION OF THE USA AS THE "BEST COUNTRY IN THE WORLD"

There is another stark example of how the population of the USA, lives under a constant delusion, reinforced by political, economic and religious leaders, about the quality of life and the perceived high ranking of the country when compared to others. This delusion is integral to the belief in the USA as the "best country" with the best political and economic systems, which plays into the acceptance of the system and overlooking the problems that are otherwise readily evident. In other words, the belief in the deluded notion of the high ranking of the USA and the nostalgia for having been born and or of having grown up there, clouds the perception, and intellectual capacity to recognize the negative state of culture, politics and economics and then to do something to improve the situation. The following is a listing of the rankings in various areas of human life showing where the USA falls in relation to other countries.

The following rankings of the United States when compared to the other countries of the world is presented as a reality check demonstrating that the USA is not even to be considered as a country ranking high in the fundamental areas of healthy and well adjusted human life since it does not rank high in positive and beneficial areas and ranks highest in negative areas:

The U.S.A. ranks 17th in happiness
World Happiness Index, 2013

The U.S.A. ranks 8th for having a nice old-age
Data from HelpAge International
http://www.helpage.org/global-agewatch/

The U.S.A. ranks 99th in peacefulness
Data from Visions of Humanity
http://www.visionofhumanity.org/#/page/indexes/global-peace-index

The U.S.A. ranks 24th in freedom from corruption
Data from Heritage Foundation
http://www.heritage.org/index/explore

The U.S.A. ranks 47th in press freedom
Reporters Without Borders

The U.S.A. ranks 22nd in freedom of the press
Data from Freedomhouse
http://www.freedomhouse.org/sites/default/files/Booklet%20for%20Website.pdf

The U.S.A. ranks 16th in manufacturing compensation costs
Data from Bureau of Labor Statistics
http://www.bls.gov/fls/#compensation

The U.S.A. ranks 23rd in wage distribution
Data from OECD
http://stats.oecd.org/Index.aspx?QueryId=7219#

The U.S.A. ranks 10th in purchasing power of minimum wage
Data from OECD
http://stats.oecd.org/Index.aspx?QueryId=7219#

The U.S.A. ranks 11th in minimum wage
Data from OECD
http://stats.oecd.org/Index.aspx?QueryId=7219#

The U.S.A. ranks 125th in GDP growth per capita
Data from World Bank
http://data.worldbank.org/indicator/NY.GDP.PCAP.KD.ZG?order=wbapi_data_value_2011+wbapi_data_value+wbapi_data_value-last&sort=desc

The U.S.A. ranks 9th in retirement security
Melbourne Mercer Global Pension Index

The U.S.A. ranks 15th in perceived press freedom
Data from Gallup
http://www.gallup.com

The U.S.A. ranks 96th in adolescent fertility
Data from UNDP
http://hdrstats.undp.org/en/indicators/36806.html

The U.S.A. ranks 22nd in gender equality
Data from World Economic Forum
http://www3.weforum.org/docs/WEF_GenderGap_Report_2012.pdf

The U.S.A. ranks 10th in economic freedom
Data from Heritage Foundation
http://www.heritage.org/index/ranking

The U.S.A. ranks 24th in freedom from corruption
Data from Heritage Foundation
http://www.heritage.org/index/explore

The U.S.A. ranks 16th in manufacturing compensation costs
Data from Bureau of Labor Statistics
http://www.bls.gov/fls/#compensation

The U.S.A. ranks 16th in where to be born
Data from Economist
http://www.economist.com/news/21566430-where-be-born-2013-lottery-life

The U.S.A. ranks 19th in state success or failure
The US is considered as a "stable" nation but not "sustainable"
Data from Fund for Peace
http://www.fundforpeace.org/global/?q=fsi-grid2012

The U.S.A. ranks 12th in prosperity
Legatum Institute

The U.S.A. ranks 24th in perceived honesty
Data from Transparency International
http://cpi.transparency.org/cpi2011/results/

The U.S.A. ranks 38th in Health Care
https://en.wikipedia.org/wiki/World_Health_Organization_ranking_of_health_systems
http://www.nejm.org/doi/full/10.1056/NEJMp0910064

The U.S.A. ranks 46th in Health Care Efficiency
Bloomberg
http://www.bloomberg.com/visual-data/best-and-worst/most-efficient-health-care-countries

The U.S.A. ranks 49th (tied with Romania) in civil liberties
Democracy Index

The USA, the supposed land of the free and home of the brave," has lost guarantees of: Habeas corpus, free speech rights, privacy, protection against torture and capital punishment without due legal process.

The USA has 4.5% of the world population and 80% of the painkillers in the entire world.[233] Another study goes further by citing the use of "semi-synthetic opioid drugs.

> Among the startling statistics, the United States now consumes 80% of the world's opioid pain medications and 99% of the world's hydrocodone (semi-synthetic opioid). The milligram per person use of prescription opioids in the United States increased from 74mg to 369mg, an increase of 402%, between 1997 and 2007. Prescription medication abuse is now only second to marijuana in terms of frequency. Prescription pharmaceuticals have become the newest – and seemingly, deadliest – gateway drug we have seen yet; nearly a third of

---

[233] http://www.dailymail.co.uk/news/article-2142481/Americans-consume-80-percent-worlds-pain-pills-prescription-drug-abuse-epidemic-explodes.html

people aged 12 and over who used drugs "recreationally" for the first time in 2009 began by using a prescription drug non-medically.[234]

Clearly, the use of prescription drugs, coupled with the use of lawful and unlawful recreational drugs, raises the concern that the USA population as a whole is in a constant state of altered mental capacity, experiencing mild to severe delusion and given to irrationality, due to intellectual incapacity if not atrophy, due to the perpetual state of drug addiction as a society.

WHAT AREAS DOES THE USA RANK HIGHEST IN

The U.S.A. ranks 1st in anxiety disorders
IFPE Congress in Vienna, Austria on April 18, 2009, on the results of World Health Organization's *World Mental Health Survey*

---

[234] http://www.theguardian.com/commentisfree/cifamerica/2011/jun/10/prescription-drug-abuse

The U.S.A. ranks 1st in small arms imports
Data from Small Arms Survey
http://www.smallarmssurvey.org/fileadmin/docs/A-Yearbook/2011/en/Small-Arms-Survey-2011-Chapter-01-Annexes-1.1-1.2-EN.pdf

The U.S.A. ranks 1st in small arms exports
Data from Small Arms Survey
http://www.smallarmssurvey.org/fileadmin/docs/A-Yearbook/2011/en/Small-Arms-Survey-2011-Chapter-01-Annexes-1.1-1.2-EN.pdf

The U.S.A. ranks 1st in horse exports
Data from FAOStat
http://faostat.fao.org/site/604/DesktopDefault.aspx?PageID=604#ancor

The U.S.A. ranks 1st in plastic surgeons
Data from ISAPS
http://www.isaps.org/files/html-contents/Downloads/ISAPS%20Results%20-%20Procedures%20in%202011.pdf

The U.S.A. ranks 1st in wine consumption
Data from Wine Institute
http://www.wineinstitute.org/files/2010_World_Wine_Consumption_By_Volume_Rank.pdf

The U.S.A. ranks 1st in locking people up
Data from ICPS
http://www.prisonstudies.org/info/worldbrief/wpb_stats.php?area=allategory=wb_poprate

The U.S.A. ranks 2nd in child poverty
From Unicef
http://www.unicef-irc.org/publications/pdf/rc10_eng.pdf

The U.S.A. ranks 2nd in CO2 emissions from consumption of energy
U.S.A. Energy Information Administration

CONCLUSIONS

It is important to understand that though, from a higher, more ideal, Maatian perspective, both the liberal as well as the conservative mind are both less than ethical mental states, the conservative mindset is least ethical and most prone to extremes of feeling, anti-intellectualism and irrationality. As such, the conservative mindset is also disposed to intellectual atrophy. When a person's ideology constantly reinforces authority, it necessarily implies obedience and that translates to non-questioning, which is an intellectual process. The conservative personality craves authority in a quest to discover purity and relieve the stress of uncertainty and fear of instability. Purity means safety, prosperity as well as freedom from anything that contradicts the ideology of what purity means to them. That can mean authority in politics, religion, commerce, etc., devoid of questioning as in questioning the fairness or harm of the political, religious or economic policies being followed. Since in that type of personality the intellect does not discern there can be no qualitative cognition to discover what is right or wrong, effective or ineffective, fair or unfair, etc.

However, it is equally important that no matter how dull the intellect, there is always a possibility of growing and learning. However, if the leadership facilitates the proliferation of prescription and non-prescription drugs, entertainments, and encourages the dull mindset by inciting fear, hatred, and base emotions through demagoguery, hate speech, acrimony, vitriol and uncompromising rhetoric, then the society will become more polarized and degraded. That polarization is a fertile environment for fear, hatred, and inaction on important social, political and economic necessities; which can actually be a political tactic, to maintain the status quo while also keeping the masses from being able to politically improve their situation. Just as a parent who does not rear the children to be thoughtful and giving allows them to develop negative habits and beliefs, so too the parents of society, the political, corporate and religious leaders also fail at leading the members of society to develop ethical conscience and peaceful demeanor as well as beneficence towards others, leading to a society that is at odds with itself, unable to grow and evolve and thus therefore, killing itself, through ignorance and bitterness.

Epilog

Politics, Government, Leadership, Virtue and Dictatorship in Modern Society

Leadership in any area of society presents the possibility for both challenge and reward to individuals. However, perhaps the greatest reward and the greatest challenge will be felt by modern professionals who would like to lead political institutions. The challenges to the modern professional and to society can be daunting and can have far reaching consequences. Logically it might be conceded that those who possess expert knowledge should have their opinions endowed with greater authority; which would seem to suggest that those with the expert knowledge are justified in having commanding roles within their communities. However, that authority may be in conflict with the higher ideals of democratic and egalitarian values of society. Nevertheless, just because a person is an expert in some field does not mean that they have the interests of the population at heart; throughout history there have been many "unethical experts" in society that have led it to ruination. The example presented earlier, of Senator Rand Paul, depicts a person who may possibly be expert in the field of western medicine but who has also demonstrated duplicity and unethical beliefs and behaviors that are detrimental to society. Then, also, there is the question; are the democratic and egalitarian ideals of modern society actually proper ideals for the wellbeing of society that it should have at all? Is inclusiveness a social value that should be supplanted in the pursuit of community or corporation efficiency? And when, if ever, might leadership in a society turn into dictatorship? The following essay will examine these issues and show that the profligate forms of government are hostile to honorable leadership, inclusiveness and to egalitarian principles. Although any number of sources might be cited in support of this thesis, the following essay will chiefly draw on the following selection of texts that contain salient conclusions about these issues and will act as complimentary commentaries along with the Maatian wisdom presented. These texts include *The Analects* of Confucius, *Tao Te Ching*, by Lao-Tzu, *The Republic*, by Plato, *On Duty*, by Cicero, *What is to be Done*, by Lenin, *The Holy Rule of St. Benedict* by St. Benedict and the Ancient Egyptian Wisdom Texts.

Prior to engaging in an investigation of the interaction of politics and the leadership of the qualified modern professional, based on expert knowledge, it would be wise to establish what expert knowledge means in leadership and how does that relate to the purpose of politics. Expert knowledge begins with philosophical understanding that can then be placed into action in the practical institutions of government. This book has been primarily concerned with the wisdom derived from the philosophy of Maat from Ancient Egypt. We will here avail ourselves of a brief comparative study to reveal expanded insights into Maat philosophy by comparing it to other similar philosophies, additionally demonstrating that Ancient Egyptian Maat philosophy in government was not the only wisdom to discover how ethical conscience in government leads to better government. Ancient Egyptian Maat Philosophy is in many respects compatible with and indeed founded on similar principles to which Confucianism is based. From the Analects of Confucius we learn that "He who exercises government by means of his virtue may be compared to the north polar star, which keeps its place and all the stars turn towards it." Compare this to the following teaching from the Ancient Egyptian Wisdom Text by Ptahotep.

> If you are a leader, setting forward your plans according to that which you decide, perform perfect actions which posterity may remember, without letting the words prevail with you which multiply flattery, which excite pride and produce vanity.

Government is supposed to be the mechanism through which people come together to cooperate to discuss and plan as well as work towards implementing the course of their society and the distribution of resources through the form of government they select through politics. Politics based on virtue is the ideal principle for good governance. This means that the supposed virtue of modern so called democracies, that anyone can become president, or prime minister, etc. is in reality the avenue through which any deviant, psychotic, sociopathic, charlatan of a personality can also get in and come to power. In this regard it would be better for there to be a clear path whereby people are vetted through a process of ethical training; the training should include world history, the humanities and social work with the addition of time served in service to humanity and not in seeking to profit from politics. Therefore, virtue is the defining characteristic that qualifies a person to become a leader. Most modern evaluators of the qualifications of a person to assume the role of leadership, such as those in a corporation who evaluate candidates for management positions, might assign the greatest weight to expert knowledge in the form of specific education in a particular vocation, profession, skill or job along with the capacity to exert authority and delegate to others with the ultimate goal of promoting higher production and higher profits for shareholders. In most societies expert knowledge is considered or valued without necessarily considering ethical conscience. A virtuous professional might be thought of as a person who is in possession of that same expert knowledge but with the understanding that the goal for humanity is the good of all and not just a segment of the community who will receive all or most of the profits and or benefits. Confucius explains that "If they be led by virtue, and uniformity sought to be given them by the rules of propriety, they will have the sense of shame, and moreover will become good." Confucius goes on to explain that failure to treat society with virtuous intent and fairness will lead to an unruly populace (which is the fear of the fascist): "The Duke Ai asked, saying, "What should be done in order to secure the submission of the people?" Confucius replied, "Advance the upright and set aside the crooked, then the people will submit. Advance the crooked and set aside the upright, then the people will not submit." Compare to the Ancient Egyptian thought:

> Punish firmly and chastise soundly, then repression of crime becomes an example. But punishment except for crime will turn the complainer into an enemy.
>
> -Ancient Egyptian Maatian Proverb

Lao-Tzu concurs with this assessment as he explains that a virtuous ruler is one who does not contrive. "The greatest virtue is to follow the Tao; how it achieves! without contriving." Thus, Lao-Tzu continues to explain that the best way of government is that which does not contrive (aspire to preeminence or fool people for selfish motives) against the people. "The second way to govern the land, is to do so without contriving. People so governed are truly blessed, for they are governed with virtue, and virtuous government is fair to all, thus leading to unity."

Plato, a long time student of the Ancient Egyptian wisdom and philosophy, concurs with the views above in that virtue should be highly valued and that those who are expert in a particular area of expertise should fill those positions. It is so in the medical disciplines as well as in politics as Plato states that "as a medicine to men, then the use of such medicines should be restricted to physicians; private individuals have no business with them." While virtue has been established as the main criteria for selecting a leader, oftentimes expert knowledge in the form of virtue, comes into conflict with the democratic and egalitarian ideals of modern society. This is because the way that democratic principles are practiced and egalitarian ideals are pursued in modern society is inherently deficient due to the lack of ethics. Democracy is defined as "Government by the people, exercised directly." But the meaning of the term has been vitiated to include "government through elected representatives" or "The common people, considered as the primary source of political power." In modern so-called democratic societies, especially in the United States of

America, there is not and has never been "Government by the people, exercised directly." A system of representatives (such as that of the USA) was setup in such a way so that people could not exercise power directly. In those societies, the concept of "democracy" has most often been equated with unregulated freedom which includes the freedom to be un-virtuous, that is, to pursue one's desires selfishly and wantonly. Plato explains that "the manifold and complex pleasures and desires and pains are generally found in children and women and servants, and in the freemen so called who are of the lowest and more numerous class." Compare the aforesaid to the following Ancient Egyptian proverbial wisdom statements.

> Complexity is the decadence of society; simplicity is the path of reality and salvation."

> "When opulence and extravagance are a necessity instead of righteousness and truth, society will be governed by greed and injustice."

> -Ancient Egyptian Maatian Proverbs

When freedom to pursue vices is practiced through or promoted by the government the society is lead to social strife. That very community which experiences social strife is the same one that will produce the leaders of the next generation of base character and that will lead to the further degeneration of subsequent generations and the eventual downfall of society. One explanation given for the setting up of a system of representative government that prevents direct democracy is that giving uneducated people the capacity to democratically decide on matters of state is simpler in a small society such as a neighborhood or even a small town; However, the argument is that when scaled up, the problems grow exponentially when there is a large community such as a country because in the larger society there will be more immature people, more "ambitious," "restless" and more "greedy" people who would unscrupulously pursue riches and power at the expense of the welfare of the whole community. Therefore, Plato concludes that the virtuous qualities necessary to rule are to be found in the smaller group of the population which has the proper temperance, upbringing and education for leadership: "Whereas the simple and moderate desires which follow reason, and are under the guidance of mind and true opinion, are to be found only in a few, and those the best born and best educated." While it is correct that due to the large number of uneducated, unethical, mentally disturbed, greedy, fearful, addicted, etc. personalities in the large society, democracy, either direct or indirect, would not work, the present system of government, government by illusion of democracy, what is in place now in the USA and Europe as well as other places, also does not and will not work as it serves to concentrate power which leads to despotism and fascism as it destroys the environment in an endless, unbridled search for profit for the few at the expense of the wellbeing of the many. The problem is that modern so-called democracies have not setup a system of representation by the wise or educated and virtuous but rather, a system by which the greedy, sociopathic elements of the society are facilitated, to enter into positions of power, change laws to their favor, propagandize the population and plunder the wealth of the nation. Therefore, leadership should be reserved for those who are virtuous and trained in the discipline of leadership just as cobblers should not take the job of warriors: "But when the cobbler or any other man whom nature designed to be a trader, having his heart lifted up by wealth or strength or the number of his followers, or any like advantage, attempts to force his way into the class of warriors, or a warrior into that of legislators and leaders, for which he is unfitted, and either to take the implements or the duties of the other; or when one man is trader, legislator, and warrior all in one, then I think you will agree with me in saying that this interchange and this meddling of one with another is the ruin of the State."

On the issue of society's leaders having the duty to raise the youth with righteousness and refrain from accumulating wealth and property to the extent that it clouds their duty to serve the society as a whole and not their own base desires and greed, the words of the Ancient Egyptian Wisdom Text teachings to Meri Ka Ra are instructive:

> (15)Raise your youths and the residence will love you,
> Increase your subjects with friendship,
> See, your city is full of new growth.
> Twenty years the youths indulge their wishes, Then they go forth as [recruits]...
> Veterans return to their children ...
>
> I raised troops from them on my accession. Advance your officials, promote your [soldiers],
> Enrich the young men who follow you,
> Provide them with goods, endow them with fields,
> Reward them with herds.

When living in society and occupying a position of leadership it is important to raise one's offspring or the youth one is responsible for with the teachings of righteousness and with good will. It is important to give abundantly according to one's means and not to hoard one's possessions or wealth. Hoarding promotes jealousy in others but more importantly it creates an obstruction to one's ability to care for others. This is because ones primary preoccupation is with acquiring wealth and property and finding ways to protect it from others instead of thinking of ways in which to help people and provide for their welfare.

Amassing material wealth and the preoccupation with possessions is the mentality of the masses. Objects do not last even when acquired righteously. Further, they cannot bring happiness or true security. Even the richest person can be swallowed up in an earthquake and what good would all the riches in the world do for that person?

On the question of leadership vs. dictatorship, based on the writings examined so far, from Ptahotep, Plato, Lao-Tzu and Confucius, we might conclude that leadership may be defined as the virtuous caring for the good of all. Dictatorship may be defined as leadership based on vice, the deviation from natural law or the deviation from the logic of doing the job one is trained for and for which one has the character to do well. From Cicero we learn that good government requires the leader to keep foremost the welfare of the nation as a whole: "Those who propose to take charge of the affairs of government should not fail to remember two of Plato's rules: first, to keep the good of the people so clearly in view that regardless of their own interests they will make their every action conform to that; second, to care for the welfare of the whole body politic and not in serving the interests of one party to betray the rest. For the administration of the government, like the office of a trustee must be conducted for the benefit of those entrusted to one's care, not of those to whom it is entrusted." So the virtue of self-denial in protecting the public trust is a principal virtue of leadership. The lack of this virtue can lead towards a leaning upon one of two other interest groups which contradict the public trust that has been conferred on the leader: "Now, those who care for the interests of a part of the citizens and neglect another part, introduce into the civil service a dangerous element - dissension and party strife."

Cicero explains that there are three forms of government. One is the "whole body politic" and the other two are the "democratic and the aristocratic parties." When the leader turns away from protecting the interests of the "whole body politic" and towards either the democratic or the aristocratic party, social strife is introduced to the political process: "The result is that some are found to be loyal supporters of the democratic, others of the aristocratic party, and few of the nation as a whole. As a result of this party spirit bitter strife arose at Athens and in our own country not only dissensions but also disastrous civil wars broke out." Caring for the "whole body politic" might be equated to some degree with the modern concept of Egalitarianism. However, the ancient ideal is not equated to the modern because the modern concept implies indiscriminate equality and humanity itself shows that people are not equal and have different abilities and needs. On this point Cicero reminds us: "in bestowing a kindness, as well as in making a requital, the first rule of duty requires us - other things being equal - to lend assistance preferably to people in proportion to their individual need." The ancient concept implies making sure that all individuals have their needs met and their capacities have a place in society that is productive and makes a contribution to society in order to also provide fulfillment and purpose in life and thereby promoting peace and harmony in the society. However, due to egoism and greed, egalitarian ideals are hard to achieve beyond the theoretical levels. Communism is an egalitarian concept based on material equality. However, the preexisting inequalities and greed produce enormous problems such as the resistance to the redistribution of wealth. Legal egalitarianism is also problematic when the society is not based on virtuous ideals since those who desire wealth or power will supplant virtue and principles of equality because they do not agree or respect those ideals as Cicero explains: "But when one begins to aspire to pre-eminence, it is difficult to preserve that spirit of fairness which is absolutely essential to justice. The result is that such men do not allow themselves to be constrained either by argument or by any public and lawful authority; but they only too often prove to be bribers and agitators in public life, seeking to obtain supreme power and to be superiors through force rather than equals through justice." Of course, in modern times we have the same types of unethical and unscrupulous, sociopathic personalities in industry and government, described by Cicero, in the form of billionaire campaign donors, bank presidents, corporate leaders and career politicians as well as the captains of industry, who wield enormous power over politics and direct the course of society regardless of supposedly "democratic" elections, regardless of the laws and regardless of ethical considerations, to their own ends and benefit, as they euphemistically spread the idea that "they are job creators," or that "they know best what is good for society", etc. while in reality many of them are self-absorbed, megalomaniacal sociopaths imposing fraud in the guise of central banking, and dictatorship in the guise of representative democracy. Additionally, regardless of the failures of capitalism and the dysfunctionality of government, which has been setup by them, the failures are neither acknowledged nor experienced by them since their wealth and power insulate them; rather, the failures are the fault of others who do not follow their dictates to the letter and implement their programs to their exact specifications. In other words, to them, the rationalization is that the failure of capitalism to provide for the needs of all members of society is due to not enough capitalism and too much caring for the environment or for helping the poor and unemployed through government programs, etc. In other words, they want more purity in the application of their disproven ideology. Thus a centralized and insulated minority runs society, enriching themselves and letting others experience the failures as their own fault instead of taking responsibility for a system that works for them, the few, and not for the masses.

Earlier in this essay it was stated that the democratic and egalitarian ideals are practiced in modern society in an inherently deficient way. Cicero included "democracy" as one of the deviations from the trust and care of the "nation as a whole" which is considered as the virtuous path of government that Lao-Tzu prefers: "virtuous government is fair to all." If the United States and similar countries are used as examples, the idea they promulgate, that democracy is the better form of government is contradicted by the outcomes of its practice. Some of the deficiencies of western democracy include some of the greatest gaps in income between rich and poor and substantial abuses of civil and corporate law, political power as well as the highest incarceration rates. As in modern society's democracies, Cicero's "democratic party," seems to represent those interest that band together in order to campaign for the interests of certain groups. In modern times those groups may be likened to the power elite, corporations and special interests.

CONCLUSION

Many people in the United States of America are amazed when they come to realize the true purpose of the Electoral College in the political process. Many other such political devises were introduced by the "Founding Fathers" of the United States of America for the purpose of preventing the direct control of the government by the people. Using a model of representative government that began to emerge years earlier in Europe, they fashioned a system of government that separates powers (among members of the power elite) and makes it difficult for changes to occur through the will of the people. One other such devise is the practice of staggered votes for elected members of congress and the executive branches of government. Thus, for the "Founding Fathers" their answer to the question of inclusiveness vs. community or corporation efficiency seems to have followed the model set forth by the writers quoted above. Clearly, the philosophers do not agree that inclusiveness should be allowed over efficiency, but here the efficiency should manifest through social fairness or meritocracy and not rule by the most wealthy, powerful or most favored. However, profligate forms of government do not allow even unethical inclusiveness of the masses to partake in the wealth of the country based on nepotism or preferential treatment based on party affiliation but rather prevent them from inclusion except to the extent that is necessary to quell their restlessness and base needs. This is accomplished by providing opportunities to acquire sufficient wealth (paycheck) to sustain basic subsistence level accommodations (rent or mortgage), food and entertainments (alcohol, drugs, sports, movies, etc.). The ancient philosophers favor all people having equal opportunity to be trained for leadership positions if they have the aptitude for such a position.

In modern society the political power and corporate wellbeing take precedence over individual rights although until recently, there had been some effort to protect individual rights, though after the attacks of 9/11/2001 and the implementation of the patriot Act", individual rights and civil liberties have steadily declined to the point where NSA whistleblower, William Binney, who supervised the development of a NSA program called "Thin Thread" that was designed to identify international networks of connections between people from their internet communications and possible threats to the USA, stated: "I resigned from the NSA in late 2001. I could not stay after the NSA began purposefully violating the Constitution."[235] Neither congress or the judiciary or the president took any action to correct the turn towards lawbreaking.

However, the "Founding Fathers" (modelers of USA society) also differ from the philosophers quoted above in that they did not set up a mechanism for promoting virtue in society beyond punishment from the judicial system for

---

[235] http://publicintelligence.net/binney-nsa-declaration/

those acts which are deemed by society to be contradictory either to individual rights or community rights. In the case of the USA, virtue was not elevated in the Declaration of Independence or in the formation of the government system. Rather the quest for personal satisfaction was elevated and the common good was equated with that: "We hold these truths to be self-evident, that all men are created equal, that they are endowed by their Creator with certain unalienable Rights, that among these are Life, Liberty and the pursuit of Happiness." Even so, that capacity to pursue happiness was not extended either to the Native American population, to women, to the slave population nor even to the non-slave population as a whole but was reserved for the power elite, the aristocracy, the white men. So from the inception of the United States of America, the supposed political ideal of all men being equal with unalienable human rights, was a sham since even at the time of this writing (Fall 3013) neither the rights of women, Native Americans or African Americans or other peoples of color, have been raised to the level of the "white man" and this condition is certainly far beneath that of Ancient Egypt wherein, for example, women had equal rights in the society, with men; something they do not have even now. The system that was setup in modern times was based on gender, and wealth, and thus rule by a power elite and an adversarial relationship between the genders and races in the form of social strife between "whites" and "blacks" and economic strife between haves and have nots that have been constant sources of conflict within and outside of the United States of America. Nevertheless, the way chosen by the "Founding Fathers" to promote virtue might be seen as a passive mode of promoting virtuous leadership whereas the philosophers quoted above promote more of a proactive approach;

> "If you are an official of high standing, and you are commissioned to satisfy the many, then hold to a straight line. When you speak don't lean to one side or to the other. Beware lest someone complain, saying to the judges, "he has distorted things", and then your very deeds will turn into a judgment of you."
> -Ancient Egyptian Proverb

The ancient philosophers promote the idea of setting up a system that would vigorously nurture and educate people, who have the right temperament, with the necessary training in philosophy and practical skills to enable them to be virtuous leaders as Plato explains, as he echoes the Ancient Egyptian teachings he studied for several decades:

Maat Philosophy Versus Fascism and the Police State

"Until philosophers are kings, or the kings and princes of this world have the spirit and power of philosophy, and political greatness and wisdom meet in one, and those commoner natures who pursue either to the exclusion of the other are compelled to stand aside, cities will never have rest from their evils..."

True democracy, the practice of government with direct control by people, as partially practiced in ancient Athens (which was also limited to certain segments of the population) for a short period of time, proved itself to be easily susceptible to corruption due to the desires of uneducated or greedy people or the designs of un-virtuous leaders, sociopathic leaders or flawed charismatic authorities who could control the feelings and opinions of the masses. It is conceivable that at the time of the establishment of the U.S.A. aristocrats, through oligarchy, patriarchy (Founding Fathers) and plutocracy, controlled the government but since the time of the industrial revolution to the present, it has been increasingly become a corpocracy. Thus, the aristocracy and the corporations have merged into a form of government in which leadership in society has turned into dictatorship based on the corporate C.E.O. model.[236] A "dictatorship" is "a government that does not allow a nation to determine its own political direction by popular election" as proven by the presidential elections of the years 1960 and 2000 in which the person who won the most votes was not installed as president but rather the person desired by the power elite was. The leaders exert control of the populace via the propaganda of a false ideal of government, i.e. the "pursuit of happiness," since there is no way for all to achieve this goal harmoniously, under the capitalist, market economic model since some will be losers at the expense of others. This is to be contrasted with the Ancient philosophical ideal of the society based on the "pursuit of virtue", which is attainable and equitable for all. Thus, one cannot conclude that democracy has actually ever been practiced in human history since the form put

---

[236] Chief Executive Officer and Board of directors who dictate policy to the employees who have no rights or say in the direction of the corporations activitites.

into practice in ancient Athens was deficient or altered as are the current forms, to be in favor of certain groups of the society. Also, it is unlikely, given the nature of humanity, that democracy as a form of government could ever be practiced in any society, let alone one wherein virtue is not promoted over greed. Just as a family needs parents to lead it, and children are not allowed to rule due to their immaturity so to a society needs wise leaders. In this context, the wise are the parents of society and the unvirtuous, the greedy, the lustful, envious, cruel, callous and sociopathic are the children who should not be allowed to operate the levers of social power as in government, corporate, religious power, and the commanding heights of the economy. Citizens can be led to understand the need to strike a balance between individual and community needs and to adopt virtuous values or their opposite as Cicero explains most succinctly:

> "Justice is, therefore, in every way to be cultivated and maintained, both for its own sake (for otherwise it would not be justice) and for the enhancement of personal honour and glory. But as there is a method not only of acquiring money but also of investing it so as to yield an income to meet our continuously recurring expenses - both for the necessities and for the more refined comforts of life - so there must be a method of gaining glory and turning it to account."

It is only in a society wherein the people are socialized to value virtue, that a social order to promote social justice, harmony, peace and progressiveness could be seriously pursued. St. Benedict controlled a community and he chose a non-democratic form of governance based on virtue and on spiritual ethics and egalitarian ideals based on equality in spirit that was to be managed through merit instead of favoritism. He explains:

> "Let him make no distinction of persons in the monastery. Let him not love one more than another, unless it be one whom he findeth more exemplary in good works and obedience."

Western philosophy forms the basis of social ethics, business ethics and the concepts of democracy and egalitarianism in Western culture. Western philosophy, unlike, Eastern, African or Native American philosophies, is not primarily based on transcendental questions of existence and a spiritual or cosmic concept of order and justice, but rather on analytical and phenomenological questions. Therefore, since its field of conscious awareness is limited to egoistic, phenomenological and mechanistic paradigms and does not take into account the expanded, spiritually and scientifically[237] proven factors of the underlying unity of Creation and humanity, Western philosophies are inadequate bases from which to consider a viable philosophical means to achieve social order, justice, peace, humanitarian ethics and harmony i.e. egalitarianism. The concept of freedom for the pursuit of happiness in Western culture implies a right to compete and hoard resources and deprive others of resources. This naturally leads to the idea of free commerce as the means to achieve and accumulate wealth and finally capitalism as a means to most efficiently achieve inordinate power and wealth. To the un-virtuous, democracy is ideal because it is the best form of government to deceive ordinary people by promoting the illusion of fairness, political equality (one person, one vote) and self-government while at the same time weakening and even adulterating their political power in order to allow free commerce and the operation of special interests using a powerless labor force. In other words, democracy is favorable to the corrupt elements of society. Lenin said that *"The theory of the class struggle"* was rejected on the grounds that it could not be applied to a strictly democratic society, governed according to the will of the majority, etc." Democracy facilitates rule of the majority over a minority, as well as political injustice and judicial inequality, thereby forming a democratic corpocracy that is, a socio-political-economic system based on finance, which supports its governmental institutions through financial backing, i.e. payoffs (campaign donations). Therefore, in a democracy while there is a veneer of self-government, actually there is government to the highest bidder; and since those who have the most wealth have the most bidding power they can get what they want and the poor have no power. This system, of financial backing by the power elite and corporations, and leaders haggling over communal interests as if they were private commodities is contradictory to egalitarianism and is highly susceptible to corruption by those who as Cicero said: "aspire to pre-eminence." The corruption manifests through disreputable political rhetoric that encourages contributions to political candidates, which degrades to bribery and extortion of political officials. In such a system the most powerful entity (the one with the most funds or influence) is able to control the agenda, which invariably is to foster favorable conditions for maintaining and becoming more wealthy and powerful as opposed to looking out for the common good of all citizens. Therefore, business serves the purpose of allowing entry into the commercial field and business ethics provide guidelines for succeeding most efficiently in that field and not the promotion of social responsibility. The adherence to these concepts cannot allow egalitarianism or true democracy to operate; they are incompatible.

---

[237] *THE TAO OF PHYSICS: AN EXPLORATION OF THE PARALLELS BETWEEN MODERN PHYSICS AND EASTERN MYSTICISM* **BY** *FRITJOF CAPRA*
DANCING WU LI MASTERS: AN OVERVIEW OF THE NEW PHYSICS **BY** *GARY ZUKAV*

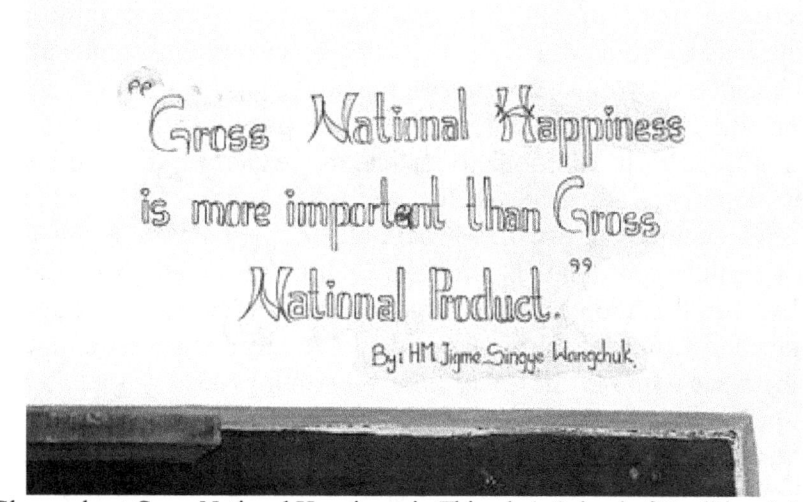

Slogan about Gross National Happiness in Thimphu's School of Traditional Arts.

The shepherding form of Government which is based on guidance, overseeing, protecting, safeguarding, supervising, and watching over the population as a whole is a more ideal form of government. In ancient Egypt the pharaoh was considered the Heka or prince who operates as a Shepherd tending over the flock, i.e. the people. The pharaoh was backed by a council of priests and priestesses who advised the pharaoh on how to conduct matters of state in keeping with the tenets of Maat or balance, righteousness, justice and truth which includes not favoring the rich over the poor or the learned over the ignorant but rather tending to the needs of individuals in accordance with their capacities and abilities just as a shepherd takes care of all the sheep but some sheep may have different needs than others. So the shepherd wisely takes differences in people into account when tending to their needs. Therefore, the governmental system used in Ancient Egypt may be classified as a Theocratic monarchy based on Maatian principles of egalitarianism, justice and politics. This ideal is similar to the kind of system used in the present day country, Bhutan, where Gross National Happiness (quality of life), which benefits people, is more important than Gross National Product (consumerism, business profits, etc), which benefits corporations. There the philosophical basis for government is not Maat, which is based on the religion of Ancient Egypt but on Dharma (ethical wisdom) which is based on the religion of Bhutan, Buddhism.

Maat Philosophy Versus Fascism and the Police State

FINALLY

We discussed the basic personality types that make up the human societies and culture. The one that tends towards the animal passions most easily falls prey to callousness, greed and lust for power and control. This type was also described in the Ancient Egyptian Wisdom Texts but in an exacerbated condition wherein the environment heightens the negative qualities of the personality; As such, that personality becomes a threat to what is righteous and just. Therefore, a society governed by virtue and balanced vision must remain vigilant so as to maintain those virtues that produce a balanced, harmonious, just and ordered society.

> *DURING the ninth dynasty, 3000 B.C.E., before the first Eurasian invasion of Egypt by the Hyksos, a Pharaoh passed on to his heir the following wisdom:*

Lo, the miserable Asiatic,
He is wretched because of the place he lives in:
Short of water, bare of wood,
Its paths are many and painful because of mountains.
He is nomadic, not dwelling in one place,
The constant need for food propels his legs,
He makes war since the time of Horus,
He is not successful in conquering nor is he conquered,
He is treacherous and does not announce the day of combat,
He is like a thief who darts around a group.
But as I live and shall be what I am,
When the Bowmen were a sealed wall,
I broke through their defenses,
I attack them with the forces from Lower Egypt,
I captured their men and women,
I took their cattle,
Until the Asiatics **despised** Egypt.
Do not worry about the Asiatic,
The Asiatic is like a crocodile on its shore,
It snatches from a lonely road,
But it cannot **capture anything** from a populous town.[238]

<u>Wisdom derived from the Teachings to Meri Ka Ra:</u>

---

[238] Ancient Egyptian Wisdom Texts. Instructions to Meri Ka Ra

Maat Philosophy Versus Fascism and the Police State

Harshness in surroundings and general environment can cause negative stress which could lead to an unsettled mind.

An unsettled mind is difficult to control. A mind that is uncontrollable will have difficulty in concentrating. Poor concentration will not allow for reflection. Reflection is necessary to make sense of one's situation and to gain intellectual understanding. A non-reflective, confused or "Wrong thinking" mind will have difficulty meditating.

A non-meditating mind will have difficulty in transcending the world of apparent dualities. One will be endlessly pulled into the "world" and the apparent thoughts going on in the mind.

As the mind will be caught up in the endless waves of joys and sorrows, it will be unable to find peace. A mind filled with too much joy or too much sorrow due to its experiences in the world will be equally agitated and one will have difficulty concentrating and calming down. One extreme (ex. Joy) leads to another (ex. Pain).

The concept of the *"Miserable Asiatic"* became known in Egypt as the concept of *"The Land of Horus and the Land of Set."* Since Set is the God of the desert, the Asiatics, who dwelt in the desert lands, became identified with Set and therefore, Setian behavior (impulsive, selfish, brute force, etc.). The teaching about the miserable Asiatic is of paramount importance because it provides an understanding of how the human mind becomes degraded and violent. A human being who is not nurtured and who is constantly experiencing stress due to lack of security, not knowing where the next meal is coming from, how to acquire and secure the needs of life and then how to hold onto them, etc. All of these worries cause a degradation in the human mind wherein the concern is not with working with others but with competing with them for food, material wealth, mates, etc. The purpose of human existence is to provide a means for the soul to experience and grow in awareness of itself as one with Creation. This feeling is blissful, supremely satisfying and universal. When the soul in a human being is not allowed to discover itself in this manner the ego in a human being is in control and this egoism fosters feelings of personal desire, separation, and animosity to anything which prevents the ego from getting what it wants. This is the source of enmity, anger, hatred and violence in human experience. Ethical conscience and spiritual values lead a human being to discover a deeper essence of life which is universal and inclusive, that is best expressed in the balance of feelings, emotions and distribution of resources. This way of ordering society leads to happiness, peace and prosperity for all members of the society. True ethical living, such as is promoted by Maat Philosophy, allows a person to understand where true happiness, peace and fulfillment in life are to be found. It shows a person that security cannot be found in the world but in that which sustains it. When the ideals of Maat Philosophy are applied to human institutions it leads to good government and well adjusted and contented societies.

Therefore, though the dire conditions related in this volume have the potential to bring down not only society and the world economy but also the world ecology, and indeed, human civilization, it is also useful to remember that there are answers to these problems. What is necessary is to have the will, as a society, to face and live by truth instead of for personal desires, delusions and ideologies. Then a proper balance will be found between the needs and desires of the many versus those of the few and a proper order and balance will also be found between humanity and nature. Such balance will produce prosperity for all and will serve as a proper foundation for the real work of human existence, not to suffer the indignities and cruelties of life, but to discover the meaning of life and a higher essence of existence which will elevate human experience to the level of exalted spirit.

A LAST WORD ON THE TERM "ETHICAL CONSCIENCE."

The term "ETHICAL CONSCIENCE" has been used throughout this volume and in summary it means a field of understanding and feeling that takes into account the MAATIAN ideal of order and balance that takes into account the wisdom of interconnectedness and complementariness that all existence founded in. With this conscience, meaning awareness, in all endeavors and calculations, then it becomes possible to create a society that has fairness for all, that provides for all and which protects the environment and promotes health in commerce and freely available healthcare services instead of promoting greed and mechanistic thinking. The mechanistic thinking is that we and the world are separate entities. This flawed idea allows the corruptions of egoism to taint the human endeavors such that the negative aspects of human consciousness with a person's ego driving aryu produce thoughts, feelings, inventions and ideologies that are self-serving, poisonous to the environment and which give license to those who want to exploit humanity and the world for their own pursuit of desire fulfillment, regardless of the consequences or harms to others or the environment. The field of consciousness embodied by "MAATIAN ETHICAL CONSCIENCE" may be likened to the field of consciousness experienced by BUDDHA CONSCIOUSNESS, CHRIST CONSCIOUSNESS, THE TAO of Lao-Tzu, MOKSHA of LORD KRISHNA, Confucianism of Confucius, etc. It is founded in the wisdom of ancient universal philosophy wisdom as expressed by the Sages of old and of modern times. It is the wisdom of interconnectedness, inclusion and peace. To live Maat is to enter into "MAATIAN ETHICAL

CONSCIENCE". Doing so is also entering into spiritual expansion and connection with the universe and its essential nature, the transcendental, the immortal and the divine. Those who experience this divine field of "MAATIAN ETHICAL CONSCIENCE" are the purveyors of worldly glories for they express that consciousness in the form of ethical conscience for all to benefit from and enjoy, not just for the present generation but for all who may come in the future. "MAATIAN ETHICAL CONSCIENCE" is not bound by the confines of egoism, sectarianism, objectivism, sociopathology, corrupted desires, politics or mechanistic ideologies; thus it is capable of resolving the issues that trouble the worldly minded and seemingly logical ideals that lead to conflict and death. If "MAATIAN ETHICAL CONSCIENCE" becomes the premise even before ideas are formulated then they will be infused with the ethical wisdom in conscious awareness and not just as a theoretical ideal but as a living dynamic matrix of life. This is the legacy of Maat in Government and the promise for the future survival and prosperity of humanity and the world.

HTP

INDEX

Abraham, 115, 173
Absolute, 161, 267
Actions, 40, 63, 64
Afghanistan, 38, 125
Africa, 38, 43, 67, 68, 78, 120, 189, 273, 283, 285, 287, 288
African American, 100, 114, 123, 250
African Proverbial Wisdom Teachings, 295
African Religion, 267, 276, 282
Air, 43, 44
Air, Clean air, 43, 44
Al Qaeda, 151
Albert Einstein, 213
Albright, Madeline, 164
Allopathic, 267
Amen, 53
Amenta, 275
Amentet, 277
American Dream, 8, 97, 129, 132, 142
American empire, 13, 161
American Heritage Dictionary, Dictionary, 33, 96, 167, 281
American Theocracy, 286
Americas, 110
Ammit, 51
Ancient Egypt, 1, 13, 14, 30, 31, 50, 52, 53, 54, 55, 58, 59, 61, 65, 66, 67, 72, 73, 74, 77, 92, 109, 153, 164, 174, 175, 181, 191, 192, 193, 200, 201, 202, 206, 207, 208, 209, 211, 212, 213, 214, 215, 217, 220, 222, 227, 241, 242, 243, 244, 245, 250, 254, 255, 267, 268, 269, 270, 271, 272, 273, 274, 275, 276, 278, 279, 280, 281, 282, 283, 284, 285, 287, 288, 292, 293, 294, 295, 296, 297, 298, 299, 300, 301, 302, 303, 304, 305, 306, 307, 308
Ancient Egyptian Book of the Dead, 201
Ancient Egyptian Wisdom Texts, 53, 174, 175, 191, 241, 255, 294
anger, 12, 15, 56, 57, 72, 93, 134, 256, 279
Ani, 67
Anu, 276
Anu (Greek Heliopolis), 276
Anubis, 51
Anunian Theology, 276
Apep serpent, 58, 59
Aramaic, 67
Ari, 55
Arjuna, 60
Aryan, 269
Asar, 202, 274, 275, 278, 279, 300, 302, 304, 306
Asar and Aset, 274
Asarian Resurrection, 273, 278, 279, 282, 306
Aset, 51, 55, 270, 274, 275, 277, 278, 279, 300, 306
Aset (Isis), 51, 55, 270, 274, 275, 277, 278, 279, 300, 306
Ashanti, 295
Asia, 42, 288
Asia Minor, 288
Asiatic, 255, 256, 285, 287, 288
Asleep, 103
Assyrians, 293
Astral, 275
Astral Plane, 275
Aten, see also Aton, 302
Atlantis, 283
Attila, 178
Attitude, 221
Avoiding, 153
Awakening, 274
baby boom, 40
baby boomer, 40
baby boomers, 40
Back, 135
BBC, 97, 108
Beatitudes, 168
Being, 61, 277
Bhagavad Gita, 60, 293
Bible, 277, 278
Black, 114, 172, 288
Black Africa, 288
black people, 105, 173
Book of Coming Forth By Day, 52, 53, 67, 274, 275
Book of Enlightenment, 201
Book of the Dead, see also Rau Nu Prt M Hru, 201, 275, 294
Brain, 221
Brazil, 39, 189
British empire, 178
bubble, real estate, 19, 80
Buddha, 60, 283, 285
Buddha Consciousness, 60
Buddhism, 254, 276, 285, 306
Buddhist, 60, 227, 273, 285
Bush administration, 198
Bush, George H., 78, 125
Bush, George W., 198
Byzantine, 74
Calm, 31
Canada, 47, 70, 85
capital punishment, 237
Capitalism, 59, 74, 75, 77, 80, 87, 188, 189

capitalist system, 7, 75, 110, 173, 187, 190
career counselor, career, job, 110, 123, 247
Caribbean, 78
Catholic, 169, 277
Catholic Church, 277
ceaseless-ness and regularity, 50, 53
celebrities, 9
Central Intelligence Agency, 107
Change, 70, 89
Cheney, Richard Bruce – vice president, 13, 234
Child, 278, 279
China, 21, 36, 37, 39, 43, 116, 119, 186, 190
Chomsky, Noam, 78, 97
Christ, 275
Christianity, 161, 169, 171, 266, 276, 277, 278
Church, 277
CIA, 128, 234
Cicero, 241, 246, 247, 252, 253
civil liberties, 132, 153, 173, 237, 249
civil service, 246
Civilization, 6, 22, 68, 124, 155, 161, 182, 269, 270, 285, 286, 287, 288, 308
Class, ruling class, 82, 185, 206
CNN, 230, 231
CNN – news reports, 230, 231
Collapse, 6, 17, 22, 68, 124, 155, 161, 182, 286
colonialism, 13
colony, 69
color, 100, 114, 123, 173, 217, 225, 250, 292, 295
Color, 291
Communism, 247
Company of gods and goddesses, 53
Conflict, 286, 296

Confucianism, 227, 242, 257
Confucius, 179, 241, 242, 243, 246, 257
Congress, 79, 88, 115, 216, 238
Conscience, 175, 257
Consciousness, 274, 295
Consciousness, human, 61, 257, 267
Conservatives, 219, 220, 221, 223
Constitution, 115, 150, 151, 159, 161, 249
contentment, 193, 212
Coptic, 274
cosmic force, 277, 284
Creation, 51, 57, 58, 59, 61, 210, 253, 256, 273, 276, 295
Crime, 176, 177
Cross, 108
Culture, 124, 189, 273, 283, 290
Cymbals, 300, 302
Danger, 45
Death, 22, 68, 124, 161, 182, 286
Debt, 18
December, 27, 115, 130, 131, 277
deficit spending, 34
Delta, 73
delusion, 62, 63, 72, 75, 90, 124, 127, 128, 129, 134, 218, 224, 235, 238
Democracy Now, 230
Democratic Party, 78, 98
Demotic, 67
Denderah, 274
Depression, 187
Desire, 296
Devotional Love, 271
Dharma, 59, 60, 61, 67, 227, 254
Dictatorship, 241, 246
Diet, 31, 268
discrimination, 133, 150, 177
DNA, 97
downfall of society., 244

drug companies, 23, 25
Drum, 300, 302
Duat, 54, 275
Earth, 31
Edfu, 274
Egyptian Book of Coming Forth By Day, 56, 64, 274
Egyptian Mysteries, 268, 280, 281, 296, 307
Egyptian Physics, 276
Egyptian proverbs, 30, 271
Egyptian Yoga, 266, 268, 273, 274, 275, 298, 299, 300, 301, 302
Egyptian Yoga see also Kamitan Yoga, 67, 266, 267, 268, 273, 274, 275, 298, 299, 300, 301, 302, 305, 306
Egyptologists, 281, 292
Electoral College, 249
Empire culture, 286
Energy, 79, 239
Enlightenment, 54, 57, 267, 268, 270, 271, 272, 274, 276, 277, 279, 280, 284, 296
Ethics, 58, 166, 209, 268, 269, 285, 287, 288, 295
Ethiocracy, 227
Ethiopia, 295
ethnicity, 204, 214
Eucharist, 275
Europe, 13, 18, 33, 42, 71, 85, 92, 130, 180, 185, 186, 244, 249
evil, 31, 66, 93, 94, 279, 281
Evil, 282
Exercise, 30, 273, 305
exploitation, 13, 224
Face, 168
Faith, 289
faith-based, 91
fascism, 6, 12, 13, 35, 50, 68, 72, 74, 75, 77, 78, 81, 83, 86, 128, 133,

142, 154, 168, 171, 172, 173, 193, 245
Fascist, 133, 150
fascist system, 153, 209
Federal Reserve System, 7, 8, 16, 17, 19, 28, 34, 35, 38, 80, 82, 83, 87, 88, 173, 186, 196, 197
Fight, 172
Food, 7
Founding Fathers, 249, 251
France, 78
free market, 68, 77, 89, 169, 170
free speech, 72, 75, 134, 135, 167, 237
free trade, 89
frustration, 62, 67, 72
Galla, 295
Galla culture, 295
Gandhi, Mahatma, 179
GDP, Gross Domestic Product, 22, 236
Geb, 274
Gender, 216
Genghis Khan, 178
Germany, 33, 96, 97, 98, 124, 203, 205
Ghana, 295
global economy, 286
Globalization, 286
God, 50, 52, 53, 54, 56, 59, 61, 62, 64, 92, 93, 94, 125, 143, 170, 174, 176, 201, 202, 204, 210, 211, 212, 256, 270, 271, 275, 276, 283, 291, 302
Goddess, 50, 52, 61, 277, 291, 298, 302
Goddesses, 61, 273, 281
Gods, 53, 61, 93, 273, 281
gods and goddesses, 50, 53, 61, 201, 276, 281, 283
Gold, 17
Good, 60, 79, 193, 200, 202, 220, 234, 282
Gospels, 277
Great Depression, 17, 187

Greece, 67, 268, 283
Greed, 192
Greek empire, 178
Greek philosophy, 266
Greeks, 293
Greenspan, Alan, 87, 88, 197
Gross National Product, 254
Guantanamo Bay, 109
Haari, 301
Haiti, 78
Hall of Maat, 55
Happiness, 71, 235, 250, 254
Harmony, 52
Hate, 73, 296
Hatha Yoga, 287
Hathor, 274, 277, 280
Hatred, 296
Health, 24, 27, 30, 31, 237, 238, 267, 276
Hearing, 116
Heart, 66, 279, 290
Heart (also see Ab, mind, conscience), 66, 279, 290
Heaven, 278
Hekau, 302
Heru, 53, 67, 73, 92, 201, 274, 275, 277, 278, 279, 282, 294, 300, 302, 306
Heru (see Horus), 53, 67, 73, 92, 201, 274, 275, 277, 278, 279, 282, 294, 300, 302, 306
Hetep, 210
Hetheru, 280, 300
HetHeru (Hetheru, Hathor), 300
Hetheru (Hetheru, Hathor), 280
Hieroglyphic, 272, 292
Hieroglyphic Writing, language, 272, 292
Hieroglyphs, 305
Hindu, 60
Hinduism, 276, 306
Hindus, 67, 281
Hitler, 98

hope, 132, 154, 290, 292
Horus, 56, 255, 300, 306
human rights, 107, 109, 129, 144, 250
Human Rights Watch, 106
HUMANITY, 280
Hussein, Saddam, 125
Hyksos, 255
Iamblichus, 293
Ignorance, 64
Ignorance, see also Khemn, 64
illusion, 62, 95, 120, 132, 134, 142, 154, 244, 253
Illusion, 132, 193, 196
Immorality, 6, 41, 119
India, 39, 119, 186, 268, 269, 270, 271, 273, 285, 287, 301
Indian Yoga, 269, 301
Indus, 269
Indus Valley, 269
Infection, 27
Initiate, 268
Intelligence, 189
intolerance, 220
Iran, 125, 128
Iraq, 38, 69, 107, 108, 125, 164
Iraqi, 107, 109
Isis, 51, 52, 55, 56, 61, 210, 270, 274, 275, 277, 300, 306
Isis, See also Aset, 51, 52, 55, 56, 61, 210, 270, 274, 275, 277, 306
Islam, 266
Jacob (and Israel), 221
Japan, 36, 41, 42, 45, 48, 92, 185, 186
Jerome, 163
Jesus, 61, 168, 275, 277, 278
Jesus Christ, 275
Jim Crow, 114, 173
Joseph, 68, 209
Joy, 256
Judaism, 266
Judgment scene, Papyrus of Ani (Any), 52

Justice, 79, 100, 106, 108, 180, 189, 234, 252
Ka, 191, 245, 255
Kabbalah, 266
Kamit (Egypt), 281
Kamitan, 268, 283
Karma, 52, 54, 55, 59, 271
Kemetic, 30, 31, 66, 67, 203, 284, 290, 297, 298, 300, 301
Khan, Genghis, 178
Khemn, see also ignorance, 281
Kill, 156, 157, 158
King, 93, 227, 278, 283
King, Dr. Martin Luther, 127, 128
Kingdom, 278
Kingdom of Heaven, 278
Kissinger, Henry, 195, 196
Knowledge, 192
Krishna, 60, 278
laissez-faire, 59, 89, 165
Land of Horus, 256
Latino, 100
Lebanon, 89
left wing, 231
Libya, 125
Life, 55, 250, 273, 283, 289, 291, 295
Life Force, 273
Love, 271
Lower Egypt, 50, 53, 255
Maat, 1, 2, 6, 14, 30, 50, 51, 52, 53, 55, 57, 58, 59, 60, 61, 62, 65, 66, 67, 68, 69, 71, 72, 73, 74, 77, 81, 91, 92, 93, 153, 163, 164, 175, 182, 192, 193, 200, 201, 202, 204, 205, 206, 208, 209, 210, 212, 213, 217, 219, 220, 222, 223, 227, 242, 254, 256, 257, 272, 277, 279, 283, 284, 290, 294, 296, 297, 307, 308
MAAT, 271

Maati, 55
MAATI, 271
Machiavellian, 196
Malawi, 295
Mandela, Nelson, 181
Manu, 52
Manufacturing Consent, 98
Martin Luther, 127, 128
Martin Luther King, 127, 128
Marx, Karl, 188
Masters, 253
Matter, 276
Matthew, 106, 221
Media, 135, 172
medical system, 26
Medicare, 26
Meditation, 268, 271, 272, 302, 303, 306
Medu Neter, 281
Memphite Theology, 276
Mer, 55
Merikara, 213
Meskhenet, 52, 53, 54, 272
Metaphysics, 276, 295
Middle East, 67, 266
Min, 274
Mind, 163
minimum wage, 186, 236
Miserable Asiatic, 256
Monarchy, 153
Moral Majority, 79
Mortality, 27
MSNBC, 12, 27, 230, 231
murder, 92, 104, 156
Murdoch, Rupert, 135
Music, 292, 300, 301, 302, 303
Mysteries, 268, 280, 281, 293, 296
mystical philosophy, 285, 294
Mysticism, 253, 269, 270, 275, 276, 280, 285, 287, 288
Mythology, 308
NAFTA, 15, 16
Napoleon, 178
nationalism, 126

Native American, 100, 110, 180, 181, 224, 250, 252
Native Americans, 110, 180, 181, 224, 250
Native American XE "Native American" s See also American Indians, 110, 180, 181, 224, 250
Nature, 48, 49
Nazi, 98
Neberdjer, 267
Nebethet, see also Nebthet, 55, 302
Nefer, 300, 302
Nefertari, Queen, 210
Nehast, 217, 281
neo-colonial, 69
neo-colonialism, 69
neo-con, 220, 224, 286
neo-conservative, 220, 224
neo-conservatives, 220
Nephthys, 55
Net, goddess, 302
Neter, 56, 271, 274, 281, 282, 285, 292, 296
Neterian, 282, 285
Neters, 31
Neteru, 56, 281, 300, 302
Netherworld, 50, 53
Nigeria, 295
Nixon, Richard, 79, 195
Noah, 20
NSA, 34, 75, 76, 97, 136, 138, 139, 232, 249
Nut, 274
Obama Administration, 33
Obama, Barack, 23, 32, 33, 107, 124, 153, 156, 157, 158, 159, 160, 168, 173, 195, 198, 199, 234
Ocean, 41, 43
Ohio, 121
Old Testament, 67
Om, 300, 301
Orion Star Constellation, 277
Orthodox, 281

Osiris, 1, 53, 55, 62, 202, 210, 274, 275, 282, 300, 302, 306
out of thin air, money, 35, 36, 69
Pain, 256
Palestinians, 120
Pan-Africanism, 308
Paul, 78, 79, 106, 128, 163, 165, 166, 226, 227, 241
Peace, 48, 195, 296
Peace (see also Hetep), 48, 195, 296
Per-aah, 66, 67
Persian Gulf, 125
Persians, 67, 293
PERT EM HERU, SEE ALSO BOOK OF THE DEAD, 275
Pharaoh, 66, 202, 208, 227, 255, 306
Philae, 274
Philosophical, 221
Philosophy, 1, 2, 6, 14, 30, 50, 54, 58, 66, 67, 68, 69, 71, 72, 73, 74, 81, 89, 91, 163, 165, 200, 201, 204, 209, 217, 219, 222, 227, 242, 256, 267, 268, 269, 270, 271, 275, 276, 279, 284, 285, 287, 288, 290, 307, 308
Physical, 221
Physiological, 221
Physiology, 221
Plato, 241, 243, 244, 246, 250
Politics, 168, 221, 241, 242
pressure, 27, 75, 82, 99, 105, 119, 163, 182, 183, 213
priests and priestesses, 66, 200, 202, 203, 208, 227, 254, 273, 282, 305
Priests and Priestesses, 268, 282
Privatization, 189, 190

Protestantism, 169
Proverbial Wisdom, 53, 295
Psychology, 221, 276
Ptah, 52, 174, 175, 276
Ptahotep, 67, 174, 175, 242, 246
Pyramid, 74
Pyramid Texts, 74
Queen, 283
Ra, 50, 51, 52, 53, 55, 58, 60, 62, 191, 210, 245, 255, 273, 300, 302, 306
race, 9, 106, 182, 186, 222, 224
racism, 114, 129, 213, 225, 296
Racism, 296
Radiation, 43
rape, 107, 173, 224
Reagan administration, 195
Reagan, Ronald, 125, 196
Reaganomics, 91
real estate market, 18
Reality, 132, 196
Realization, 270
Recession, 19
Red, 108
Reflection, 256
Relax, 303
Relaxation, 303
Religion, 267, 269, 270, 275, 276, 278, 279, 282, 283, 285, 287, 288, 300, 308
Rennenet, 52, 54
Republican Party, 229
Resentment, 93
reserve currency, 34, 35, 36, 37, 40, 69
Resurrection, 273, 275, 277, 278, 279, 282
retribution, 166
rich and powerful, 12, 35, 77, 203
Right wing, 231
RITUAL, 280
Rituals, 277
Roman, 13, 74, 188, 293
Roman Empire, 188

Romans, 293
Rome, 13, 283
Roosevelt, Franklin D., 185
Rwanda, 205
Saa (spiritual understanding faculty), 56
Sages, 54, 64, 67, 257, 267, 274, 275, 279, 284
Saints, 275
San, 106
School, 47, 103, 254
Sebai, 201, 284, 291
See also Ra-Hrakti, 50, 51, 52, 53, 55, 58, 60, 62, 191, 210, 245, 255, 273, 300, 302, 306
See Nat, 302
Self (see Ba, soul, Spirit, Universal, Ba, Neter, Heru)., 50, 53, 54, 56, 63, 64, 221, 269, 270, 272, 274, 280, 291
Self-created lifestyle, lifestyle, 21, 30, 133, 210, 225
Sema, 2, 283, 296
Set, 256, 282
Seti I, 273, 302
Setian, 256
Sex, 274
sexism, 129, 296
Sexism, 296
Shai, 52, 54
Shedy, 268
Shemsu Hor, 56
Shepherd, 202, 254
Shetaut Neter, 274, 281, 282, 285, 296, 307, 308
Shetaut Neter See also Egyptian Religion, 274, 281, 282, 285, 296, 307, 308
Silver, 17
Sirius, 277
skin, 225
slavery, 8, 92, 110, 115, 117, 119, 129, 142,

181, 189, 198, 224, 281
Slavery, 110, 120, 188
Social Security, 203
Societal philosophy, 227
Society, 6, 180, 189, 200, 221, 241
Soul, 55, 58, 63, 212, 282
South America, 43, 195
Soviet Union, 97, 98, 178
Spirit, 202, 234
Spiritual discipline, 268
SPIRITUALITY, 268, 290
Study, 44, 97, 106
Sublimation, 274
Superpower, 286
superpower mindset, 125
Superpower Syndrome, 286
Superpower Syndrome Mandatory Conflict Complex, 286
Supreme Being, 52, 56, 57, 277
Supreme Court, 196
Survival, 79
Syria, 69, 124, 125
TANTRA, 274
TANTRA YOGA, 274
Tao, 59, 241, 243, 253
Tao Te Ching, 241
Taoism, 266
Taxes, 21, 188
Television, 49, 230
Television, TV, 49
Temple, 61, 201, 274, 280
Temple of Aset, 274
Temu, 53
Ten Commandments, 168
Texas, 102, 103, 143
The Absolute, 267
The Black, 288
The God, 93, 94, 153, 201, 273
The Gods, 273
Theban Theology, 267
Thebes, 267, 273
Themis, 50
Theocracy, 286
Theology, 267, 276
Thoreau, Henry David, 126, 206

Thoth, 51
Thoughts, 64
Thoughts (see also Mind), 64
Time, 135
time and space, 54, 61, 63, 64, 218, 282
tolerance, 221
Tomb, 208, 210, 273, 302
Tomb of Seti I, 273, 302
Torture, 108
Tradition, 172
transcendental reality, 282
Tree, 295
Tree of Life, 295
Triad, 267
Trinity, 275, 302
Truth, 172, 206
Turkey, 196
Unconscious, 219
Understanding, 1, 52, 130, 282
United Kingdom, 130
United Nations, 126
United States of America, 115, 184, 185, 244, 249, 250, 286
Universal Consciousness, 274
Upanishads, 275, 293
USA, West, 6, 7, 8, 13, 15, 16, 17, 18, 19, 21, 23, 26, 28, 31, 32, 34, 35, 36, 37, 39, 40, 41, 42, 43, 47, 68, 69, 71, 74, 75, 76, 78, 80, 81, 85, 87, 88, 92, 95, 97, 98, 99, 104, 109, 110, 113, 114, 115, 116, 117, 119, 120, 123, 124, 125, 126, 127, 128, 129, 144, 152, 156, 158, 160, 161, 162, 172, 179, 182, 186, 193, 195, 196, 197, 203, 220, 232, 235, 237, 238, 244, 249
Usage, 101
Vatican, 169

Vedanta, 60
Vedic, 269
Vice, 125
Vietnam, 128
Violence, 189, 296
Wall Street, 19, 20, 34, 35, 40, 80, 87, 88, 90, 134, 149, 162, 166, 168, 173, 197
Wal-Mart, 79, 132
wars, 16, 38, 40, 42, 69, 89, 91, 92, 118, 119, 125, 128, 160, 161, 182, 206, 207, 219, 246
Waset, 267
Washington, George, 196
Wealth, Money, 19, 20, 74, 176, 228
West Bank, 120
Western, West, 52, 120, 169, 172, 173
White, 6
white people, 119
Will, 43, 157
Wisdocracy, 227
Wisdom, 31, 67, 209, 211, 227, 242, 245, 255, 271, 273, 293, 294
Wisdom (also see Djehuti, Aset), 31, 67, 209, 211, 227, 242, 245, 255, 271, 273, 293, 294
World Ba, 177
World Ba XE "World Ba" nk, 177
World Trade Center, 14, 28
World War II, 98, 164, 286
Yoga, 54, 56, 59, 266, 267, 268, 269, 270, 273, 274, 275, 276, 279, 283, 285, 287, 288, 298, 299, 300, 301, 302, 308
Yoga of Action, 56
Yogic, 287, 296
Yoruba, 295

Maat Philosophy Versus Fascism and the Police State

OTHER BOOKS FROM C M BOOKS
P.O.Box 570459
Miami, Florida, 33257
(305) 378-6253 Fax: (305) 378-6253

Prices subject to change.

1. *EGYPTIAN YOGA: THE PHILOSOPHY OF ENLIGHTENMENT* An original, fully illustrated work, including hieroglyphs, detailing the meaning of the Egyptian mysteries, tantric yoga, psycho-spiritual and physical exercises. Egyptian Yoga is a guide to the practice of the highest spiritual philosophy which leads to absolute freedom from human misery and to immortality. It is well known by scholars that Egyptian philosophy is the basis of Western and Middle Eastern religious philosophies such as *Christianity, Islam, Judaism,* the *Kabala*, and Greek philosophy, but what about Indian philosophy, Yoga and Taoism? What were the original teachings? How can they be practiced today? What is the source of pain and suffering in the world and what is the solution? Discover the deepest mysteries of the mind and universe within and outside of your self. 8.5" X 11" ISBN: 1-884564-01-1 Soft $19.95

Maat Philosophy Versus Fascism and the Police State

2. *EGYPTIAN YOGA: African Religion Volume 2-* Theban Theology U.S. In this long awaited sequel to *Egyptian Yoga: The Philosophy of Enlightenment* you will take a fascinating and enlightening journey back in time and discover the teachings which constituted the epitome of Ancient Egyptian spiritual wisdom. What are the disciplines which lead to the fulfillment of all desires? Delve into the three states of consciousness (waking, dream and deep sleep) and the fourth state which transcends them all, Neberdjer, "The Absolute." These teachings of the city of Waset (Thebes) were the crowning achievement of the Sages of Ancient Egypt. They establish the standard mystical keys for understanding the profound mystical symbolism of the Triad of human consciousness. ISBN 1-884564-39-9 $23.95

3. *THE KEMETIC DIET: GUIDE TO HEALTH, DIET AND FASTING* Health issues have always been important to human beings since the beginning of time. The earliest records of history show that the art of healing was held in high esteem since the time of Ancient Egypt. In the early 20th century, medical doctors had almost attained the status of sainthood by the promotion of the idea that they alone were "scientists" while other healing modalities and traditional healers who did not follow the "scientific method' were nothing but superstitious, ignorant charlatans who at best would take the money of their clients and at worst kill them with the unscientific "snake oils" and "irrational theories". In the late 20th century, the failure of the modern medical establishment's ability to lead the general public to good health, promoted the move by many in society towards "alternative medicine". Alternative medicine disciplines are those healing modalities which do not adhere to the philosophy of allopathic medicine. Allopathic medicine is what medical doctors practice by an large. It is the theory that disease is caused by agencies outside the body such as bacteria, viruses or physical means which affect the body. These can therefore be treated by medicines and therapies The natural healing method began in the absence of extensive technologies with the idea that all the answers for health may be found in nature or rather, the deviation from nature. Therefore, the health of the body can be restored by correcting the aberration and thereby restoring balance. This is the area that will be covered in this volume. Allopathic techniques have their place in the art of healing. However, we should not forget that the body is a grand achievement of the spirit and built into it is the capacity to maintain itself and heal itself. Ashby, Muata ISBN: 1-884564-49-6 $28.95

4. INITIATION INTO EGYPTIAN YOGA Shedy: Spiritual discipline or program, to go deeply into the mysteries, to study the mystery teachings and literature profoundly, to penetrate the mysteries. You will learn about the mysteries of initiation into the teachings and practice of Yoga and how to become an Initiate of the mystical sciences. This insightful manual is the first in a series which introduces you to the goals of daily spiritual and yoga practices: Meditation, Diet, Words of Power and the ancient wisdom teachings. 8.5" X 11" ISBN 1-884564-02-X   Soft Cover $24.95 U.S.

5. *THE AFRICAN ORIGINS OF CIVILIZATION, RELIGION AND YOGA SPIRITUALITY AND ETHICS PHILOSOPHY* HARD COVER EDITION Part 1, Part 2, Part 3 in one volume 683 Pages Hard Cover First Edition Three volumes in one. Over the past several years I have been asked to put together in one volume the most important evidences showing the correlations and common teachings between Kamitan (Ancient Egyptian) culture and religion and that of India. The questions of the history of Ancient Egypt, and the latest archeological evidences showing civilization and culture in Ancient Egypt and its spread to other countries, has intrigued many scholars as well as mystics over the years. Also, the possibility that Ancient Egyptian Priests and Priestesses migrated to Greece, India and other countries to carry on the traditions of the Ancient Egyptian Mysteries, has been speculated over the years as well. In chapter 1 of the book *Egyptian Yoga The Philosophy of Enlightenment,* 1995, I first introduced the deepest comparison between Ancient Egypt and India that had been brought forth up

to that time. Now, in the year 2001 this new book, *THE AFRICAN ORIGINS OF CIVILIZATION, MYSTICAL RELIGION AND YOGA PHILOSOPHY,* more fully explores the motifs, symbols and philosophical correlations between Ancient Egyptian and Indian mysticism and clearly shows not only that Ancient Egypt and India were connected culturally but also spiritually. How does this knowledge help the spiritual aspirant? This discovery has great importance for the Yogis and mystics who follow the philosophy of Ancient Egypt and the mysticism of India. It means that India has a longer history and heritage than was previously understood. It shows that the mysteries of Ancient Egypt were essentially a yoga tradition which did not die but rather developed into the modern day systems of Yoga technology of India. It further shows that African culture developed Yoga Mysticism earlier than any other civilization in history. All of this expands our understanding of the unity of culture and the deep legacy of Yoga, which stretches into the distant past, beyond the Indus Valley civilization, the earliest known high culture in India as well as the Vedic tradition of Aryan culture. Therefore, Yoga culture and mysticism is the oldest known tradition of spiritual development and Indian mysticism is an extension of the Ancient Egyptian mysticism. By understanding the legacy which Ancient Egypt gave to India the mysticism of India is better understood and by comprehending the heritage of Indian Yoga, which is rooted in Ancient Egypt the Mysticism of Ancient Egypt is also better understood. This expanded understanding allows us to prove the underlying kinship of humanity, through the common symbols, motifs and philosophies which are not disparate and confusing teachings but in reality expressions of the same study of truth through metaphysics and mystical realization of Self. (HARD COVER) ISBN: 1-884564-50-X $45.00 U.S. 8 1/2" X 11"

6. *AFRICAN ORIGINS BOOK 1 PART 1* African Origins of African Civilization, Religion, Yoga Mysticism and Ethics Philosophy-<u>Soft Cover</u> $24.95 ISBN: 1-884564-55-0

7. *AFRICAN ORIGINS BOOK 2 PART 2* African Origins of Western Civilization, Religion and Philosophy (Soft) -<u>Soft Cover</u> $24.95 ISBN: 1-884564-56-9

Maat Philosophy Versus Fascism and the Police State

8.   EGYPT AND INDIA AFRICAN ORIGINS OF *Eastern Civilization, Religion, Yoga Mysticism and Philosophy*-<u>Soft Cover</u> $29.95 (Soft) ISBN: 1-884564-57-7

9.   THE MYSTERIES OF ISIS: **The Ancient Egyptian Philosophy of Self-Realization** - There are several paths to discover the Divine and the mysteries of the higher Self. This volume details the mystery teachings of the goddess Aset (Isis) from Ancient Egypt- the path of wisdom. It includes the teachings of her temple and the disciplines that are enjoined for the initiates of the temple of Aset as they were given in ancient times. Also, this book includes the teachings of the main myths of Aset that lead a human being to spiritual enlightenment and immortality. Through the study of ancient myth and the illumination of initiatic understanding the idea of God is expanded from the mythological comprehension to the metaphysical. Then this metaphysical understanding is related to you, the student, so as to begin understanding your true divine nature. ISBN 1-884564-24-0 $22.99

Maat Philosophy Versus Fascism and the Police State

10. *EGYPTIAN PROVERBS:* collection of —Ancient Egyptian Proverbs and Wisdom Teachings -How to live according to MAAT Philosophy. Beginning Meditation. All proverbs are indexed for easy searches. For the first time in one volume, ——Ancient Egyptian Proverbs, wisdom teachings and meditations, fully illustrated with hieroglyphic text and symbols. EGYPTIAN PROVERBS is a unique collection of knowledge and wisdom which you can put into practice today and transform your life. $14.95 U.S   ISBN: 1-884564-00-3

11. *GOD OF LOVE: THE PATH OF DIVINE LOVE The Process of Mystical Transformation and The Path of Divine Love*   This Volume focuses on the ancient wisdom teachings of "Neter Merri" –the Ancient Egyptian philosophy of Divine Love and how to use them in a scientific process for self-transformation. Love is one of the most powerful human emotions. It is also the source of Divine feeling that unifies God and the individual human being. When love is fragmented and diminished by egoism the Divine connection is lost. The Ancient tradition of Neter Merri leads human beings back to their Divine connection, allowing them to discover their innate glorious self that is actually Divine and immortal. This volume will detail the process of transformation from ordinary consciousness to cosmic consciousness through the integrated practice of the teachings and the path of Devotional Love toward the Divine. 5.5"x 8.5" ISBN 1-884564-11-9 $22.95

12. *INTRODUCTION TO MAAT PHILOSOPHY: Spiritual Enlightenment Through the Path of Virtue*   Known commonly as Karma in India, the teachings of MAAT contain an

extensive philosophy based on ariu (deeds) and their fructification in the form of shai and renenet (fortune and destiny, leading to Meskhenet (fate in a future birth) for living virtuously and with orderly wisdom are explained and the student is to begin practicing the precepts of Maat in daily life so as to promote the process of purification of the heart in preparation for the judgment of the soul. This judgment will be understood not as an event that will occur at the time of death but as an event that occurs continuously, at every moment in the life of the individual. The student will learn how to become allied with the forces of the Higher Self and to thereby begin cleansing the mind (heart) of impurities so as to attain a higher vision of reality. ISBN 1-884564-20-8 $22.99

13. *MEDITATION The Ancient Egyptian Path to Enlightenment*   Many people do not know about the rich history of meditation practice in Ancient Egypt. This volume outlines the theory of meditation and presents the Ancient Egyptian Hieroglyphic text which give instruction as to the nature of the mind and its three modes of expression. It also presents the texts which give instruction on the practice of meditation for spiritual Enlightenment and unity with the Divine. This volume allows the reader to begin practicing meditation by explaining, in easy to understand terms, the simplest form of meditation and working up to the most advanced form which was practiced in ancient times and which is still practiced by yogis around the world in modern times. ISBN 1-884564-27-7 $22.99

14. *THE GLORIOUS LIGHT MEDITATION* TECHNIQUE OF ANCIENT EGYPT New for the year 2000. This volume is based on the earliest known instruction in history given for the practice

of formal meditation. Discovered by Dr. Muata Ashby, it is inscribed on the walls of the Tomb of Seti I in Thebes Egypt. This volume details the philosophy and practice of this unique system of meditation originated in Ancient Egypt and the earliest practice of meditation known in the world which occurred in the most advanced African Culture. ISBN: 1-884564-15-1 $16.95 (PB)

15. *THE SERPENT POWER: The Ancient Egyptian Mystical Wisdom of the Inner Life Force.* This Volume specifically deals with the latent life Force energy of the universe and in the human body, its control and sublimation. How to develop the Life Force energy of the subtle body. This Volume will introduce the esoteric wisdom of the science of how virtuous living acts in a subtle and mysterious way to cleanse the latent psychic energy conduits and vortices of the spiritual body. ISBN 1-884564-19-4 $22.95

16. *EGYPTIAN YOGA The Postures of The Gods and Goddesses* Discover the physical postures and exercises practiced thousands of years ago in Ancient Egypt which are today known as Yoga exercises. Discover the history of the postures and how they were transferred from Ancient Egypt in Africa to India through Buddhist Tantrism. Then practice the postures as you discover the mythic teaching that originally gave birth to the postures and was practiced by the Ancient Egyptian priests and priestesses. This work is based on the pictures and teachings from the Creation story of Ra, The Asarian Resurrection Myth and the carvings and reliefs from various Temples in Ancient Egypt 8.5" X 11" ISBN 1-884564-10-0 Soft Cover $21.95 Exercise video $20

17. *SACRED SEXUALITY: ANCIENT EGYPTIAN TANTRA YOGA: The Art of Sex* Sublimation and Universal Consciousness This Volume will expand on the male and female principles within the human body and in the universe and further detail the sublimation of sexual energy into spiritual energy. The student will study the deities Min and Hathor, Asar and Aset, Geb and Nut and discover the mystical implications for a practical spiritual discipline. This Volume will also focus on the Tantric aspects of Ancient Egyptian and Indian mysticism, the purpose of sex and the mystical teachings of sexual sublimation which lead to self-knowledge and Enlightenment. ISBN 1-884564-03-8 $24.95

18. *AFRICAN RELIGION Volume 4: ASARIAN THEOLOGY: RESURRECTING OSIRIS* The path of Mystical Awakening and the Keys to Immortality NEW REVISED AND EXPANDED EDITION! The Ancient Sages created stories based on human and superhuman beings whose struggles, aspirations, needs and desires ultimately lead them to discover their true Self. The myth of Aset, Asar and Heru is no exception in this area. While there is no one source where the entire story may be found, pieces of it are inscribed in various ancient Temples walls, tombs, steles and papyri. For the first time available, the complete myth of Asar, Aset and Heru has been compiled from original Ancient Egyptian, Greek and Coptic Texts. This epic myth has been richly illustrated with reliefs from the Temple of Heru at Edfu, the Temple of Aset at Philae, the Temple of Asar at Abydos, the Temple of Hathor at Denderah and various papyri, inscriptions and reliefs. Discover the myth which inspired the teachings of the *Shetaut Neter* (Egyptian Mystery System - Egyptian Yoga) and the Egyptian Book of Coming Forth By Day. Also,

discover the three levels of Ancient Egyptian Religion, how to understand the mysteries of the Duat or Astral World and how to discover the abode of the Supreme in the Amenta, *The Other World* The ancient religion of Asar, Aset and Heru, if properly understood, contains all of the elements necessary to lead the sincere aspirant to attain immortality through inner self-discovery. This volume presents the entire myth and explores the main mystical themes and rituals associated with the myth for understating human existence, creation and the way to achieve spiritual emancipation - *Resurrection.* The Asarian myth is so powerful that it influenced and is still having an effect on the major world religions. Discover the origins and mystical meaning of the Christian Trinity, the Eucharist ritual and the ancient origin of the birthday of Jesus Christ. Soft Cover ISBN: 1-884564-27-5 $24.95

19. *THE EGYPTIAN BOOK OF THE DEAD MYSTICISM OF THE PERT EM HERU* " I Know myself, I know myself, I am One With God!–From the Pert Em Heru "The Ru Pert em Heru" or "Ancient Egyptian Book of The Dead," or "Book of Coming Forth By Day" as it is more popularly known, has fascinated the world since the successful translation of Ancient Egyptian hieroglyphic scripture over 150 years ago. The astonishing writings in it reveal that the Ancient Egyptians believed in life after death and in an ultimate destiny to discover the Divine. The elegance and aesthetic beauty of the hieroglyphic text itself has inspired many see it as an art form in and of itself. But is there more to it than that? Did the Ancient Egyptian wisdom contain more than just aphorisms and hopes of eternal life beyond death? In this volume Dr. Muata Ashby, the author of over 25 books on Ancient Egyptian Yoga Philosophy has produced a new translation of the original texts which uncovers a mystical teaching underlying the sayings and rituals instituted by the Ancient Egyptian Sages and Saints. "Once the philosophy of Ancient Egypt is understood as a mystical tradition instead of as a religion or primitive mythology, it reveals its secrets which if practiced today will lead anyone to discover the glory of spiritual self-discovery. The Pert em Heru is in every way comparable to the Indian Upanishads or the Tibetan Book of the Dead." ? $28.95 ISBN# 1-884564-28-3 Size: 8½" X 11

20. *African Religion VOL. 1- ANUNIAN THEOLOGY THE MYSTERIES OF RA* The Philosophy of Anu and The Mystical Teachings of The Ancient Egyptian Creation Myth Discover the mystical teachings contained in the Creation Myth and the gods and goddesses who brought creation and human beings into existence. The Creation myth of Anu is the source of Anunian Theology but also of the other main theological systems of Ancient Egypt that also influenced other world religions including Christianity, Hinduism and Buddhism. The Creation Myth holds the key to understanding the universe and for attaining spiritual Enlightenment. ISBN: 1-884564-38-0 $19.95

21. *African Religion VOL 3: Memphite Theology: MYSTERIES OF MIND* Mystical Psychology & Mental Health for Enlightenment and Immortality based on the Ancient Egyptian Philosophy of Menefer -Mysticism of Ptah, Egyptian Physics and Yoga Metaphysics and the Hidden properties of Matter. This volume uncovers the mystical psychology of the Ancient Egyptian wisdom teachings centering on the philosophy of the Ancient Egyptian city of Menefer (Memphite Theology). How to understand the mind and how to control the senses and lead the mind to health, clarity and mystical self-discovery. This Volume will also go deeper into the philosophy of God as creation and will explore the concepts of modern science and how they correlate with ancient teachings. This Volume will lay the ground work for the understanding of the philosophy of universal consciousness and the initiatic/yogic insight into who or what is God? ISBN 1-884564-07-0 $22.95

Maat Philosophy Versus Fascism and the Police State

22. *AFRICAN RELIGION VOLUME 5: THE GODDESS AND THE EGYPTIAN MYSTERIESTHE PATH OF THE GODDESS THE GODDESS PATH* The Secret Forms of the Goddess and the Rituals of Resurrection The Supreme Being may be worshipped as father or as mother. *Ushet Rekhat* or *Mother Worship*, is the spiritual process of worshipping the Divine in the form of the Divine Goddess. It celebrates the most important forms of the Goddess including *Nathor, Maat, Aset, Arat, Amentet and Hathor* and explores their mystical meaning as well as the rising of *Sirius,* the star of Aset (Aset) and the new birth of Hor (Heru). The end of the year is a time of reckoning, reflection and engendering a new or renewed positive movement toward attaining spiritual Enlightenment. The Mother Worship devotional meditation ritual, performed on five days during the month of December and on New Year's Eve, is based on the Ushet Rekhit. During the ceremony, the cosmic forces, symbolized by Sirius - and the constellation of Orion ---, are harnessed through the understanding and devotional attitude of the participant. This propitiation draws the light of wisdom and health to all those who share in the ritual, leading to prosperity and wisdom. $14.95 ISBN 1-884564-18-6

23. *THE MYSTICAL JOURNEY FROM JESUS TO CHRIST* Discover the ancient Egyptian origins of Christianity before the Catholic Church and learn the mystical teachings given by Jesus to assist all humanity in becoming Christlike. Discover the secret meaning of the Gospels that were discovered in Egypt. Also discover how and why so many Christian churches came into being. Discover that the Bible still holds the keys to mystical

Maat Philosophy Versus Fascism and the Police State

realization even though its original writings were changed by the church. Discover how to practice the original teachings of Christianity which leads to the Kingdom of Heaven. $24.95   ISBN# 1-884564-05-4 size: 8½" X 11"

24.   *THE STORY OF ASAR, ASET AND HERU:* An Ancient Egyptian Legend (For Children) Now for the first time, the most ancient myth of Ancient Egypt comes alive for children. Inspired by the books *The Asarian Resurrection: The Ancient Egyptian Bible* and *The Mystical Teachings of The Asarian Resurrection, The Story of Asar, Aset and Heru* is an easy to understand and thrilling tale which inspired the children of Ancient Egypt to aspire to greatness and righteousness. If you and your child have enjoyed stories like *The Lion King* and *Star Wars you will love The Story of Asar, Aset and Heru.* Also, if you know the story of Jesus and Krishna you will discover than Ancient Egypt had a similar myth and that this myth carries important spiritual teachings for living a fruitful and fulfilling life. This book may be used along with *The Parents Guide To The Asarian Resurrection Myth: How to Teach Yourself and Your Child the Principles of Universal Mystical Religion.* The guide provides some background to the Asarian Resurrection myth and it also gives insight into the mystical teachings contained in it which you may introduce to your child. It is designed for parents who wish to grow spiritually with their children and it serves as an introduction for those who would like to study the Asarian Resurrection Myth in depth and to practice its teachings. 8.5" X 11"   ISBN: 1-884564-31-3 $12.95

Maat Philosophy Versus Fascism and the Police State

25. *THE PARENTS GUIDE TO THE AUSARIAN RESURRECTION MYTH:* How to Teach Yourself and Your Child the Principles of Universal Mystical Religion. This insightful manual brings for the timeless wisdom of the ancient through the Ancient Egyptian myth of Asar, Aset and Heru and the mystical teachings contained in it for parents who want to guide their children to understand and practice the teachings of mystical spirituality. This manual may be used with the children's storybook *The Story of Asar, Aset and Heru* by Dr. Muata Abhaya Ashby. ISBN: 1-884564-30-5 $16.95

26. *HEALING THE CRIMINAL HEART.* Introduction to Maat Philosophy, Yoga and Spiritual Redemption Through the Path of Virtue   Who is a criminal? Is there such a thing as a criminal heart? What is the source of evil and sinfulness and is there any way to rise above it? Is there redemption for those who have committed sins, even the worst crimes?   Ancient Egyptian mystical psychology holds important answers to these questions. Over ten thousand years ago mystical psychologists, the Sages of Ancient Egypt, studied and charted the human mind and spirit and laid out a path which will lead to spiritual redemption, prosperity and Enlightenment.   This introductory volume brings forth the teachings of the Asarian Resurrection, the most important myth of Ancient Egypt, with relation to the faults of human existence: anger, hatred, greed, lust, animosity, discontent, ignorance, egoism jealousy, bitterness, and a myriad of psycho-spiritual ailments which keep a human being in a state of negativity and adversity   ISBN: 1-884564-17-8 $15.95

27. *TEMPLE RITUAL OF THE ANCIENT EGYPTIAN MYSTERIES--THEATER & DRAMA OF THE ANCIENT EGYPTIAN MYSTERIES*: Details the practice of the mysteries and ritual program of the temple and the philosophy an practice of the ritual of the mysteries, its purpose and execution. Featuring the Ancient Egyptian stage play-"The Enlightenment of Hathor' Based on an Ancient Egyptian Drama, The original Theater -Mysticism of the Temple of Hetheru 1-884564-14-3 $19.95 By Dr. Muata Ashby

28. *GUIDE TO PRINT ON DEMAND: SELF-PUBLISH FOR PROFIT, SPIRITUAL FULFILLMENT AND SERVICE TO HUMANITY* Everyone asks us how we produced so many books in such a short time. Here are the secrets to writing and producing books that uplift humanity and how to

get them printed for a fraction of the regular cost. Anyone can become an author even if they have limited funds. All that is necessary is the willingness to learn how the printing and book business work and the desire to follow the special instructions given here for preparing your manuscript format. Then you take your work directly to the non-traditional companies who can produce your books for less than the traditional book printer can. ISBN: 1-884564-40-2 $16.95 U. S.

29.   *Egyptian Mysteries: Vol. 1,* Shetaut Neter What are the Mysteries? For thousands of years the spiritual tradition of Ancient Egypt, *Shetaut Neter,* "The Egyptian Mysteries," "The Secret Teachings," have fascinated, tantalized and amazed the world. At one time exalted and recognized as the highest culture of the world, by Africans, Europeans, Asiatics, Hindus, Buddhists and other cultures of the ancient world, in time it was shunned by the emerging orthodox world religions. Its temples desecrated, its philosophy maligned, its tradition spurned, its philosophy dormant in the mystical *Medu Neter*, the mysterious hieroglyphic texts which hold the secret symbolic meaning that has scarcely been discerned up to now. What are the secrets of *Nehast* {spiritual awakening and emancipation, resurrection}. More than just a literal translation, this volume is for awakening to the secret code *Shetitu* of the teaching which was not deciphered by Egyptologists, nor could be understood by ordinary spiritualists. This book is a reinstatement of the original science made available for our times, to the reincarnated followers of Ancient Egyptian culture and the prospect of spiritual freedom to break the bonds of *Khemn,* "ignorance," and slavery to evil forces: *Såaa* . ISBN: 1-884564-41-0 $19.99

30.   *EGYPTIAN MYSTERIES VOL 2:* Dictionary of Gods and Goddesses This book is about the mystery of neteru, the gods and goddesses of Ancient Egypt (Kamit, Kemet). Neteru

Maat Philosophy Versus Fascism and the Police State

means "Gods and Goddesses." But the Neterian teaching of Neteru represents more than the usual limited modern day concept of "divinities" or "spirits." The Neteru of Kamit are also metaphors, cosmic principles and vehicles for the enlightening teachings of Shetaut Neter (Ancient Egyptian-African Religion). Actually they are the elements for one of the most advanced systems of spirituality ever conceived in human history. Understanding the concept of neteru provides a firm basis for spiritual evolution and the pathway for viable culture, peace on earth and a healthy human society. Why is it important to have gods and goddesses in our lives? In order for spiritual evolution to be possible, once a human being has accepted that there is existence after death and there is a transcendental being who exists beyond time and space knowledge, human beings need a connection to that which transcends the ordinary experience of human life in time and space and a means to understand the transcendental reality beyond the mundane reality. ISBN: 1-884564-23-2 $21.95

31.   *EGYPTIAN MYSTERIES VOL. 3* The Priests and Priestesses of Ancient Egypt This volume details the path of Neterian priesthood, the joys, challenges and rewards of advanced Neterian life, the teachings that allowed the priests and priestesses to manage the most long lived civilization in human history and how that path can be adopted today; for those who want to tread the path of the Clergy of Shetaut Neter. ISBN: 1-884564-53-4 $24.95

32.   *The War of Heru and Set:* The Struggle of Good and Evil for Control of the World and The Human Soul This volume contains a novelized version of the Asarian Resurrection myth that is based on the actual scriptures presented in the Book Asarian Religion (old name –Resurrecting Osiris). This volume is prepared in the form of a screenplay and can be easily adapted to be used as a stage play. Spiritual seeking is a mythic journey that has many emotional highs and lows, ecstasies and depressions, victories and

frustrations. This is the War of Life that is played out in the myth as the struggle of Heru and Set and those are mythic characters that represent the human Higher and Lower self. How to understand the war and emerge victorious in the journey o life? The ultimate victory and fulfillment can be experienced, which is not changeable or lost in time. The purpose of myth is to convey the wisdom of life through the story of divinities who show the way to overcome the challenges and foibles of life. In this volume the feelings and emotions of the characters of the myth have been highlighted to show the deeply rich texture of the Ancient Egyptian myth. This myth contains deep spiritual teachings and insights into the nature of self, of God and the mysteries of life and the means to discover the true meaning of life and thereby achieve the true purpose of life. To become victorious in the battle of life means to become the King (or Queen) of Egypt.Have you seen movies like The Lion King, Hamlet, The Odyssey, or The Little Buddha? These have been some of the most popular movies in modern times. The Sema Institute of Yoga is dedicated to researching and presenting the wisdom and culture of ancient Africa. The Script is designed to be produced as a motion picture but may be addapted for the theater as well. $21.95   copyright 1998 By Dr. Muata Ashby ISBN 1-8840564-44-5

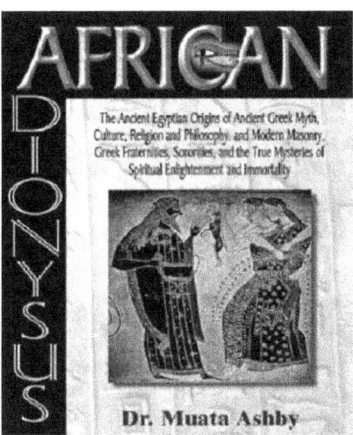

33. *AFRICAN DIONYSUS: FROM EGYPT TO GREECE:* The Kamitan Origins of Greek Culture and Religion ISBN: 1-884564-47-X   FROM EGYPT TO GREECE   This insightful manual is a reference to Ancient Egyptian mythology and philosophy and its correlation to what later became known as Greek and Rome mythology and philosophy. It outlines the basic tenets of the mythologies and shoes the ancient origins of Greek culture in Ancient Egypt. This volume also documents the origins of the Greek alphabet in Egypt as well as Greek religion, myth and philosophy of the gods and goddesses from Egypt from the myth of Atlantis and archaic period with the Minoans to the Classical period. This volume also acts as a resource for Colleges students who would like to set up fraternities and sororities based on the original Ancient Egyptian principles of Sheti and Maat philosophy. ISBN: 1-884564-47-X $22.95 U.S.

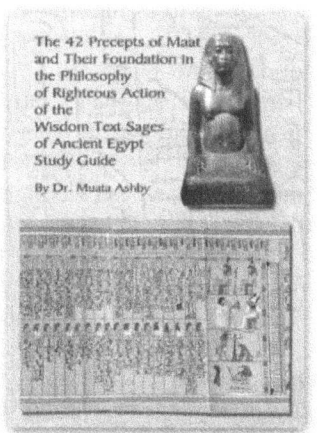

34.   *THE FORTY TWO PRECEPTS OF MAAT, THE PHILOSOPHY OF RIGHTEOUS ACTION AND THE ANCIENT EGYPTIAN WISDOM TEXTS* <u>ADVANCED STUDIES</u>
This manual is designed for use with the 1998 Maat Philosophy Class conducted by Dr. Muata Ashby. This is a detailed study of Maat Philosophy. It contains a compilation of the 42 laws or precepts of Maat and the corresponding principles which they represent along with the teachings of the ancient Egyptian Sages relating to each. Maat philosophy was the basis of Ancient Egyptian society and government as well as the heart of Ancient Egyptian myth and spirituality. Maat is at once a goddess, a cosmic force and a living social doctrine, which promotes social harmony and thereby paves the way for spiritual evolution in all levels of society. ISBN: 1-884564-48-8 $16.95 U.S.

35.   THE SECRET LOTUS: Poetry of Enlightenment
Discover the mystical sentiment of the Kemetic teaching as expressed through the poetry of Sebai Muata Ashby. The teaching of spiritual awakening is uniquely experienced when the poetic sensibility is present. This first volume contains the poems written between 1996 and 2003. **1-884564--16 -X $16.99**

Maat Philosophy Versus Fascism and the Police State

36. The Ancient Egyptian Buddha: The Ancient Egyptian Origins of Buddhism

This book is a compilation of several sections of a larger work, a book by the name of African Origins of Civilization, Religion, Yoga Mysticism and Ethics Philosophy. It also contains some additional evidences not contained in the larger work that demonstrate the correlation between Ancient Egyptian Religion and Buddhism. This book is one of several compiled short volumes that has been compiled so as to facilitate access to specific subjects contained in the larger work which is over 680 pages long. These short and small volumes have been specifically designed to cover one subject in a brief and low cost format. This present volume, The Ancient Egyptian Buddha: The Ancient Egyptian Origins of Buddhism, formed one subject in the larger work; actually it was one chapter of the larger work. However, this volume has some new additional evidences and comparisons of Buddhist and Neterian (Ancient Egyptian) philosophies not previously discussed. It was felt that this subject needed to be discussed because even in the early 21st century, the idea persists that Buddhism originated only in India independently. Yet there is ample evidence from ancient writings and perhaps more importantly, iconographical evidences from the Ancient Egyptians and early Buddhists themselves that prove otherwise. This handy volume has been designed to be accessible to young adults and all others who would like to have an easy reference with documentation on this important subject. This is an important subject because the frame of reference with which we look at a culture depends strongly on our conceptions about its origins. in this case, if we look at the Buddhism as an Asiatic religion we would treat it and it's culture in one way. If we id as African [Ancient Egyptian] we not only would see it in a different light but we also must ascribe Africa with a glorious legacy that matches any other culture in human history and gave rise to one of the present day most important religious philosophies. We would also look at the culture and philosophies of the Ancient Egyptians as having African insights that offer us greater depth into the Buddhist philosophies. Those insights inform our knowledge about other African traditions and we can also begin to understand in a deeper way the effect of Ancient Egyptian culture on African culture and also on the Asiatic as well. We would also be able to discover the glorious and wondrous teaching of mystical philosophy that Ancient Egyptian Shetaut Neter religion offers, that is as powerful as any other mystic system of spiritual philosophy in the world today. ISBN: 1-884564-61-5 $28.95

Maat Philosophy Versus Fascism and the Police State

37. The Death of American Empire: Neo-conservatism, Theocracy, Economic Imperialism, Environmental Disaster and the Collapse of Civilization

This work is a collection of essays relating to social and economic, leadership, and ethics, ecological and religious issues that are facing the world today in order to understand the course of history that has led humanity to its present condition and then arrive at positive solutions that will lead to better outcomes for all humanity. It surveys the development and decline of major empires throughout history and focuses on the creation of American Empire along with the social, political and economic policies that led to the prominence of the United States of America as a Superpower including the rise of the political control of the neo-con political philosophy including militarism and the military industrial complex in American politics and the rise of the religious right into and American Theocracy movement. This volume details, through historical and current events, the psychology behind the dominance of western culture in world politics through the "Superpower Syndrome Mandatory Conflict Complex" that drives the Superpower culture to establish itself above all others and then act hubristically to dominate world culture through legitimate influences as well as coercion, media censorship and misinformation leading to international hegemony and world conflict. This volume also details the financial policies that gave rise to American prominence in the global economy, especially after World War II, and promoted American preeminence over the world economy through Globalization as well as the environmental policies, including the oil economy, that are promoting degradation of the world ecology and contribute to the decline of America as an Empire culture. This volume finally explores the factors pointing to the decline of the American Empire economy and imperial power and what to expect in the aftermath of American prominence and how to survive the decline while at the same time promoting policies and social-economic-religious-political changes that are needed in order to promote the emergence of a beneficial and sustainable culture. **$25.95soft** 1-884564-25-9, Hard Cover **$29.95** 1-884564-45-3

38. The African Origins of Hatha Yoga: And its Ancient Mystical Teaching

The subject of this present volume, The Ancient Egyptian Origins of Yoga Postures, formed one subject in the larger works, African Origins of Civilization Religion, Yoga Mysticism and Ethics Philosophy and the Book Egypt and India is the section of the book African Origins of Civilization. Those works contain the collection of all correlations between Ancient Egypt and India. This volume also contains some additional information not contained in the previous work. It was felt that this subject needed to be discussed more directly, being treated in one volume, as opposed to being contained in the larger work along with other subjects, because even in the early 21st century, the idea persists that the Yoga and specifically, Yoga Postures, were invented and developed only in India. The Ancient Egyptians were peoples originally from Africa who were, in ancient times, colonists in India. Therefore it is no surprise that many Indian traditions including religious and Yogic, would be found earlier in Ancient Egypt. Yet there is ample evidence from ancient writings and perhaps more importantly, iconographical evidences from the Ancient Egyptians themselves and the Indians themselves that prove the connection between Ancient Egypt and India as well as the existence of a discipline of Yoga Postures in Ancient Egypt long before its practice in India. This handy volume has been designed to be accessible to young adults and all others who would like to have an easy reference with documentation on this important subject. This is an important subject because the frame of reference with which we look at a culture depends strongly on our conceptions about its origins. In this case, if we look at the Ancient Egyptians as Asiatic peoples we would treat them and their culture in one way. If we see them as Africans we not only see them in a different light but we also must ascribe Africa with a glorious legacy that matches any other culture in human history. We would also look at the culture and philosophies of the Ancient Egyptians as having African insights instead of Asiatic ones. Those insights inform our knowledge bout other African traditions and we can also begin to understand in a deeper way the effect of Ancient Egyptian culture on African culture and also on the Asiatic as well. When we discover the deeper and more ancient practice of the postures system in Ancient Egypt that was called "Hatha Yoga" in India, we are able to find a new and expanded understanding of the practice that constitutes a discipline of spiritual practice that informs and revitalizes the Indian practices as well as all spiritual disciplines. $19.99 ISBN 1-884564-60-7

39. The Black Ancient Egyptians

This present volume, The Black Ancient Egyptians: The Black African Ancestry of the Ancient Egyptians, formed one subject in the larger work: The African Origins of Civilization, Religion, Yoga Mysticism and Ethics Philosophy. It was felt that this subject needed to be discussed because even in the early 21st century, the idea persists that the Ancient Egyptians were peoples originally from Asia Minor who came into North-East Africa. Yet there is ample evidence from ancient writings and perhaps more importantly, iconographical evidences from the Ancient Egyptians themselves that proves otherwise. This handy volume has been designed to be accessible to young adults and all others who would like to have an easy reference with documentation on this important subject. This is an important subject because the frame of reference with which we look at a culture depends strongly on our conceptions about its origins. in this case, if we look at the Ancient Egyptians as Asiatic peoples we would treat them and their culture in one way. If we see them as Africans we not only see them in a different light but we also must ascribe Africa with a glorious legacy that matches any other culture in human history. We would also look at the culture and philosophies of the Ancient Egyptians as having African insights instead of Asiatic ones. Those insights inform our knowledge bout other African traditions and we can also begin to understand in a deeper way the effect of Ancient Egyptian culture on African culture and also on the Asiatic as well. ISBN 1-884564-21-6 $19.99

40. The Limits of Faith: The Failure of Faith-based Religions and the Solution to the Meaning of Life

Is faith belief in something without proof? And if so is there never to be any proof or discovery? If so what is the need of intellect? If faith is trust in something that is real is that reality historical, literal or metaphorical or philosophical? If knowledge is an essential element in faith why should there by so much emphasis on believing and not on understanding in the modern practice of religion? This volume is a compilation of essays related to the nature of religious faith in the context of its inception in human history as well as its meaning for religious practice and relations between religions in modern times. Faith has come to be regarded as a virtuous goal in life. However, many people have asked how can it be that an endeavor that is supposed to be dedicated to spiritual upliftment has led to more conflict in human history than any other social factor? ISBN 1884564631 SOFT COVER - $19.99, ISBN 1884564623 HARD COVER - $28.95

41. Redemption of The Criminal Heart Through Kemetic Spirituality and Maat Philosophy

Special book dedicated to inmates, their families and members of the Law Enforcement community. ISBN: 1-884564-70-4
$5.00

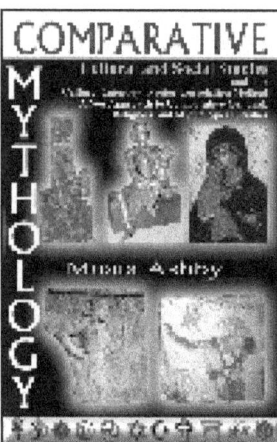

42. COMPARATIVE MYTHOLOGY

What are Myth and Culture and what is their importance for understanding the development of societies, human evolution and the search for meaning? What is the purpose of culture and how do cultures evolve? What are the elements of a culture and how can those elements be broken down and the constituent parts of a culture understood and compared? How do cultures interact? How does enculturation occur and how do people interact with other cultures? How do the processes of acculturation and cooptation occur and what does this mean for the development of a society? How can the study of myths and the elements of culture help in understanding the meaning of life and the means to promote understanding and peace in the world of human activity? This volume is the exposition of a method for studying and comparing cultures, myths and other social aspects of a society. It is an expansion on the Cultural Category Factor Correlation method for studying and comparing myths, cultures, religions and other aspects of human culture. It was originally introduced in the year 2002. This volume contains an expanded treatment as well as several refinements along with examples of the application of the method. the apparent. I hope you enjoy these art renditions as serene reflections of the mysteries of life.
ISBN: 1-884564-72-0
Book price $21.95

43. CONVERSATION WITH GOD: Revelations of the Important Questions of Life
$24.99 U.S.

This volume contains a grouping of some of the questions that have been submitted to Sebai Dr. Muata Ashby. They are efforts by many aspirants to better understand and practice the teachings of mystical spirituality. It is said that when sages are asked spiritual questions they are relaying the wisdom of God, the Goddess, the Higher Self, etc. There is a very special quality about the Q & A process that does not occur during a regular lecture session. Certain points come out that would not come out otherwise due to the nature of the process which ideally occurs after a lecture. Having been to a certain degree enlightened by a lecture certain new questions arise and the answers to these have the effect of elevating the teaching of the lecture to even higher levels. Therefore, enjoy these exchanges and may they lead you to enlightenment, peace and prosperity. Available Late Summer 2007 ISBN: 1-884564-68-2

44. MYSTIC ART PAINTINGS
(with Full Color images) This book contains a collection of the small number of paintings that I have created over the years. Some were used as early book covers and others were done simply to express certain spiritual feelings; some were created for no purpose except to express the joy

of color and the feeling of relaxed freedom. All are to elicit mystical awakening in the viewer. Writing a book on philosophy is like sculpture, the more the work is rewritten the reflections and ideas become honed and take form and become clearer and imbued with intellectual beauty. Mystic music is like meditation, a world of its own that exists about 1 inch above ground wherein the musician does not touch the ground. Mystic Graphic Art is meditation in form, color, image and reflected image which opens the door to the reality behind the apparent. I hope you enjoy these art renditions and my reflections on them as serene reflections of the mysteries of life, as visual renditions of the philosophy I have written about over the years. ISBN 1-884564-69-0 $19.95

45. **ANCIENT EGYPTIAN HIEROGLYPHS FOR BEGINNERS**
This brief guide was prepared for those inquiring about how to enter into Hieroglyphic studies on their own at home or in study groups. First of all you should know that there are a few institutions around the world which teach how to read the Hieroglyphic text but due to the nature of the study there are perhaps only a handful of people who can read fluently. It is possible for anyone with average intelligence to achieve a high level of proficiency in reading inscriptions on temples and artifacts; however, reading extensive texts is another issue entirely. However, this introduction will give you entry into those texts if assisted by dictionaries and other aids. Most Egyptologists have a basic knowledge and keep dictionaries and notes handy when it comes to dealing with more difficult texts. Medtu Neter or the Ancient Egyptian hieroglyphic language has been considered as a "Dead Language." However, dead languages have always been studied by individuals who for the most part have taught themselves through various means. This book will discuss those means and how to use them most efficiently. ISBN 1884564429 **$28.95**

Maat Philosophy Versus Fascism and the Police State

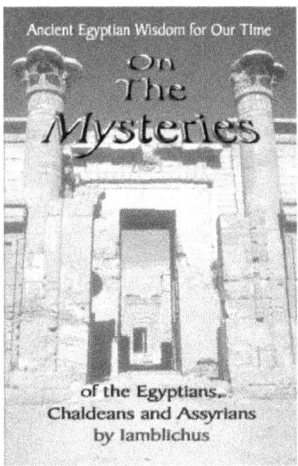

46. ON THE MYSTERIES: Wisdom of An Ancient Egyptian Sage -with Foreword by Muata Ashby
This volume, On the Mysteries, by Iamblichus (Abamun) is a unique form or scripture out of the Ancient Egyptian religious tradition. It is written in a form that is not usual or which is not usually found in the remnants of Ancient Egyptian scriptures. It is in the form of teacher and disciple, much like the Eastern scriptures such as Bhagavad Gita or the Upanishads. This form of writing may not have been necessary in Ancient times, because the format of teaching in Egypt was different prior to the conquest period by the Persians, Assyrians, Greeks and later the Romans. The question and answer format can be found but such extensive discourses and corrections of misunderstandings within the context of a teacher - disciple relationship is not usual. It therefore provides extensive insights into the times when it was written and the state of practice of Ancient Egyptian and other mystery religions. This has important implications for our times because we are today, as in the Greco-Roman period, also besieged with varied religions and new age philosophies as well as social strife and war. How can we understand our times and also make sense of the forest of spiritual traditions? How can we cut through the cacophony of religious fanaticism, and ignorance as well as misconceptions about the mysteries on the other in order to discover the true purpose of religion and the secret teachings that open up the mysteries of life and the way to enlightenment and immortality? This book, which comes to us from so long ago, offers us transcendental wisdom that applied to the world two thousand years ago as well as our world today. ISBN 1-884564-64-X $25.95

Maat Philosophy Versus Fascism and the Police State

47. The Ancient Egyptian Wisdom Texts -Compiled by Muata Ashby
The Ancient Egyptian Wisdom Texts are a genre of writings from the ancient culture that have survived to the present and provide a vibrant record of the practice of spiritual evolution otherwise known as religion or yoga philosophy in Ancient Egypt. The principle focus of the Wisdom Texts is the cultivation of understanding, peace, harmony, selfless service, self-control, Inner fulfillment and spiritual realization. When these factors are cultivated in human life, the virtuous qualities in a human being begin to manifest and sinfulness, ignorance and negativity diminish until a person is able to enter into higher consciousness, the coveted goal of all civilizations. It is this virtuous mode of life which opens the door to self-discovery and spiritual enlightenment. Therefore, the Wisdom Texts are important scriptures on the subject of human nature, spiritual psychology and mystical philosophy. The teachings presented in the Wisdom Texts form the foundation of religion as well as the guidelines for conducting the affairs of every area of social interaction including commerce, education, the army, marriage, and especially the legal system. These texts were sources for the famous 42 Precepts of Maat of the Pert M Heru (Book of the Dead), essential regulations of good conduct to develop virtue and purity in order to attain higher consciousness and immortality after death. ISBN1-884564-65-8 $18.95

48. THE KEMETIC TREE OF LIFE

Maat Philosophy Versus Fascism and the Police State

THE KEMETIC TREE OF LIFE: Newly Revealed Ancient Egyptian Cosmology and Metaphysics for Higher Consciousness The Tree of Life is a roadmap of a journey which explains how Creation came into being and how it will end. It also explains what Creation is composed of and also what human beings are and what they are composed of. It also explains the process of Creation, how Creation develops, as well as who created Creation and where that entity may be found. It also explains how a human being may discover that entity and in so doing also discover the secrets of Creation, the meaning of life and the means to break free from the pathetic condition of human limitation and mortality in order to discover the higher realms of being by discovering the principles, the levels of existence that are beyond the simple physical and material aspects of life. This book contains color plates   **ISBN: 1-884564-74-7** $27.95 U.S.

49-MATRIX OF AFRICAN PROVERBS: The Ethical and Spiritual Blueprint
This volume sets forth the fundamental principles of African ethics and their practical applications for use by individuals and organizations seeking to model their ethical policies using the Traditional African values and concepts of ethical human behavior for the proper sustenance and management of society. Furthermore, this book will provide guidance as to how the Traditional African Ethics may be viewed and applied, taking into consideration the technological and social advancements in the present. This volume also presents the principles of ethical culture, and references for each to specific injunctions from Traditional African Proverbial Wisdom Teachings. These teachings are compiled from varied Pre-colonial African societies including Yoruba, Ashanti, Kemet, Malawi, Nigeria, Ethiopia, Galla, Ghana and many more. ISBN 1-884564-77-1

50- **Growing Beyond Hate: Keys to Freedom from Discord, Racism, Sexism, Political Conflict, Class Warfare, Violence, and How to Achieve Peace and Enlightenment**---
INTRODUCTION: WHY DO WE HATE? Hatred is one of the fundamental motivating aspects of human life; the other is desire. Desire can be of a worldly nature or of a spiritual, elevating nature. Worldly desire and hatred are like two sides of the same coin in that human life is usually swaying from one to the other; but the question is why? And is there a way to satisfy the desiring or hating mind in such a way as to find peace in life? Why do human beings go to war? Why do human beings perpetrate violence against one another? And is there a way not just to understand the phenomena but to resolve the issues that plague humanity and could lead to a more harmonious society? Hatred is perhaps the greatest scourge of humanity in that it leads to misunderstanding, conflict and untold miseries of life and clashes between individuals, societies and nations. Therefore, the riddle of Hatred, that is, understanding the sources of it and how to confront, reduce and even eradicate it so as to bring forth the fulfillment in life and peace for society, should be a top priority for social scientists, spiritualists and philosophers. This book is written from the perspective of spiritual philosophy based on the mystical wisdom and sema or yoga philosophy of the Ancient Egyptians. This philosophy, originated and based in the wisdom of Shetaut Neter, the Egyptian Mysteries, and Maat, ethical way of life in society and in spirit, contains Sema-Yogic wisdom and understanding of life's predicaments that can allow a human being of any ethnic group to understand and overcome the causes of hatred, racism, sexism, violence and disharmony in life, that plague human society. ISBN: 1-884564-81-X

52. Guide to Creating a Kemetic Marriage Contract

This marital contract guide reflects actual Ancient Egyptian Principles for Kemetic Marriage as they are to be applied for our times. The marital contract allows people to have a framework with which to face the challenges of marital relations instead of relying on hopes or romantic dreams that everything will workout somehow; in other words, love is not all you need. The latter is not an evolved, mature way of handling one of the most important aspects of human life. Therefore, it behooves anyone who wishes to enter into a marriage to explore the issues, express their needs and seek to avoid costly mistakes, and resolve conflicts in the normal course of life or make sure that their rights and dignity will be protected if any eventuality should occur. Marital relations in Ancient Egypt were not like those in other countries of the time and not like those of present day countries. The extreme longevity of Ancient Egyptian society, founded in Maat philosophy, allowed the social development of marriage to evolve and progress to a high level of order and balance. Maat represents truth, righteous, justice and harmony in life. This meant that the marital partner's rights were to be protected with equal standing before the law. So there was no disparity between rights of men or rights of women. Therefore, anyone who wants to enter into a marriage based on Kemetic principles must first and foremost adhere to this standard…equality in the rights of men and women. This guide demonstrates procedures for following the Ancient Egyptian practice of formalizing marriage with a contract that spells out the important concerns of each partner in the marital relationship, based on Maatian principles [of righteous, truth, harmony and justice] so that the rights and needs of each partner may be protected within the marriage. It also allows the partners to think about issues that arise out of the marital relations so that they may have a foundation to fall back on in the event that those or other unforeseen issues arise and cause conflict in the relationship. By having a document of expressed concerns, needs and steps to be taken to address them, it is less likely that issues which affect the relationship in a negative way will arise, and when they do, they will be better handled, in a more balanced, just and amicable way.

EBOOKISBN 978-1-937016-59-3 HARDCOPYBOOKISBN: 1-884564-82-8

Maat Philosophy Versus Fascism and the Police State

MUSIC BASED ON THE PRT M HRU AND OTHER KEMETIC TEXTS

Available on Compact Disc $14.99 and Audio Cassette $9.99

Adorations to the Goddess- Vol. 1

Music for Worship of the Goddess based on the goddess teachings and words of power of Ancient Egypt

NEW Egyptian Yoga Music CD
by Sehu Maa
Ancient Egyptian Music CD

©1999 By Muata Ashby
CD $14.99 –

Maat Philosophy Versus Fascism and the Police State

MERIT'S INSPIRATION
NEW Egyptian Yoga Music CD
by Sehu Maa
Ancient Egyptian Music CD
Instrumental Music played on
reproductions of Ancient Egyptian Instruments– Ideal for meditation and
reflection on the Divine and for the practice of spiritual programs and Yoga exercise sessions.
©1999 By
Muata Ashby
CD $14.99 –
UPC# 761527100429

Maat Philosophy Versus Fascism and the Police State

ANORATIONS TO RA AND HETHERU
NEW Egyptian Yoga Music CD
By Sehu Maa (Muata Ashby)
Based on the Words of Power of Ra and HetHeru
played on reproductions of Ancient Egyptian Instruments **Ancient Egyptian Instruments used: Voice, Clapping, Nefer Lute, Tar Drum, Sistrums, Cymbals – The Chants, Devotions, Rhythms and Festive Songs Of the Neteru – Ideal for meditation, and devotional singing and dancing.**

©1999 By Muata Ashby
CD $14.99 –
UPC# 761527100221

SONGS TO ASAR ASET AND HERU
NEW
Egyptian Yoga Music CD
By Sehu Maa
played on reproductions of Ancient Egyptian Instruments– **The Chants, Devotions, Rhythms and
Festive Songs Of the Neteru - Ideal for meditation, and devotional singing and dancing.
Based on the Words of Power of Asar (Asar), Aset (Aset) and Heru (Heru)** Om Asar Aset Heru is the third in a series of musical explorations of the Kemetic (Ancient Egyptian) tradition of music. Its ideas are based on the Ancient Egyptian Religion of Asar, Aset and Heru and it is designed for listening, meditation and worship. ©1999 By Muata Ashby
CD $14.99 –
UPC# 761527100122

Maat Philosophy Versus Fascism and the Police State

HAARI OM: ANCIENT EGYPT MEETS INDIA IN MUSIC
NEW Music CD
By Sehu Maa

The Chants, Devotions, Rhythms and Festive Songs Of the Ancient Egypt and India, harmonized and played on reproductions of ancient instruments along with modern instruments and beats. Ideal for meditation, and devotional singing and dancing.

Haari Om is the fourth in a series of musical explorations of the Kemetic (Ancient Egyptian) and Indian traditions of music, chanting and devotional spiritual practice. Its ideas are based on the Ancient Egyptian Yoga spirituality and Indian Yoga spirituality.

©1999 By Muata Ashby
CD $14.99 –
UPC# 761527100528

RA AKHU: THE GLORIOUS LIGHT
NEW

Maat Philosophy Versus Fascism and the Police State

Egyptian Yoga Music CD
By Sehu Maa

The fifth collection of original music compositions based on the Teachings and Words of The Trinity, the God Asar and the Goddess Nebethet, the Divinity Aten, the God Heru, and the Special Meditation Hekau or Words of Power of Ra from the Ancient Egyptian Tomb of Seti I and more...

played on reproductions of Ancient Egyptian Instruments and modern instruments - **Ancient Egyptian Instruments used: Voice, Clapping, Nefer Lute, Tar Drum, Sistrums, Cymbals – The Chants, Devotions, Rhythms and Festive Songs Of the Neteru – Ideal for meditation, and devotional singing and dancing.**

©1999 By Muata Ashby
CD $14.99 –
UPC# 761527100825

GLORIES OF THE DIVINE MOTHER
Based on the hieroglyphic text of the worship of Goddess Net.
The Glories of The Great Mother
©2000 **Muata Ashby**
CD $14.99 UPC# 761527101129`

<u>*NEW RELEASE*</u>

Maat Philosophy Versus Fascism and the Police State

©2002 Music based on the Ancient Egyptian tradition of birth music and sounds for the ceremony of giving birth.

NEW RELEASE

©2003 Music for Meditation and Relaxation

NEW RELEASE

Maat Philosophy Versus Fascism and the Police State

©2005 Dua Asar

Music based on the Asarian tradition and more Ancient Egyptian traditions. Includes remixes and new releases

Maat Philosophy Versus Fascism and the Police State

MAIN VIDEOS

Egyptian Yoga Exercise Class Level 1
Muata Ashby (Writer), Muata Ashby (Producer), Muata Ashby (Director)

List Price: $25.00
80 minutes, NTSC
UPC: 883629024394
Discover the practice of Egyptian Yoga postures based on the posture system practiced by the Ancient Egyptian priests and priestesses of Ancient Egypt. This is a practice for physical health but also for mental mythological and spiritual journey to higher consciousness.

Introduction to Ancient Egyptian Hieroglyphs
Muata Ashby (Writer), Muata Ashby (Producer), Muata Ashby (Director)

List Price: $25.00
60 minutes, NTSC
UPC: 883629113227
Introduction to Ancient Egyptian Hieroglyphs Class 1

Introduction to Egyptian Yoga
Muata Ashby (Writer), Muata Ashby (Producer), Muata Ashby (Director)

List Price: $25.00
60 minutes, NTSC

Maat Philosophy Versus Fascism and the Police State

UPC: 883629113159
Introduction to Egyptian Yoga philosophy and its influence on other world religions as well as its implications for spiritual evolution as conceived by the Ancient Egyptian sages Lecture by Dr. Muata Ashby

Glorious Light Meditation System of Ancient Egypt
Muata Ashby (Writer), Muata Ashby (Producer), Muata Ashby (Director)

List Price: $25.00
60 minutes, NTSC
UPC: 883629113104
Glorious Light Meditation System of Ancient Egypt is the oldest practice of formal meditation before Buddhism, Hinduism and Taoism. Ra Akhu, the glorious light was commissioned by the Pharaoh Sety 1 and it was enjoined for men and women to practice. This DVD is an introduction to the system and a practice session.

Asarian Resurrection: Myth of Asar, Aset and Heru (Osiris, Isis and Horus)
Muata Ashby (Writer), Muata Ashby (Producer), Muata Ashby (Director)

List Price: $25.00
60 minutes, NTSC
UPC: 883629111247
Audiovisual lecture by Dr. Muata Ashby on the most important myth of ancient Egypt based on the myth of Osiris, Isis and Horus, and its spiritual implications for attaining spiritual enlightenment

Ancient Egyptian Music Session Live Performances
Muata Ashby (Writer), Muata Ashby (Producer), Muata Ashby (Director)

Maat Philosophy Versus Fascism and the Police State

List Price: $25.00
60 minutes, NTSC
UPC: 883629113241
Ancient Egyptian Music Session Live Performances using Ancient Egyptian musical instrument reproductions and original lyric from ancient Egyptian hymbs and texts

Introduction to Maat Philosophy
Muata Ashby (Writer), Muata Ashby (Producer), Muata Ashby (Director)

List Price: $25.00
60 minutes, NTSC
UPC: 883629113234
Introduction to Maat Philosophy, the Ancient Egyptan philosophy of social order, justice and truth

Introduction to Shetaut Neter Part 1 -Egyptian Mysteries
Muata Ashby (Writer), Muata Ashby (Producer), Muata Ashby (Director)

List Price: $25.00
60 minutes, NTSC
UPC: 883629113166

Maat Philosophy Versus Fascism and the Police State

Audiovisual with powerpoint presentation on Shetaut Neter philosophy, the Egyptian mysteries, the Ancient Egyptian religious principles of metaphysics and mysticism. Lecture by Dr. Muata Ashby

Pan-Africanism in Light of Maat Philosophy
Muata Ashby (Writer), Muata Ashby (Producer), Muata Ashby (Director)

List Price: $25.00
60 minutes, NTSC
UPC: 883629113173
Pan-Africanism in Light of Maat Philosophy relates to how the concept of seein African culture in its totality relates to the promotion of African political, economic and social wellbeing under African principles of spiritual ethics Lecture by Dr. Muata Ashby

Mythology of the Ancient Egyptian Yoga Postures
Muata Ashby (Writer), Muata Ashby (Producer), Muata Ashby (Director)

List Price: $25.00
60 minutes, NTSC
UPC: 883629113265
Lecture series by Dr. Muata Ashby-Course traces the African Origins of Civilization, Religion and Philosophy. This video traces the origins and development of the Ancient Egyptian Yoga Postures. Contains slide presentation with actual original photos of the original postures from Ancient Egypt.